A Trip Too Far

A TRIP TOO FAR
ECOTOURISM, POLITICS AND EXPLOITATION

Rosaleen Duffy

Earthscan Publications Ltd
London • Sterling, VA

First published in the UK and USA in 2002
by Earthscan Publications Ltd

ISBN: 1 85383 759 8 paperback
      1 85383 758 X hardback

Typesetting by PCS Mapping & DTP, Gateshead
Printed and bound in the UK by Creative Print and Design Wales, Ebbw Vale
Cover design by Danny Gillespie

For a full list of publications please contact:
Earthscan Publications Ltd
120 Pentonville Road, London, N1 9JN, UK
Tel: +44 (0)20 7278 0433
Fax: +44 (0)20 7278 1142
Email: earthinfo@earthscan.co.uk
Web: **www.earthscan.co.uk**

22883 Quicksilver Drive, Sterling, VA 20166-2012, USA

Earthscan is an editorially independent subsidiary of Kogan Page Ltd and
publishes in association with WWF-UK and the International Institute for
Environment and Development

A catalogue record for this book is available from the British Library

Library of Congress Cataloging-in-Publication Data
Duffy, Rosaleen.
    A trip too far : ecotourism, politics, and exploitation / Rosaleen Duffy.
        p. cm.
    Includes bibliographical references (p.   ).
    ISBN 1-85383-758-X (hardback) — ISBN 1-85383-759-8 (pbk.)
    1. Ecotourism. I. Title.

    G156.5.E26 D84 2002
    338.4'79104—dc21
                                                            2001007665

CONTENTS

ACKNOWLEDGEMENTS

This book began life as a research project at Edinburgh University, which focused on the environmental attitudes of tourists who visited Belize. However, within a week or so of fieldwork it became clear that tourists were only one part of a much bigger picture of tourism, and that their responses could not be separated out from the broader landscape of tourism development. The funding of this research came from the Economic and Social Research Council, while I was a research fellow at Edinburgh University 1997–1999 (grant number L320253245), and at Lancaster University 1999–2000 (grant number R000223013). I would like to thank Professor Liz Bondi at Edinburgh University for her support on an academic and personal level. At Edinburgh, the feedback from the Feminist Geography Reading Group was especially helpful, with particular thanks to Dr Susan Lilley, Dr Gillian Rose, Dr Lynda Johnston, Dr Joyce Davidson, Hannah Avis, Anja Maaike-Green and Nichola Wood. The network of feminist geographers provided an invaluable source of support during my time at Edinburgh. At Edinburgh, a great deal of support was also provided by Maeve O'Donohue, Kate Benstead, Nicolas Regnauld and Alastair Edwards. At Lancaster University, the staff at the Department of Politics and International Relations have been instrumental in the development of this book, and in providing me with an environment where a large research and writing project could be completed. I would like to thank Professor Christopher Clapham for his constant help with reading drafts of papers, listening to my tales from fieldwork and always managing to come up with excellent suggestions and constructive comments. Within the Department, my colleagues have been very supportive, and

constantly had to put up with 'just one more story from Belize....'
For their patience I thank Dr Feargal Cochrane, Dr Alan
Warburton, Ann McAleer, Dr Jan Selby and our Head of
Department, Gordon Hands.

I cannot count the number of people who helped me in Belize.
However, it should be made clear that the opinions contained in
this book are entirely my own and not the responsibility of anyone
who facilitated this research. In addition, any errors are mine and
not theirs. Having said that, Aline Harrisson and the Harrisson
family, and Mary Vasquez and the Vasquez family were great hosts
who not only provided hospitality but also talked over much of the
research findings and listened to me when I was homesick. At the
University of Belize, the staff of the Marine Research Centre were
very welcoming and provided me with facilities to undertake the
research. I would like to thank Pio Saqui, Philip Morgan, Dwight
Neal and Dr Vincent Palacio (now at Programme for Belize). I
remain indebted to Karie Holtermann and Eden Garcia for their
willingness to accommodate me and this research at the Marine
Research Station on Calabash Caye, when they were clearly under
a great deal of pressure. I admired their ability to carry out their
duties in a professional manner under the most difficult circumstances. On Ambergris Caye, I would like to thank Julie Seldon
and Gary Peacock, Gaz Coopers dive shop, Daniel and Elodia
Nunez, Ruby's hotel and the staff of Fido's bar, all of whom made
my stays very enjoyable and informative. On Caye Caulker, I would
like to thank Ellen MacCrae, Nino Rosado, Dean Baldwin,
Chocolate, Trends Hotel, the staff of Oceanside and Sand Box as
well as Shady Shores from Vancouver Island. In Toledo District, I
must thank Gregory Ch'oc of the Kekchi Council of Belize; his
insights into ecotourism and Mayan issues were instrumental in the
development of this research. Likewise, the help provided by Chet
Schmidt, Pio Coc and Rafael Cal of Medina Bank Village was
invaluable. Peter Eltringham, author of numerous guidebooks to
the region also provided me with lots of very useful information
and contacts. My stays in Belize City and elsewhere were also made
enjoyable and productive by a number of people, but I would like
to thank Chidi Metu and the staff at Amandala, Luz Hunter from
Tubroos Tree books, Dave Vernon of Toadal Adventures, Linda

Werthrus of Seasports Belize, Augustin Flores at Pal's Guesthouse, as well as Dr Ilka Feller at the Smithsonian Institute for her help with the research. Likewise, numerous tour operators, NGOs and journalists in Britain and in Belize provided critical information. I cannot name them all for reasons of confidentiality and to ensure their safety, but I would like to thank them especially for taking a risk to tell me their version of the story on the politics of ecotourism in Belize. Finally, a thanks has to go to the tourists who let me interview them in Belize. I am sure that, for some of them, my presence was a real imposition on their holiday fun. Interviewing tourists was a key personal experience for me that changed my outlook on socialising and on travel in the developing world. While it was sometimes very frustrating, difficult and even upsetting, in retrospect I do not think I would have changed any of it. And although the conclusions I make in Chapter 2 of this book are critical of tourist attitudes and behaviours, I did meet some really great people who were committed to the idea of making tourism environmentally sustainable and culturally sensitive.

Finally, a mention must be made of my family. They had to follow me through the highs and lows of this research, and they allowed me to flit off to the other side of the world during Christmas and New Year. So a big thanks goes to Mum and Dad, Carmel and Simon, Joanna, Thomas and Peter, Terry and Liza, Orla, Liam and Kathy, Luke and Liam, Katherine and Dennis, and Annabel and Chris. A special thanks goes to my sister Mary who visited me on fieldwork in Belize. She had her holidays constantly interrupted by my zeal for interviewing tourists and it is because of her that I learned to scuba dive – which I am now mad keen on. She also gave me a crucial space to rest after fieldwork, when I turned up at her flat looking dusty and dishevelled.

INTRODUCTION

With increasing frequency, ecotourism is proposed as a way of ensuring environmental conservation while enabling economic development. Developing countries, in particular, are being encouraged by a set of diverse interest groups to consider ecotourism as a solution to their environmental and economic challenges. The supporters of ecotourism as a development strategy include international financial institutions, global environmental organizations, global tourism businesses, national governments and local community organizations, as well as individuals who regard themselves as ecotourists. In many ways ecotourism is being proposed as a tool for negotiating complicated relationships between these potentially conflicting interest groups. For example, ecotourism is often thought to provide a resolution to conflicts over the reservation of land for national parks, because it enables local communities and private businesses to derive financial benefits from engaging with conservation.

Ecotourism can be broadly defined as nature-based tourism that does not result in the negative environmental, economic and social impacts that are associated with mass tourism. Ecotourism is promoted as a form of travel that brings only benefits to the host societies, because ecotourists are thought to be culturally aware 'ethical travellers' who are keen to reduce negative impacts on the environment. Such perceptions of ecotourism are characteristic of tourists from Northern industrialized countries who believe that they are saving the lemurs of Madagascar, or the iguanas of the Galapagos, by travelling to see them. Ecotourists, environmental non-governmental organizations (NGOs) and tour operators all suggest that such tourism brings revenue to cash-strapped developing countries. The implication is that ecotourist holidays pay directly for conservation initiatives to save the animals, or landscapes, that the ecotourists visit.

This book is intended as a critique of the nature of ecotourism. A key strand in the argument is that ecotourism creates both positive and negative impacts, and the book offers an analysis of the ways in which different parts of Belizean society cope with those effects. The intention is to place ecotourism in its political context in order to examine whether it is really capable of providing environmentally sustainable development. In particular, I will argue that ecotourism is firmly locked into notions of 'green capitalism', and thus it cannot provide radical sustainable development, contrary to its supporters' claims. Ecotourism is a business that has to compete alongside other businesses, and it focuses on profit rather than conservation. On the positive side, a strategy based on ecotourism encourages governments to ensure that conservation is financially sustainable, even in developing countries in which many sectors must compete for scarce governmental resources. However, ecotourism is not the cost-free business option that its supporters suggest.

The promoters of ecotourism suggest that it is an apolitical business, a simple consumer choice that will benefit development and environmental conservation, while conveniently providing some revenue for the host country as well. In fact, ecotourism involves deeply political choices by those who create the demand (ecotourists) and by the interest groups that cater for them (primarily businesses, governments and NGOs). Ecotourism is part of a broader system of 'blue-green' thought, which defines the environment as a resource with a distinct economic value, and so differs from more left-wing 'red-green' ideas and ecocentric 'deep-green' philosophies. Ecotourism also fits neatly with dominant development theories based on neoliberal economics and notions of comparative advantage. It is clear that ecotourism is of a piece with the free market, business-oriented strategies favoured by those who lend money to developing countries, for example the World Bank and governments in industrialized states. It does not require a fundamental reshaping of the global economic and political system, but rather works within existing structures. As such, ecotourism is favoured because it does not constitute a threat to the dominant economic and political patterns that characterize the post-Cold-War world. Instead, ecotourism is part of the 'liberal peace', in which neoliberal ideas about politics and economics have become globalized. As ecotourism does have this strong neoliberal ideological strand, it is important to examine the beliefs that underpin its use as a development and conservation strategy. This book will examine the differing strands of environmental thought and analyse them in relation to ecotourism. In the course of this examination I will argue that ecotourism can be regarded as a part of a global capitalist system rather than any kind of challenge to it.

The politics of ecotourism are clear at all levels of the business. I intend to provide an analysis of ecotourism that considers the environmental attitudes of the ecotourists themselves, as well as the ways in which ecotourism intersects with globalization. The ways in which ecotourists construct and view the environment, and their impacts on host societies, are vitally important to an understanding of how ecotourism can be thought of as 'green greed'. I will suggest that ecotourists are not so concerned about their own interaction with the environment, or about mitigating the negative effects of their vacation choices. Instead, they are more concerned with journeys of self-development; their decisions to deny themselves the luxuries of other forms of tourism just reflect the roles they play within their peer groups. In interviews, ecotourists reveal that they are primarily concerned about the ways in which their holidays affect them as individuals. This emphasis on the self links up with theories of self-reflexivity, in which individuals exercise consumer power in relation to global corporations. This is very different from collective, organized political protests that are aimed at influencing governments. In a sense, the way in which the individual makes green choices about vacationing removes the political context from ecotourism. As a result, the rest of this book consists of an analysis of the political implications of ecotourism, using Belize as an example.

It also investigates the impacts that ecotourism has on host societies. This is especially important, because the promoters of ecotourism claim that it involves a relationship of equal power between the host society and the guest, and that negative social impacts are minimized because ecotourism businesses and ecotourists themselves are 'culturally aware'. This book focuses on the impact spiral created by ecotourism, and shows how it brings social, economic and environmental transformations to developing societies. These transformations are driven by the need to serve the demands of individual ecotourists, who are part of a wider system of travel over which they have little control. Ecotourists, like conventional tourists, need restaurants, bars, shops and accommodation. Because ecotourism often takes place in relatively remote areas and small communities, the effects of establishing a small-scale hotel or food outlet can have the same impact as building a Hilton in a large town or city. The direct personal relationship between host and guest is a microcosm of the wider politics of ecotourism.

In a critically important way, ecotourism also relies on a politically laden image of the destination country. This book will examine the political implications of this image of the exotic nation state, created for external consumption. Ecotourism is a global business, and each destination is effectively in competition with other potential vacation spots, so countries must carve out specific identities. The image of the host society and its natural environment plays a key part in understanding how ecotourism can be regarded as part of green capitalism. The host societies are packaged and commodified for consumption by an external audience, promising the exotic, the unspoilt, the pristine and – even worse – the primitive. These images feed back into domestic politics through their use by political and economic elites. The development of an ecotourism image affects national politics and policy making deeply, particularly policy decisions that might affect visitor numbers. Policies that are not favoured by external interest groups, such as tour operators, environmental NGOs and ecotourists themselves, are swiftly taken off the political agenda.

An examination of the ways in which political problems can affect ecotourism images is an important component of this book. Indigenous communities engage with ecotourism operations in complex ways. It is a type of commerce that is intended to benefit indigenous communities and foster genuine local participation, and has been promoted as a way of enabling local communities to become meaningful partners in revenue-generation schemes, as well as ensuring that benefits are equitably shared. Many indigenous communities around the world have tried to set up their own ecotourism ventures to bring development and environmental conservation to their areas. However, ecotourism is part of a bigger political and economic system that directly frustrates genuine development for indigenous communities. This is especially the case when ecotourism has to compete with other development interests that lay claim to the environments that indigenous communities wish to exploit for ecotourism.

Finally, this book will provide an analysis of how other development interests compete with ecotourism, and how they all intersect with globalization. Tourism and ecotourism are usually regarded as examples of globalization; however, in the Central American region the industry is linked to global networks in a peculiar way. Legitimate business interests are heavily dependent on illicit networks dealing in drugs or money laundering, or even illegally caught lobsters or stolen Mayan archeological artefacts. Ecotourism's dependence on such illegitimate, global business networks means that environmental protection legislation is not properly enforced. In effect, globalization has undermined the ability of national governments to formulate and enforce policies to control ecotourism development and secure environmental conservation. The visible structures of governance, such as political departments and ministries, remain, but they are rendered ineffective by global networks that determine the pace and direction of ecotourism development. Individual ecotourists choosing their holiday destinations are entirely unaware of these processes, and cannot control them through consumer power or self-reflexivity.

Thus, this book will provide a critique of ecotourism's operation in the South. Belize is used as a case study, but many of the arguments surrounding ecotourism in Belize are equally applicable to other societies. The fieldwork was carried out during three visits to Belize over the period 1997–2000, and was funded by the Economic and Social Research Council.[1] Fifty-three semi-structured interviews were undertaken, mostly with individual ecotourists, but occasionally with couples and groups of friends travelling together. Key representatives from the ecotourism industry were also interviewed. A total of 89 semi-structured interviews were carried out with tour operators, guides, academics and journalists, as well as representatives from conservation organizations, community organizations and government departments. The interviews were tailored to the interviewee's specific area of expertise. Any mistakes are my responsibility rather than that of the interviewees.

The material gleaned from the interviews was vitally important. Interviews provide information that cannot be strictly defined as 'true' or 'untrue'; they are alternative narratives on the same topic or political event. They may provide an explanation of the interviewee's world-view, or simply their version of events. They are often the only means of obtaining certain kinds of information, especially about illegal activities. In talking about events, organizations and each other, people may provide a more accurate record of events than written sources are able to. At the very least, the interviews show how people construct the world around them. In particular, discussions about opposing interest groups reveal the fragility of political reputations, and the stories that people tell about themselves (and others) indicate a kind of flexible truth, which is significant because people believe it. It became clear – through the interviewing process and the examination of local press reports, government documents and NGO reports – that the problems associated with ecotourism in Belize definitely have implications for other developing countries that are considering it as a new policy direction.

CHAPTER 1

GREEN GREED: ECOTOURISM AND ENVIRONMENTAL IDEOLOGIES

Introduction

Ecotourism has been proposed by a number of interest groups as a new way forward for environmentally sustainable development. Its supporters believe it provides the answer to complex conflicts surrounding resource use and management. Ecotourism is presented as beneficial for the South because it enables the generation of profit from environmental resources without resorting to polluting, smoke-stack industries. Northern environmental campaigners say that it sidesteps the difficulties associated with industrial development in their own countries. After all, what negative impact can a few environmentally aware and culturally sensitive travellers have on the developing world? This outlook fails to acknowledge the deeply political nature of ecotourism as a development strategy. The theoretical basis of ecotourism means that it does have an enormous impact on host societies in the South, both positive and negative.

The issue of environmental care has emerged as one of the most important debates in developing countries. In particular, there has been an increased interest in tourism as a potential vehicle for development that is both economically beneficial and environmentally sustainable, and this is encapsulated in the buzzword 'ecotourism'. Despite continuing debate about the precise nature of ecotourism, it can be broadly defined as nature tourism that consists of travelling to a relatively undisturbed or uncontaminated natural area with the specific object of studying, admiring and enjoying the scenery, wild plants and animals, as well as cultural characteristics of the areas (Boo, 1990, pp1–3; see also Bottrill, 1995, pp45–54). However, the debates surrounding ecotourism have masked the important ideological content of ecotourism as a development strategy. The way in which the environment is defined determines the policies that are used to manage or conserve it; the 'environment' is negotiated using sets of competing ideas. Environmentalism is not a single perspective, but rather encompasses widely differing ideas. This variety reveals the extent of disagreement within the environmental critique of science and science policy. While environmental care is often presented as an uncontested and positivist science, the environmental debate demonstrates that decisions regarding the environment are politically, socially and economically informed.

Ecotourism has been promoted by multilateral lending agencies, governments of the North and South, private businesses and non-governmental organizations (NGOs). This book takes a critical stance towards ecotourism and argues that it forms part of the central legitimizing argument for the switch to free-market policies favoured by numerous global interest groups. The ideological content of ecotourism has been masked; interest groups seek to depoliticize their position by claiming that it would enable the South to develop economically without the attendant problems of environmental degradation. However, ecotourism is intensely ideological, and the decision to develop an ecotourism industry involves decisions that deeply affect numerous political interest groups, ranging from the private tour industry to indigenous community organizations and even criminal networks of traffickers and money launderers. This chapter will examine the strands of political ideology within ecotourism, and will show how ecotourism is closely related to free-market, business-oriented strategies popular with Northern states and multilateral lending agencies. In particular, it asks whether ecotourism constitutes genuine sustainable development with minimal negative social, political, environmental and economic impacts.

Contested Ideas of Environmental Sustainability

In the 1990s the idea of sustainability began to permeate discussions of development in the South; the call went out that development strategies must minimize their negative impacts on the environment. Debates about environment and development crystallized around the Brundtland Report of 1987. The Brundtland Commission defined sustainability as 'meeting the needs of the present without compromising the ability of future generations to meet their own needs' (WCED, 1987, p8). However, there remains a great deal of disagreement over what this really means. Beck argues that our technologically advanced society is characterized by situations in which large-scale environmental hazards have been forced upon citizens by states, and the management of these hazards has led to confusion (Beck, 1995, pp1–13). This confusion is clearly demonstrated by disputes over the definition of sustainability and the kinds of policies that will be required to achieve it.

Beck suggests that hazards in contemporary society differ from those of industrial society. These new hazards cannot be delimited spatially, temporally or socially; they cross national boundaries and encompass all social classes. They do not fit the theory of the single causal factor, nor can particular institutions be held liable; numerous anonymous actors cause hazards. Beck argues that the lack of proper planning for environmental catastrophes exposes the paradigm error: society is prepared for industrial disasters, which can be contained and their effects reversed, but environmental catastrophes have now started to have an irreversible impact. As we enter the 21st century, it seems that these environmental problems may not be resolved in the foreseeable future (Beck,

1995). In this 'risk society', the bases and forms of modernity are open to scrutiny by all. Giddens argues that the processes of globalization have generalized modernity, so that remote agencies or events influence individual actions, and individual actions have a global impact. As a result, modernity is characterized by hazards that are simultaneously our own doing and beyond our control (Giddens, 1994, pp57–62).

A key characteristic of the risk society is that science has ceased to be an uncontested arena. This is nowhere more apparent than in the environmental movement, with its disagreements over the speed and direction of environmental change. The increasing uncertainty about the causes, extent and rates of environmental change is, in some ways, the result of the risk society. For example, there is no consensus about whether global warming exists, or – if it does exist – about how the impacts can be managed or reduced (Redclift, 1992, pp37–39). Such decisions about such environmental problems and policies are determined by social constructions of risk, and the failure to recognize the value judgements involved in environmental policy distorts the public debate and the relationship between expert knowledge and public value-choices (Wynne, 1992, pp114–116; see also Shrader-Frechette and McCoy, 1994, pp107–109).

The risk society has also affected the way in which individuals think about their places in society and the impacts of their actions. Modern society is dissolving the contours of industrial society and opening the way to another construction of modernity. This is what Beck terms 'reflexive modernization', which occurs when we are confronted with risk-society effects that cannot be dealt with or assimilated in an industrial society. In a reflexive society there is uncertainty: in debates about risks no-one is an expert, and yet at the same time everyone is an expert (Beck, 1994, pp5–13; Smith, 1996, pp25–47; and Cohan, 1999). As a result, control over the form and direction of discussions about environmental issues is wrested from scientific experts and enjoyed by the wider public. A number of approaches, with differing vocabularies, have been developed to manage controversies arising from differing points of view. It is clear that scientific discourses have become highly contested by political and social discourses (Myerson and Rydin, 1996, pp19–23; Rydin, 1999).

This transformation has become apparent in the growth of the environmental movement. The bases of modern society, and particularly its reliance on technology, have been exposed and confronted. In particular, the twin concerns of economic growth and technological development have been criticized as the root causes of environmental problems. For example, those social groups most involved in environmental organizations are also more likely to be sceptical about the ability of an uncontested or positivist brand of science and technological innovation to solve global problems (Cotgrove and Duff, 1980, pp333–338). According to Beck, the environmental critique of the Enlightenment approach to science and knowledge constitutes the most powerful brake on industrial momentum, and as such it provides a system of thought that is intended to guide the way human society should be organized (Beck, 1995, pp53–57; Szerzynski, 1999).

However, environmental decision making is essentially determined by the distribution of power in society, and also within the environmental movement. The deep ideological divisions within the environmental movement are voiced in society by differing interest groups. Debates about the environment reveal the environmental agenda; and as they appear, change and are contested, they demonstrate the dynamics of that agenda (Myerson and Rydin, 1996, pp4–7). For example, the language used to justify environmental arguments resonates to the tune of a culture. These voices overlap, contest a world view or address a common topic, so that the word *population* reveals a terrain of voices that includes varieties of Malthusian and anti-Malthusian perspectives, all of which claim to be green viewpoints (Myerson and Rydin, 1996, pp203–206; Petrucci, 2000). These views range from those who do not challenge the existing global structures to those who advocate a fundamental reorganization of society on every level. In terms of political ideology, the environmental perspective can be divided into three strands: blue-green (or light green), red-green and deep green, and each proposes different policies designed to protect or manage the environment. It is clear from these divisions that the 'environment' is a social, cultural, economic and political construct.

Blue-greens can be found at the conservative or right-wing end of the environmental spectrum. They are often associated with concepts of weak sustainability or light green policies intended to ensure environmental protection within existing social, economic and political structures (Beckerman, 1994, pp194–198; Dobson, 1996, pp406–410; Miller, 2000). Blue-green thought has its historical antecedents in the writings of Bacon, Malthus and Darwin, and draws heavily on Adam Smith and John Stuart Mill (Mill, 1863; Smith, 1776; Beckerman, 1994, pp191–209). It is reformist: many blue-greens suggest that environmental care is possible within existing structures. This reflects a commitment to conservatism, the preservation of the status quo. This is translated into ideas about natural balance in society, economics and politics. It is also characterized by the belief that man-made capital is a perfect substitute for natural capital (Dobson, 1996, pp406–409).

Such ideas have fed into other areas of conservation policy, such as the maintenance of existing social, political and economic structures. Blue-green methods of environmental care are drawn from utilitarianism, liberalism and free-market principles. The utilitarian principle of the greatest good for the greatest number has been translated into methods of environmental management (Mill, 1863). Environmental economics relies on the idea that the free market is the most efficient allocator of resources, and will maximize pleasure for the greatest number of people (Sagoff, 1994, pp285–310; Pearce, Barbier and Markandya, 1990; Winpenny, 1991). Blue-green beliefs have proved particularly popular with the business community, and have been adopted by the International Chamber of Commerce as the guiding principles for sustainable development in the future (Eden, 1994, pp160–167). Blue-green ideas certainly constitute the reformist side of the environmental movement. A commitment to weak sustainability does not require a fundamental reorganization of social, economic and political structures; it assumes that sustainability can be achieved within existing structures.

Red-greens can be found on the left wing of the environmental debate, but they share with the blue-greens a commitment to sustainable development. However, their analysis of the causes of environmental degradation and the policies that are required to implement sustainable development is very different. In general, red-greens argue that the environment is a social construct; they do not adhere to the idea of authentic nature, untouched by humanity. Current debates centred on social ecology and ecosocialism tend to be more homogenous than blue-green ideas, but red-greens do include diverse groups such as ecofeminists (McIntosh, 1996, pp3–30; Eckersley, 1992, pp63–71).

Bookchin argues that when environmentalists advocate protecting the planet from humanity, they are masking important hierarchical social-power relations, and that the ecological impact of human reason, science and technology depends enormously on the type of society in which these forces are shaped and employed (Bookchin, 1991, p32). For red-greens, social organization is the most important factor in explaining the state of the environment. For example, instead of laying the blame for ecological degradation on the individual, social ecologists highlight the activities of industry and elites. In terms of the development debate, social ecologists point to over-consumption in the North rather than population growth, poverty or industrialization in the South as the source of global environmental ills (Bryant, 1997, pp5–19; Drummond and Marsden, 1995, pp58–62). Such radical accounts of the causes behind ecological degradation beg radical solutions, which can be politically unpopular and immensely difficult to carry out.

Ecosocialists such as Andre Gorz argue that a radical break with economic rationality and capitalism (a system of competition with profit as the goal) is necessary. For Marxists and ecosocialists, over-accumulation is the problem for the environment, and this involves a situation where the level of capital needed to produce the same goods is so high that they cannot be reproduced at a normal level, and so productivity declines. Over-accumulation may occur among certain groups (industrial elites), at a national or regional scale, or at the global scale along the North–South divide. The response to over-accumulation is thought to involve the search for new markets, or more sophisticated goods; one strategy is built-in obsolescence (Gorz, 1980, pp20–28). For ecosocialists, an end to over-consumption is crucial for the maintenance of an environment capable of supporting human life, and this will mean an inversion of capitalist logic, so that better may mean less. Social ecologists, ecofeminists and ecosocialists share a hostility to the market: they believe it is an inefficient and unjust allocator of natural resources, and that it can never reflect the true value of a resource (Dryzek and Lester, 1989, pp314–330).

There is also a strong sense of anthropocentrism in ecosocialism, which angers animal rights activists and deep greens who emphasize that humanity is just a part of the ecosystem rather than its dominator. Ecosocialists argue for the use of the environment for human benefit, so long as it does not cause irreversible damage or depletion. Unlike Marxists, ecosocialists argue that the root of hierarchical human societies lies in human domination of non-human nature (Eckersley, 1992, pp179–186). This anthropocentric approach divides red-greens from deep greens.

The deep green position claims to be a third way, after socialist and capitalist conceptions of society, politics, economics and the environment. Deep greens are associated with a belief in strong sustainability, which involves a radical break with existing social, economic and political structures in order to give environmental protection the highest priority (Beckerman, 1994, pp191–209). In contrast to blue-green and red-green approaches, which derive from established political traditions, the deep greens claim to have a commitment to the environment itself, and to follow whatever paths, however radical, the maintenance of the environment requires. While they see the other approaches as ultimately human-centred, they perceive their own as environment-centred. There is also a light green position, which shares some elements of other green thinking but remains committed to the principle that humans are only one part of the ecosystem and do not have special licence to exploit or dominate non-human nature (Sterba, 1994, pp229–244; Peterson and Peterson, 1996, pp123–126; Berthold-Bond, 2000). It is this ecocentrism, rather than anthropocentrism, which is the distinguishing feature of deep greens. However, it is not politically neutral: deep greens have more in common with red-greens than blue-greens. James Lovelock's 'Gaia hypothesis' has been very influential in the deep-green debate. He suggests that the whole planet, including the mountains, seas and atmosphere, is a living organism (Gaia), which is a self-regulating, self-organizing system, the greatest manifestation of life. Lovelock is thus interested in preserving the health of the whole organism rather than one component of it (human beings) (Lovelock, 1988, pp181–182;

1979). Gaia also informs much radical sustainable development literature in relation to the South, because it calls for the redefinition of humanity's relationship with the Earth. Aldo Leopold's 'land ethic' and the Gaia hypothesis are useful for environmentalists because they offer a new basis from which to argue in favour of environmental care: everything has intrinsic value, and the preservation of all components is necessary to maintain the overall health of the planet (Leopold, 1986, pp73–82).

The animal liberation movement developed independently from the green movement but is now integral to it. In particular, it shares common concerns with deep-greens about the welfare of all species, albeit for different reasons. The animal rights issue is now defined as part of environmentalism, and as such it has a role to play in defining 'environment'. In many ways the ideology of animal liberation is derived from the writings of Jeremy Bentham on the extension of moral obligations to all beings who are capable of experiencing pleasure or pain. Animal liberationists argue that all sentient beings are capable of experiencing pleasure and pain, and argue that animals should not be killed or exploited for human benefit. Ecocentrics view nature as an inter-related web, a view that has echoes of romantic notions of the environment, the land ethic and the Gaia hypothesis (Hettinger and Throop, 1999). For deep greens, organisms are not simply a part of an ecosystem; they actually constitute it. It is clear that deep green philosophy would give rise to policies that would fundamentally reorganize social, economic and political structures to ensure a sustainable world. However, Beckerman notes that the policies required are extreme, and he refers to deep ecology as 'absurdly strong sustainability' (Beckerman, 1994, pp191–209).

Discussions about how to manage the environment clearly have important social, political and economic dimensions; they are not confined to a depoliticized scientific discourse and neutral decision making. As Gorz suggests, although these discussions are presented to the public as matters for science and technology, this is based on erroneous assumptions about the nature of the debate (Gorz, 1980, pp17–20). For the purposes of public policy discussions, environmental questions are presented in a simplistic way, and subtle ethical doctrines are translated into generalized principles, which thus lose impact and importance (Goodin, 1983, pp3–21). Environmentalists disagree about policies to achieve an ecological society, but they agree about the common commitment to a broad idea of sustainable development, despite disagreements over what this actually means. Most environmentalists and conservationists agree that the main objective of policy should be a sustainable relationship between humanity and the environment (Caulfield, 1989, pp13–57). This relationship is at the heart of debates about the potential for ecotourism as a pathway to sustainable development.

A Trip Too Far?

The idea that environmentally sustainable tourism can contribute to development in the South is clearly related to blue-green environmental concepts. Like other blue-green forms of environmental management, the attempt to develop resources while not degrading them through a policy of ecotourism does not challenge existing political, economic and social structures. Instead, the blue-green strategy of ecotourism operates within current norms and, crucially, within existing business or market logic. Ecotourism also relies on the individual exercising power through choices about consumption, rather than acting as a citizen engaged in collective and organized protest. In this way ecotourism, as a subset of the global tourism industry, is firmly embedded in green capitalism, where the individual bears responsibility for environmental conservation or degradation rather than governments or private industry.

The increased interest in tourism as a development strategy is part of the global re-emergence of neoliberalism expressed through global governance and the shift towards a 'liberal peace'. As a part of this global governance project, tourism is clearly a highly politicized policy choice. It is essentially political because the pursuit of tourism development raises questions about the economic, political and social dimensions of the development process. Tourism also means that overt and covert development objectives are pursued at the expense of other objectives, and the selection and implementation of certain political and economic values will depend on the winners and losers in the development of tourism (Hall, 1994, pp108–112). The interest in tourism can be related to neoliberal theories of modernization and their emphasis on the importance of internal factors as facilitators or inhibitors of business-oriented development. The ideological basis of development through tourism growth reveals that tourism is very much a political process and part of a global shift towards political and economic liberalism, rather than a private or individualized activity (Matthews and Richter, 1991, pp120–123).

The renewed emphasis on outward-oriented growth and the rise of neoliberal development strategies has focused attention on tourism as a potential growth sector. The central core of neoliberal development strategies is an emphasis on economic diversification, particularly a commitment to non-traditional exports such as tourism (Brohman, 1996, pp48–52). This approach has also been favoured by international lending agencies such as the World Bank and the International Monetary Fund (IMF), and by bilateral donors, who have made loans available in return for reforms that favour market-oriented growth (World Bank, 1994). For example, tourism in the Central American and Caribbean regions has received considerable levels of assistance from the US and the European Union through the Mundo Maya project and the Caribbean Basin Initiative (CBI) (Stonich, Sorensen and Hundt, 1995, pp1–5).

Supporters of tourism as a development strategy also point out that it fits snugly with neoliberal strategies of basing economies on comparative advantage. Advocates of this position argue that each state should concentrate on exporting the goods that it is naturally best at producing (Amsden, 1990, pp5–32; Porter, 1990). For example, in the Caribbean, tourism was actively promoted in order to make up for the diminishing profitability of banana production in the 1990s (Pattullo, 1996, pp6–8). It is difficult to fit tourism into traditional notions of import and export because it is an exported good, consumed by people from the North in the countries of the South. However, it is generally viewed as a foreign-exchange earner in much the same way as traditional exports. Developing countries are considered to have a comparative advantage in tourism because they attract tourists from the North who are seeking the sunshine, beaches and other natural and cultural attractions to be found in the South. Governments in the South, facing financial problems and an end to secure markets for their goods in former colonial countries, have looked to tourism as an answer to their problems (Lynn, 1992, pp371–372). Most governments, regardless of their political ideology, see tourism as being economically important and so it has experienced significant levels of state intervention. This is unusual for business, which is primarily regarded as a matter for private enterprise (Hall, 1994, pp28–32). National tourism policies tend to be geared towards the generation of economic growth, and the concept of tourism development is almost synonymous with economic growth, Westernization and modernization, because tourism means employment, balance of payments, regional development and foreign exchange (Hall, 1994, pp112–120; Harrison, 1992, pp8–11).

Tourism development is also closely bound up with the private sector at the local, national and global level. Many governments are keen to couch public-sector tourism development in pro-business rhetoric and policy (Matthews and Richter, 1991, pp123–125). Tourism development has proved particularly attractive to local elites in developing countries, whether they are involved in government or the private sector. Elites tend to favour tourism for much the same reasons as businesses in the developed world and global lending agencies (Hall, 1994, pp120–123). Modernization theorists view elites as the modernizers with a developing society. The activities of international tour operators open up new economic opportunities within developing countries, meaning that local entrepreneurs with existing businesses are able to take advantage of new tourism developments. Elites tend to promote tourism because the profits from it flow towards them (Harrison, 1992c, pp22–26; Van de Berghe, 1995, pp568–588). On a broader level, tourism is credited with being a major provider of employment in developing states, often in areas where there are few other opportunities. Tourism provides employment in direct and indirect ways. Direct employment is provided within the services and industries that make up what is collectively known as the tourism industry, including hotels, tour operators and casinos. Indirect employment is provided in sectors that are affected by tourism, such as local transport, craft production, restaurants and bars used by locals and visitors alike. However, a great deal of direct and indirect employment that is created by tourism is in the informal sector. In the informal sector, local people provide services to tourists on a casual basis, such as selling local crafts as souvenirs (Pattullo, 1996, pp52–56; Hitchcock and Teague, 2000; Abbot-Cone, 1995, pp314–327). The extent of employment creation in the informal sector is unquantifiable, but even so such opportunities can make a significant contribution to household finances in developing countries (Pattullo, 1996, pp56–61).

The commitment to tourism as a development strategy is related to wider debates about development, which have been influenced by neoliberal economics and modernization theory. It is favoured by international business because it allows expansion into long-haul markets, and by governments and developing-country elites because it is a means of improving the balance of payments, earning foreign exchange and providing employment.

Conventional tourism development can be a positive force for development, but it can also have negative impacts. The interest in tourism as a development strategy is closely linked to the resurgence of neoliberal ideas about the causes of underdevelopment and the policies needed to overcome these difficulties. The arguments about tourism as a development strategy are related to wider theories of development, and conventional tourism has been criticized on economic, political and social grounds. The environmental impact of tourism has caused concern among environmental groups, the tourism industry and those interested in development. The problems associated with tourism have encouraged the development of ideas about how tourism can be made more socially, culturally and environmentally sensitive.

Tourism and the Sustainability Debate

One of the challenges facing the tourism industry is how to develop without destroying the environment. Tourism in developing states is often reliant on the environment, the attraction for Western tourists, and so mitigating the impact of tourism on that key attraction is critical. The environmental problems caused by conventional mass tourism development have provided a clear example of how tourism can be the cause of its own demise. The impacts associated with mass tourism development, including building infrastructure such as roads, airports, hotel complexes and restaurants, have led to calls for a smaller and more environmentally friendly form of tourism.

Cater suggests that the poorest countries are the least capable of withstanding the adverse impacts on their potential for sustainability, and so they are the most in need of sustainable tourism development (Cater, 1994, pp80–85). The natural environment is critical to the attractiveness of a tourist destination because it provides the backdrop to commercial service areas and recreation sites (Farrell and Runyan, 1991, pp26–40). As a result, it is important to plan for sustainable tourism development. One of the fundamental truths about tourism is that, as an industrial activity, tourism consumes resources, creates waste and has specific infrastructure needs, and that as a consumer of resources it has the potential to over-consume. Over time, with incremental change, tourism development has the capacity to transform local environments (McKercher, 1993, pp6–10).

The expansion of tourism around the globe has led to fears about the environmental impact of millions of people moving around the world. It is clear that tourism will not disappear, and so the issue is not whether tourism is beneficial or not, but how it can be carried out in a more environmentally, socially and culturally sensitive manner (Wilkinson, 1992, pp386–395). The fact that the continued success of tourism depends on the protection of the environment means that the tourism industry and other interested parties should have a stakehold in conservation. Given its reliance on natural habitats, tourism and the interests of the environment ought to have mutually reinforcing objectives. Pressure to develop a more environmentally sensitive form of tourism has come from within the tourism industry and from NGOs, but there has often been a mismatch between their viewpoints. Campaigning organizations have promoted ethical or responsible tourism, while those involved in the tourism industry regard this as unrealistic and divorced from the realities of the business world. In addition, campaigning organizations argue that regulation needs to come from an independent body or from the state, whereas the tourism industry is very much in favour of the idea of self-regulation (Forsyth, 1995, pp210–231). However, as Cater suggests, given the multiple interests involved in tourism and the environment, a completely sustainable outcome is likely to be an ideal rather than a reality (Cater, 1995, pp21–23).

Nevertheless, there has been an increasing interest in alternative forms of tourism development. Many of the criticisms of conventional tourism, such as foreign domination and nature of the tourism-related employment, also apply to alternative forms of tourism. However, alternative tourisms such as ecotourism are meant to reduce the negative effects of tourism and contribute to positive social, cultural, economic and environmental developments. Ecotourism still relies on the notion that developing states have a comparative advantage in terms of the variety and extent of unspoilt natural environments (Cater, 1992, pp69–72). Developing states have turned to ecotourism as a means of earning foreign exchange while ensuring that the environment is not degraded. Ecotourism has become an increasingly popular label attached to various forms of alternative tourism. While a definitive standard of what constitutes ecotourism has not yet been developed, there is loose agreement on the kinds of effects that ecotourism should have.

There is no single definition of ecotourism; instead, debates revolve around the environmental impact of a particular tourist development, or the environmental credentials of a tourist company that defines itself as ecologically sound. In general, ecotourism should satisfy conservation and development objectives (Lindberg, Enriquez and Sproule, 1996, pp543–547). It is often defined as travel to natural areas that conserves the environment and improves the welfare of local people. In theory, ecotourism should satisfy a number of key objectives.

The most obvious effect that ecotourism should have is that it should conserve the environment that is the basis of its business. This is linked to environmental economics theories in which the interests of the market and the environment can be compatible if resources are subject to wise use. Advocates of ecotourism point out that public interest in the environment can be used to market a product, and at the same time this interest can be used to conserve the resources on which the product relies (Wight, 1994, pp39–41). Ecotourism implies resource use that minimizes negative environmental impacts and contributes to conservation (Wallace and Pierce, 1996, pp848–851). Environmental impacts can be reduced in a number of ways. One of the most direct forms of control in protected areas is the use of barriers and marked footpaths; permits, licences and charges prohibit or restrict certain types of behaviour. These direct measures can be used alongside indirect control, such as interpretation, to reduce inappropriate behaviour on a voluntary basis (Orams, 1995, pp83–85). It is important to ensure that such controls also take account of issues of equity. If pricing mechanisms, such as increased entry fees to a protected area, are used to restrict access, this can raise problems with social equity, since charges can exclude local people from their own national heritage while allowing easy access for overseas visitors.

The ecotourism label has been attached to many types of tourism ventures, ranging from 'soft' to 'hard' ecotourism. Operators in the Caribbean who offer a day or two of nature-based activities, while continuing to provide the traditional Caribbean sea, sand and sun product, are seen as exponents of soft ecotourism. Hard ecotourism is more closely associated with areas that cannot accommodate conventional tourism development, such as offshore reefs, mountainous interiors or undeveloped coastal areas (Weaver, 1994, pp162–164). Ecotourism and other forms of nature-based tourism may also result in negative environmental impacts. In areas that are remote and underdeveloped, overcrowding by tourists can cause significant environmental damage. For example, nature-based tourism in the Himalayas of Nepal has led to deforestation in the Annapurna Sanctuary as local people attempt to provide fuel-wood for trekker lodges (Boo, 1990, pp19–21).

It is clear that there are different types of businesses that lay claim to ecotourism. Cruise-Malloy and Fennel argue that ecotourism businesses conform to one of three types of organizational culture. 'Market ecotourism' refers to businesses that are characterized by ethical conduct and a commitment to sustainability, but only as a means of avoiding external punishment or receiving rewards. 'Socio-bureaucratic ecotourism' is equally concerned with financial viability, but the manner in which goals are pursued differs significantly from conventional businesses (for example, local customs will be important to the tour operators). 'Principled ecotourism' (or 'post-conventional') represents the most advanced moral archetype, which values sustainable and unobtrusive ecotourism, and expands its notions of justice by operating with global ecology in mind (Cruise-Malloy and Fennell, 1997, pp9–12).

The ways in which tour operators have taken the environmental perspective on board mean that, in effect, ecotourism has become a buzzword that assists businesses in marketing their products. Wight points out that the term is tacked on to promotional materials, usually for remote destinations. The tour in question may be a conventional trip that has merely been repackaged, providing the potential client with no basis on which to judge its environmental credentials (Wight, 1994, pp41–44). Businesses generally operate on the principle of maximizing profits; they will tend to emphasize the short-term economic benefit, which may or may not conflict with long-term environmental interests (Forsyth, 1995, pp225–228). Nevertheless, there is broad agreement about the kinds of positive benefits that ecotourism should bring to any locality.

In contrast to mass or conventional tourism development, ecotourism should have only positive financial impacts. In theory, ecotourism should reduce leakages and create tourism-related employment (Lindberg, Enriquez and Sproule, 1996, pp553–557). Ecotourism should also aim to direct economic benefits, which should complement rather than overwhelm or replace traditional practices, to local people; examples are farming and fishing. This means that the local economy will be more diversified and able to cope with changes or a reduction in tourism (Wallace and Pierce, 1996, pp848–851). Apart from direct employment in ecotourism developments, local people should also be able to take advantage of tourist demand for local crafts. One of the least-explored options for revenue capture is the sale of tourist merchandise; the motivations for buying local crafts are varied, ranging from souvenir hunting to the search for authenticity, or for an intrinsically beautiful object (Healy, 1994, pp137–140; Hitchcock and Teague, 2000; Stiles, 1994, pp106–111). It is also important to examine the sustainability of local craft production, particularly if crafts are made from wildlife products or scarce local woods. Ecotourism is often associated with allowing local communities a greater degree of participation in the planning and management of developments in their area. For example, local people can provide critical information to tourists if they are allowed to participate in interpretation services in protected areas (Bramwell and Lane, 1993, pp73–75). By allowing participation and providing real economic benefits, ecotourism is intended to increase support for conservation among residents living near protected areas and other fragile natural systems (Lindberg, Enriquez and Sproule, 1996, pp553–557). As part of this, ecotourism is intended to allow visitors the chance to learn about local culture, history and environment.

Ecotourism developments also imply smaller-scale and more specialist forms of accommodation. One of the criticisms of mass tourism is the effect that tourist accommodation has on the environment. Accommodation for ecotourists is intended to be more in keeping with local culture and heritage. Lodges are often sited in wilderness areas, and they tend to be small, locally owned, provide local employment and are spread over an area rather than being clustered in one resort (Moscardo, Morrison and Pearce, 1996, pp29–33). However, because ecotourism tends to be developed on a smaller scale, it can have significant impacts on the local economy but little impact on regional or national development (Boo, 1990, pp15–19). This means that under certain circumstances ecotourism fails to achieve one of the objectives that attract developing states – development with environmental care.

While a definition of ecotourism remains elusive, there is broad agreement on the types of impacts that environmentally sensitive tourism should have. In general, it should provide local economic benefits, conserve the environment, allow local participation in planning and management and be developed in a socially and culturally sensitive manner.

Conclusion

Tourism presents the developing world with a series of challenges that include costs and benefits. The advocates of tourism as a development strategy are very closely allied to neoliberal development theories that focus on market-led measures, such as liberalization, earning foreign exchange through international trade and privatization. The emphasis on tourism as a potential engine for growth and development is part of the resurgence in the popularity of theories of modernization and neoliberal economics. The criticisms of tourism as culturally, economically and environmentally damaging have led to an interest in alternative forms of tourism. This intersected with greater demand from the North for environmentally sensitive tours in developing countries. Ecotourism is promoted as an attempt to create a form of tourism that is environmentally sustainable, as well as culturally sensitive and economically beneficial. Ecotourism has been viewed by the tourism industry and by developing states as a means of conserving valuable environmental resources while encouraging economic growth. However, as with conventional tourism, ecotourism is associated with some negative impacts. Nevertheless, while ecotourism does not represent a radical departure in terms of development strategies, it is a significant shift in emphasis for the private sector and state agencies involved in tourism management.

It is clear that the environmental perspective contains a number of different ideologies. Debates about sustainable development often mask important ideological differences between various forms of environmental thought. 'Environmentalism' is a term that has been used to describe those who advocate a fundamental reshaping of social, political and economic structures, as well as those who express a commitment to environmental sustainability within current structures. The commitment to ecotourism as a means to develop and conserve natural resources simultaneously is closely related to a particular environmental ideology. The development of an ecotourism strategy does not challenge existing political, economic and social structures. Rather, it can be devised and implemented by businesses and governments with relative ease. Ecotourism constitutes a blue-green environmental policy, and can be categorized as weak sustainability. This book will now examine closely the politics of ecotourism and explore how it is firmly locked into neoliberal development strategies that necessarily require a shift to weak sustainability rather than strong sustainability.

CHAPTER 2

MISERY, SELF-INDULGENCE AND SELF-DENIAL

Introduction

Tourism and ecotourism are often discussed in terms of their structural organization, economic impact or the environmental credentials of green businesses. However, a vital part of any study of tourism is an examination of the attitudes and behaviour of the individual tourists. This chapter is concerned with an analysis of the attitudes ecotourists have towards their destinations and the behaviours they exhibit while on vacation. The increasing interest in environmentally sustainable holidays is clearly related to wider social, political, economic and environmental changes in industrialized societies. Broadly, these changes have been conceptualized as part of the switch to a period of reflexive modernization, in which modern society, through further processes of modernization, is dissolving the contours of industrial society and opening the way to another modernity, the risk society (see Chapter 1). Reflexive modernization means that people reflect upon and confront themselves with the effects of the risk society that cannot be dealt with or assimilated within industrial society (Beck, 1994, pp5–13; Smith, 1996, pp25–47). A belief in people's capacity to reflect on their own position and behaviour is important, because it implies that further environmental regulation by the state and private sector is unnecessary. Notions of self-reflexivity are particularly pertinent to ecotourism because proponents of that industry claim that ecotourists are keen to limit their consumption of environmental resources in order to minimize the negative impacts of their holiday-making.

Critiques levelled at conventional tourism development in developing societies portray it as an example of the over–consumption that characterizes Western societies, and is environmentally unsustainable and socially and culturally damaging to developing countries. Ecotourism is often hailed as a form of tourism development that avoids such pitfalls, and Belize promotes itself as the ecotourism destination for travellers with environmental and social concerns. Ecotourists are thought to be a new type of tourist, distinct from mass tourists because they are environmentally conscious as well as socially and culturally aware. Ecotourists are often defined as travellers who are willing to engage in self-denial in order to preserve the environment and reduce the social and economic impacts of their holiday-making activities. In theory they will reduce their consumption of natural resources, such as water and fuel-wood, and they are concerned to ensure that the local populace, and not multinational corporations, receive maximum financial benefits from tourism.

This chapter will firstly examine the notion of self-reflexivity and the risk society. Secondly, it will investigate the relevance of the idea of reflexivity by using a case study of ecotourists in Belize. It will explore the extent to which ecotourists in Belize reflect on their own position in the ecotourist economy and their own impact on the environment, and the motivations behind choosing independent forms of travel. However, while they are self-denying, ecotourists also engage in a form of ultimate self-indulgence, because they enjoy the rustic and basic nature of their travel experience, which provides a complete contrast to their home lifestyle. This chapter, then, will examine the notion of the self-denying ecotourist as the self-indulgent ecotourist.

The Risk Society and Self-reflexivity

Beck suggests that hazards in contemporary society differ from those in industrial society. These new hazards cannot be delimited spatially, temporally or socially; they cross national boundaries and encompass all social classes. They do not have a single causal factor, nor can particular institutions be held liable; instead, numerous anonymous actors cause hazards. As seen in Chapter 1, Beck argues that the lack of provision for catastrophes exposes a paradigm error: the belief that society remains prepared for industrial disasters which can be contained and their effects reversed. However, in the late 20th century environmental catastrophes began to have an irreversible impact, and in the 21st century it may become clear that they will not end in the foreseeable future. Beck terms this the 'risk society' (Beck, 1995; Szerzynski, 1999). In this kind of society, the bases and forms of modernity are open to scrutiny by all individuals. The shift to a risk society has also affected the way in which individuals think about their place in society and the impact of their actions. 'Reflexive' may be defined as 'marked by or capable of reflection' (Czyzewski, 1994, pp161–163). It also implies the capacity to confront one's own actions and modify one's behaviour to take account of the potential impacts of those actions (Beck, 1994, p5). Giddens argues that humans have the capacity to understand what they do while they do it, and their knowledge is crucial in determining behaviour towards the environment (Giddens cited in Redclift, 1992, p39). So, reflexivity is a layer of thinking that requires people to consider what they do naturally or unconsciously (Myerson and Rydin, 1996, pp1–4; Rydin, 1999).

Self-reflexivity is intimately bound up with ecotourism: ecotourists are thought to be sensitive travellers who seek to reduce the negative impacts of their holiday-making. The self-reflexive tourist has the potential to form the basis of environmentally sustainable tourism; if ecotourists are able to confront their own actions and modify their own behaviour towards the environment, it will reduce the need for institutional control over natural resources (Smith, 1996, pp25–27). For example, if self-reflexive ecotourists are given information about water shortages, they should be able to limit their consumption. Such self-limiting behaviour could encourage the sustainable development of natural resources, without the need for coercive controls from the state or private sector. In this way the concept of a self-reflexive ecotourist is closely related to blue-green ideas about the free-market management of the environment, because it casts the individual as a consumer rather than as a citizen. Ecotourists are expected to exercise political and economic power through individual choices about consumption, thereby contrasting with red-green notions of the individual exercising power through collective protest. Rather like blue-green ideas of environmental management, self-reflexivity is an individual rather than an collective activity and within the context of ecotourism it does not necessarily imply a fundamental reshaping of political and economic structures. Instead, self-reflexivity has much in common with rational-actor analysis, in which the individual is regarded as constantly engaged in complex cost–benefit calculations that inform their daily decisions. It means that individuals have a much greater part to play in decision making.

Cotgrove and Duff suggest that the increasing interest in environmental issues is partly due to the development of new social groups, interests and values that cut across traditional class-based alignments. These new social groups have attempted to challenge the central values of industrial society, particularly the emphasis on economic growth (Cotgrove and Duff, 1980, pp333–338). However, in general, the emergence of these new values has been linked with the middle classes in industrial society (Cotgrove and Duff, 1980, pp341–348; Munt, 1994a, pp101–105; Beck, 1995, pp53–57). Social changes in Western society have resulted in an expansion of the middle class and a contraction of the conventional working class. This means that there is an increased proportion of people with higher levels of education and professional or managerial jobs. These people also tend to be relatively mature, and this has led to a heightened interest in the environment and certain kinds of tourism. Ecotourists are generally defined as those with an interest in outdoor pursuits, and are financially comfortable, well-educated, older people with free time to travel (Ballantine and Eagles, 1994, pp210–212). There has been a decline in interest in highly structured and planned mass or package tours, and an increased demand for more flexible tourism that posits the environment as a major attraction (Urry, 1992, pp7–10). Ecotourism is attractive to certain social groups, and the demand for ecotourist holidays is directly linked to the rise in the environmental movement, which constitutes a new radicalism in the middle classes of the Western industrialized world. This is reflected in the switch from mass tourism to more individualized travel (Urry, 1990, pp47–50).

The increased interest in new forms of tourism is reflected in the growth of individuated, flexible, ecologically focused holidays. Munt suggests that this indicates a desire for holidays that are in keeping with postmodern culture. For example, tourism practices may no longer be simply about sightseeing, but include other activities such as trekking or mountain biking. Tourism has become interwoven with education and learning new skills. This is clear from the development of art and cultural tours, and of skiing and diving (Urry, 1990, p154). Similarly, Mowforth and Munt suggest that mass tourist interest in sea, sun and sand has been replaced by the enthusiasm of the independent tourist for trekking, trucking and travelling (Mowforth and Munt, 1998, pp125–155). The growth in environmental awareness in industrial societies has been accompanied by an expansion of the romantic gaze as tourism spreads worldwide; people increasingly search out, gaze upon and compare different places (Urry, 1992, pp13–16).

Postmodern societies are often concerned with notions of 'otherness', and ecotourism concerns itself with discovering the cultures of the developing world (Munt, 1994a, pp101–105). Ballantine and Eagles argue that ecotourists are more likely to want vacations that provide opportunities to learn about host cultures, societies or environments; they like to visit wilderness areas and see as much as possible in the time available (Ballantine and Eagles, 1994, pp210–212). This search for novelty and an 'authentic' pre-industrial nature distinguishes ecotourists from those who prefer mass tourism. Ecotourists also seek out experiences as an individual rather than as part of a group. This contributes to the romantic gaze, which is reliant upon being far removed from the crowd. Notions of the 'remote', the 'untouched', the 'unspoilt' and even the 'primitive' are used as markers of ecotourist desirability, and the destinations are presented as being the antithesis of industrial society. Local host cultures are often portrayed as extensions of the natural world (Edwards, 1996, pp200–204; Dann, 1996b, pp67–71; Mowforth and Munt, 1998, pp44–83). In industrialized societies the desire for holidays has become a felt need. This need turns into motivations, which translate into expectations. For example, tourists fully expect their trip to be a getting-away-from-it-all experience (Gnoth, 1997, pp286–300). Of course, people travel for a number of different reasons. Travel is conceptualized as escape, a means of exploring other cultures; it broadens the mind, and acts as a means of self-discovery; it represents a period of hedonism, happiness or freedom (Krippendorf, 1987, pp22–28; Dann, 1996a, pp101–134). People travel to seek a temporary refuge from the cycle of everyday life, which revolves around work, home and free time (Krippendorf, 1987, pp3–19). Novelty-seeking has been identified as one of the major motivations for tourists; they travel because they want to experience something new or different. This motivation is particularly important for ecotourists, who specifically seek out new experiences, but it also serves another purpose, because it can be complementary to the need for status recognition from others (Lee and Crompton, 1992 pp732–738). However, turning to the case of ecotourists in Belize, the purpose of this chapter is to examine the environmental attitudes and behaviours of ecotourists, and their relationship to the concepts of self-reflexivity and the risk society.

Interviewing People at Leisure

Firstly, it is necessary to discuss some of the difficulties encountered in exploring ecotourists' capacity for self-reflexive behaviour. The difficulties associated with self-reflexivity and vacationing were especially interesting. In particular, the reluctance of many ecotourists to engage in interviews indicated that one of the major motivations for ecotourist holidays was relaxation, getting away from it all and a desire to engage in hedonistic pursuits. In this respect, ecotourists differ little from the mass tourists they want to distinguish themselves from. Since ecotourists are assumed to be self-reflexive and concerned about their environmental, economic and cultural impact on the host society, it might have been expected that they would be more than willing to engage with a study aimed at reducing the environmental effects of their vacationing. However, ecotourists were keen to point out that they were just in Belize to relax and the idea of being interviewed by an academic about environmental problems was not a priority. For example, one ecotourist stated that he wanted reading time on his vacation because he did not have the time in his everyday working life.[1] Similarly, another ecotourist justified her vacation as a time to relax because she worked in a high-pressure environment on Wall Street and had felt the need to take a break.[2] Thus, ecotourists felt (justifiably) able to refuse to participate in anything that might require consideration, mental effort or reflecting on problems. For example, one ecotourist, in response to questions about how she viewed the impact of ecotourism on developing countries, remarked: 'Oh no, now you are going to make me think'.[3] Similarly, a group of conservation volunteers who perceived themselves as ecotourists were also recalcitrant interviewees. This was partially because of a deteriorating relationship between their organization, Coral Cay Conservation, and the University of Belize. However, the difficulties faced by the researcher are related to the idea of a conservation holiday that is supposed to be a change from the normal pattern of everyday life and the expected pattern of holiday-making. One volunteer explained her initial reticence thus: 'We just seem to be doing everything for everybody here and we just don't feel like doing anyone else a favour.'[4]

Ecotourists in Belize were quite clear about their intention of forgetting about the everyday problems they faced at home. This was significant because it demonstrated the level of importance ecotourists give to their 'right' to relax. It is clear that they regard a holiday as essential for mental and physical health, and as a key part of coping with working life.

At another level there were entirely practical reasons for ecotourists declining to be interviewed. One of the main difficulties in the more expensive resorts was that the clients were nervous that any person who directly approached them had a hidden agenda. This was understandable since one important theme in Ambergris Caye was property speculation by foreign (mainly US) interests. A significant proportion of the ecotourists who visited Belize were wealthy and were worried about being approached with property deals or by tour guides offering trips to the reef. For example, one ecotourist commented that since he had had an opportunity to interact with the researcher socially for a couple of days, he knew that it was safe to allow an interview to proceed, but prior to that he had been concerned that it would ultimately lead to a sales and marketing agenda.[5]

Since the strategy of directly approaching ecotourists failed to produce many interviews, the research required a new and creative approach. This involved establishing social links with ecotourists by taking trips and meeting them in bars and restaurants. In general, ecotourists were able to talk at length in the evenings in a relaxed social atmosphere. This also meant that the interview had to be presented as a light and entertaining set of questions that would not prevent them relaxing. Interviewing one ecotourist in a social setting often meant that other tourists became interested in what was going on. Days on which trips were cancelled due to poor weather conditions also proved to be fruitful because ecotourists were left with nothing to occupy their time.

Image and Desire in Ecotourism

The question about why ecotourists had chosen Belize as a destination was very important. Travel is partially motivated by representations of destinations through, for example, photographs, advertisements and postcards. Often, the exoticism contained in a photograph influences and is shaped by the ecotourist process itself; the photograph helps to create and sustain tourist desire and fantasy, and the expansion of long-haul travel to developing countries is highly dependent on such imagery to attract visitors (Edwards, 1996, pp197–204; Markwell, 1997, pp151–155; Dann, 1996b, pp67–71). Part of this is to do with the postmodern search for authenticity, which is particularly evident in ecotourism; it relies on promoting unspoilt and remote wildernesses. Such images enhance the belief that the ecotourist will be able to leave the concerns of home society behind and have an authentic wilderness experience (Dann, 1996a, pp247–249).

Broadly, ecotourists had been attracted to Belize through contact with friends or relatives who had previously travelled to the country, rather than as a result of advertising and marketing, which had played a minor role. This was reflected in ecotourists' interest in reading about a destination before they arrived, and they were generally informed about Belize by guidebooks, especially from the Lonely Planet and Rough Guide series, which provide much more information than travel agents.[6] Another source of information was the internet: a number of interviewees stated that they had looked up various websites for information about where to stay and where to visit, as well as using email to book hotels.[7] However, a number of those interviewed also remarked that they did not know a great deal about Belize before they arrived, and had expected it to be more like the rest of Central America. This was particularly the case with ecotourists who were travelling through from Mexico, Honduras or Guatemala to Belize.[8]

A significant number of those interviewed stated that their primary motivation for coming to Belize was to dive on the coral reefs.[9] There were some tourists who were on a longer trip through Central America, and they mentioned that the attraction of Belize was that it is a Caribbean beach on which they could have a break and relax during their travels through the region.[10] Some of this latter category did dive while in Belize, but others were satisfied with snorkelling on the reef or river trips to see manatees (indigenous sea cows) and Mayan ruins.[11]

Regardless of the types of activities that they engaged in, it was clear that the natural environment and archaeological sites were the major attraction for visitors. However, their image of Belize as a vacation destination was informed by stereotyped representations of the Caribbean and Central America. Ecotourist expectations and the imagery they used to describe the islands definitely reflected the stereotyped representations of the Caribbean as a destination with silver sand, palm trees and turquoise water. For example, a number of ecotourists stated that Belize had conformed to their expectations of the Caribbean, as constituted by islands and sunshine.[12] For example, one ecotourist remarked, 'My image was pirates, seriously, and palm trees.'[13] Another part of the image is of the Caribbean as filled with reggae music and as a 'relaxed place to chill out',[14] or as 'unhurried, where tourists are forced to relax'.[15] It was notable that, in general, ecotourists wanted to see certain images, including palm trees. Beaches (or the lack of them) were mentioned frequently, and another recurrent theme was the desire to gaze upon 'exotic' peoples, whom they identified as indigenous Mayans and Rastafarians.[16]

The lists of things to see and do handed out by tour operators turned out to be significant. When diving or snorkelling, ecotourists were keen to see the spectacular marine life on the list, rather than a general coral reef scene with numerous small fish. There was a noticeable desire to see larger or more brightly coloured marine life, such as lobster, barracuda, sharks or parrotfish.[17] The desire to see large fish or wrecks is rather like the marine equivalent of the 'African Big Five' on which the wildlife safari industry depends. Those involved in ecotourism and conservation in Belize have recognized the importance of allowing ecotourists easy access to spectacular marine life. The importance of Shark Ray Alley and Hol Chan Marine Reserve trips for snorkellers, and the Amigos Wreck dive or Blue Hole dive for divers, illustrate this. Shark Ray Alley and the Amigos Wreck are well known in San Pedro town (Ambergris Caye) for the relative ease of shark- and ray-spotting. In addition, the Amigos Wreck was specifically sunk by the Amigos Del Mar Dive Shop because ecotourists enquired about whether there were any wreck dives in the vicinity of the island, and it was intended to reduce pressure on other popular dive sites that were becoming over-crowded. The Amigos Wreck is currently one of the most requested ecotourist dives.[18] When the weather was unsuitable for diving and snorkelling, there was a feeling of frustration and a pent-up demand for diving among ecotourists. As a result they requested that dive shops should continue to run a tour even during very poor weather conditions because they had come specifically to dive every day.[19] In response to this problem, tour operators and conservation groups were involved in a plan to create an artificial reef to attract marine life on the sheltered mangrove side of Ambergris Caye, because it would allow ecotourists to dive and snorkel regardless of the weather and sea conditions.[20]

Ecotourists have a list of sights that they want to see in Belize before they return home with new tales to share with their families and peer groups. One ecotourist remarked that before coming to Belize he had 'done the tubing in a river in San Ignacio, we saw Mayan ruins in Yucatan (Mexico) and we can tell you all about the pyramids at Tikal (Guatemala) and Caracol (Belize)'.[21] Similarly, another ecotourist stated that his trip to Belize was motivated by his wish to see a big cat: 'that was the reason for coming to Belize, I want to see a jaguar. It is that thing of ruins, rainforest and reef.'[22] The phrase 'ruins, rainforest and reef' is significant because it is a marketing slogan used by the Belize Tourist Board (BTB) and private ecotour operators to promote the country internationally as an ecotourism destination.

For divers, the trip to the Blue Hole can be an all-important experience. One recently qualified diver expressed great disappointment that his inability to equalize the pressure in his ears to that of the surrounding water (resulting in ear and sinus problems) meant that he had to abandon his attempt to dive the Blue Hole.[23] Similarly, another ecotourist remarked: 'I like wreck diving and deep diving. I have seen enough fish now. I like the adrenaline really.'[24] For some ecotourists it is the experience of diving or snorkelling on the reef in Belize, rather than the marine life they can see, which is of importance. For example, one interviewee suggested that she liked to look at the coral formations rather than the fish to experience the beauty of the marine world, which she found to be a very spiritual experience.[25]

Reflecting on the Impact of Tourism

In order to investigate whether people demonstrated their knowledge as agents, it was important to find out whether ecotourists confronted the impacts of their own presence in a developing country. With a few exceptions, the majority of ecotourists interviewed did not reflect on and confront the results of their own actions. One ecotourist stated that if he were given information about a particular country that implied that his visit would spoil the country, he would not go on holiday there. In fact he decided not to go to the Galapagos because he had seen a report about the negative impact that an increase in tourism had had on the islands.[26]

What was striking was the degree of similarity between ecotourist responses to questions about the advantages and disadvantages of ecotourism. It was particularly difficult to elicit negative attitudes to ecotourism from ecotourists, because if they were concerned by the impact of their travel to another country then they might not have travelled to Belize in the first place. Ecotourism was perceived and constructed in interviews as economically beneficial, a source of employment and foreign exchange for developing countries.[27] Ecotourism was favourably perceived as a clean industry that avoided the environmental costs of more traditional smoke-stack industries.[28] It was clear in interviews that ecotourists talked of their destinations and experiences mainly in terms of their own benefits. One interviewee summed it up as a case of ecotourists wanting to see somewhere different and less developed than their home countries; but he wanted a certain level of comfort. While it was refreshing that an American drink, Gatorade, was not in all the shops, it did not stop him from actually buying Gatorade in Belize.[29] This was nowhere more apparent than when ecotourists were invited to consider the possible problems associated with choosing a developing country as a holiday destination. The very fact that ecotourists were in Belize meant that they were in a sense obliged to think of ecotourism as beneficial to themselves and to the country they were visiting.

However, some ecotourists did reflect on the fact that they were, as ecotourists, being asked to offer opinions on ecotourism and its drawbacks.[30] Where criticisms were offered of the tourist industry it was in terms of the need to control resort construction to prevent Belize becoming like 'another Cancun'. In fact Cancun was commonly constructed and presented by interviewees as an example of the kind of tourist resort that travellers to Belize did not favour.[31] Where the industry was criticized it was for failing to meet an ideal image of ecotourism development as expressed by ecotourists themselves. For example, one ecotourist expressed her desire to see Belize City reworked to fit tourist images of a cute colonial town with quaint inns and shops that maximized its charm for visitors.[32] A number of ecotourists complained about the highly visible litter problem on the islands, but their own role in creating the litter was not reflected upon. Instead, local people were singled out for criticism for failing to address the problem and dispose of it properly.[33]

This also intersected with ideas about how ecotourism might be affecting the local culture. One ecotourist was concerned by the cultural impact of ecotourism on local society, and she expressed sadness about what she termed a 'bastardized' culture in Thailand as a result of the growth in tourism. She noted that as a result of such cultural changes it was not worth visiting Thailand any more because it could not give an authentic experience of a different culture.[34] It was clear from the interviews that, with few exceptions, ecotourists did not reflect on and confront the impacts of their own actions as ecotourists. They preferred to gloss over the apparent problems and realities of a development strategy based on their desire to travel overseas.

Ecotourists can replicate the same problems as the mass tourists that they are expected to replace. In particular, the problems created by the meeting of very different cultures have been highlighted. New forms of tourism such as ecotourism, adventure tourism and cultural tourism have become increasingly intrusive and dependent on the destination community, and this intrusion has resulted in the development of uneven power relationships between the host and origin communities (Craik, 1995, pp87–89). Ecotourists are thought to be interested in finding out about local cultures and experiencing social exchanges with host societies. Indeed, ecotourists in Belize did express an interest in meeting local people as part of a real and authentic experience of Belizean culture, as opposed to engaging only in staged events for ecotourists. For example, one interviewee stated that because ecotourism was underdeveloped in Belize one had to meet local people instead of other ecotourists, and that it was interesting to interact with another culture.[35] Local people, as defined by ecotourists, were very friendly and easy to meet.[36] However, it was clear that ecotourists were also hesitant about actually meeting local people, and, to a degree, some ecotourists resorted to negative racial stereotypes of local people as the exotic 'other' and a danger to travellers. For example, one interviewee remarked that he did not want to meet black Belizeans because other travellers had forewarned him that they could be aggressive and annoying.[37]

Similarly, the Rastafarian community suffered from negative stereo-typing.

Krippendorf argues that people do not really leave their every-day life behind while on holiday. They do not suddenly become different people when they travel; their behaviour on holiday is shaped by everyday styles of living (Krippendorf, 1987, pp30–34). However, it was clear from the behaviour of ecotourists in Belize that they felt free from the everyday constraints on their behav-iour, and enjoyed the sense of letting off steam. For example, divers were a difficult group for the researcher to find, since they were busy diving as many times as was possible in their vacation, and as a result they were not to be found socializing in the evening until their final night.[38] Yet when their final night came, divers were to be found drinking to excess in the bars to make up for lost time. This was also the case with the ecotourist volunteers brought to Belize by Coral Cay Conservation; they indulge in purely hedonis-tic activities including excessive drinking on a regular basis. This, coupled with an atmosphere of sexual freedom, led to complaints from the host organization, University College of Belize, and an attempt to make the island alcohol-free.[39] The fondness for exces-sive drinking and for drug-taking (especially marijuana, but occasionally cocaine) caused some concern among island dwellers. The reputation of Caye Caulker as a laid-back place where marijuana is freely available and controls are lax limited its proposed development as a family destination for high-spending ecotourists. In addition, because of the demands of ecotourists, an interest group that is economically dependent on the drug trade and politically and financially backed by the 'coke and party set' of expatriates has developed on the islands.[40]

The importance of the self and of self-indulgence to ecotourists was also apparent in the obvious engagement with the sex industry in Belize. Rather than being culturally sensitive, a number of ecotourists replicate the difficulties associated with mass tourism and its attendant problems of sex tourism and drug culture. Much has been written about the expansion of sex tourism in developing countries. Pearce argues that culture shock is inevitable with tourism, and that rule-breaking by visitors may be unintentional and thus forgiven by hosts. However, when visitors continue with their own social rules while disregarding the sensitivities of the local populace, that is cultural arrogance (Pearce, 1995, pp143–145; Brown, 1992, pp361–370; Pattullo, 1996, pp84–92). Drug-use by ecotourists and sexual contact between local people and ecotourists were two themes that were not easily accessible in interviews. However, it was clear from observation and interviews with tour guides that drug-use and sex tourism were regularly engaged in by ecotourists.[41] Occasionally the topics did arise in interviews, mainly when ecotourists complained of constant offers of drugs or sex.[42] One ecotourist was keen to demonstrate that his ecotourism was based around the desire to take cocaine and smoke marijuana for two weeks.[43] The cultural impact of the advent of tourism on the islands of Belize was self-evident; the ecotourists' search for sexual adventure intersected with the macho male culture in Belize, which values the ability to simultaneously maintain a number of girlfriends. This was nowhere more apparent than in the regularly repeated phrase used by male tour guides on the islands, 'Don't you want a vacation boyfriend?'[44]

The search for the exotic by white Western ecotourists as well as Belizean tour guides explained the prevalence of sex tourism. Ecotourists and locals alike commented on the highly visible and extremely common holiday relationships between ecotourists and locals, or between two ecotourists. For example, one ecotourist indicated the ease of meeting local men as 'a girl on your own', and she also expressed a desire for sexual adventure on the island with a black or Hispanic (rather than a white) man.[45] Other female ecotourists found the attitude of male ecotourists and male locals difficult to cope with. One stated that she thought the attitude was barbaric and indicated that men in the ecotourist resorts (locals and ecotourists) felt they could behave any way they liked.[46] Indeed the researcher herself was constantly proposi-tioned; in general a polite refusal was sufficient, but on some occasions the situation very quickly became hostile and volatile. For example, the researcher had a lemon wedge from a drink violently pushed in her mouth by a male ecotourist attempting to proposition her, while another male tourist felt able to shove a camera down the researcher's T-shirt in his search for adventur-ous holiday photos.

It was clear that ecotourist and locals alike perceived this to be normal behaviour in an ecotourist resort. Ecotourists were divorced from the everyday social constraints of home and so they felt they would suffer no long-term consequences as a result of bad behaviour. This was confirmed by the perception that local tour guides had of ecotourists. For example, one tour guide pointed out a particular ecotourist and remarked that she was just like all the other white women that came to the islands: she said she was 'good' but in fact she was 'bad' (his terminology) and would have sex with anyone.[47] Whether this was accurate is not important; the significance of this remark is that this is the perception of ecotourists held by those who worked in the ecotourism industry. This view was also expressed by a hotel manager who commented on the prevalence of holiday relationships between white women tourists and male Rastas on the island. She stated that such relationships were extremely common, and that it was clear that the island gigolos merely waited for fresh groups of ecotourists to arrive on planes and boats each week and targeted a particular woman (usually one travelling alone or with another woman) from the moment they arrived.[48] In fact one ecotourist stated that he could see there were lots of ecotourists who came to the coastal areas of Belize 'just to get laid by the island people.'[49] One interviewee stated that he was looking for local women prostitutes as part of his vacation experience, and he justified this to himself and fellow travellers as contributing to the island economy.[50]

Such behaviour is normally associated with mass tourism resorts rather than with the supposedly more socially and culturally aware independent traveller who is concerned about minimizing the impact of his or her presence in developing countries. Ecotourists have been hailed as a new form of tourists, but their cultural impact in Belize is still highly visible. Rather like their mass tourism counterparts, some ecotourists travel to developing countries to sexually exploit local male, female, adult or child bodies. Any separation into ecotourists, sex tourists and drug tourists does not provide a very accurate account of the types of activities engaged in by ecotourists, and fails to acknowledge that ecotourists often replicate the problems associated with mass tourism even if it is on a smaller scale.

Environmental Beliefs and Behaviours

The environmental attitudes of ecotourists were also explored in interviews. Obviously, the degree to which an individual is environmentally aware will determine the extent to which he or she will behave in an environmentally responsible manner. As a result, a great deal of writing about environmentalism is concerned with the development of environmental awareness. Beck suggests that the shift to a risk society has also affected the way in which individuals think about their place in society and the impact of their actions (Beck, 1994, pp5–13; Smith, 1996, pp25–47). This transformation has become apparent in the rise of the environmental movement. However, while some environmentalists have concentrated on the use of political, economic and technological instruments to solve environmental problems, it has become clear that a change in individual behaviour is also necessary. Debates about environmentally sustainable tourism have concentrated on the ways in which tour operators and state agencies can modify their practices to produce a more environmentally friendly form of travel. Yet Krippendorf suggests that the responsibility for creating a more sustainable form of tourism lies with individuals, who must become aware of their own motives for travelling, their personal desires and the concerns of other people (Krippendorf, 1987, pp140–148). This has led to studies that examine the nature of environmental attitudes and how they are reflected in environmentally friendly behaviour. This also forms part of the debate about the shift from citizen to consumer (Lengkeek, 1993, pp7–32). The emphasis on consumer roles means that individual behaviour, rather than group behaviour, has become an important area. This behaviour must be evaluated to determine whether environmental care and sustainability can be achieved without coercive means.

The specifics of people's attitudes towards the environment are important in understanding behaviour; they help to determine whether individuals take action to protect the environment (Hagvar, 1994, pp515–518). Numerous studies have attempted to categorize environmental beliefs, and to find out why certain social groups are more likely to hold such beliefs than others (Cotgrove and Duff, 1980, pp333–338; Schultz and Stone, 1994, pp25–28;

Stern, Dietz and Kalof, 1995, pp322–348; Schahn and Holzer, 1990, pp767–786; Wall, 1995, pp294–316; Davidson and Freudenburg, 1996, pp302–339). In addition, theories of altruistic behaviour have been extended into arguments that a person is more likely to act in a environmentally responsible way if they are aware of the potentially harmful consequences of a particular behaviour (Stern, Dietz and Kalof, 1993, pp322–348; Sparks and Shepherd, 1992, p398). The difficulty of evaluating environmental attitudes is that it relies on self-reported behaviour. People tend to over-report the extent of their environmentally friendly attitudes and actions in order to be perceived as engaging in socially desirable behaviours (Scott and Willits, 1994, pp248–250).

Various attempts have been made to measure the extent of people's environmental beliefs; the set of criteria used by Dunlap and Van Liere has come to be accepted as a means of doing this. Dunlap and Van Liere argue that the dominant social paradigm (DSP) consists of traditional values, including belief in the abundance of environmental resources, economic growth and prosperity, faith in science and technology and limited government. The DSP has been challenged by what they term the new environmental paradigm (NEP), which encompasses ideas about 'Spaceship Earth' and steady-state economics. The NEP scale is a series of statements that are used to test a respondent's acceptance of environmental ideas. The scale includes statements such as: 'humans are serious abusers of the environment'; 'when humans interfere with nature it often produces disastrous consequences'; and 'humans have the right to modify nature to suit their own needs' (Dunlap and Van Liere, 1978, pp10–19; Dunlap and Van Liere, 1984, pp1013–1028; Luzar, Diagne, Gan and Henning, 1995, pp544–555). However, this method should be treated with caution. The criteria in the NEP reveal whether a particular individual subscribes to a particular environmental ideology, rather than demonstrating whether they are environmentally aware per se. People can cite a number of reasons for a particular belief or behaviour, and these reasons can often be in conflict with each other. It is important not to assume that a certain type of behaviour can be consistently attributed to a particular reason or motivation.

Ecotourists were asked about the extent of their environmental knowledge of Belize, and the NEP scale was used to provide a degree of information about their broad environmental attitudes. The ecotourists who visited Belize were generally not members of any environmental organizations, and they described themselves as broadly interested in the environment but not at all activists.[51] It was that the environmental debate had had an impact on the way in which they perceived their environment and the problems that face it. When asked to respond to the NEP statements, most ecotourists had difficulty in deciding whether they strongly agreed or disagreed. The fact that the environmental debate has become more complex over the last 20 years was also reflected. Rather than providing a rapid response, interviewees offered criticisms of the statements. Indeed, some ecotourists said that they thought the environmental debate had clearly moved on from the statements (which were drawn up in the 1970s).[52] 'Human beings have the right to modify the natural environment to suit their own needs' was the statement that prompted most discussion. The tourists were concerned to point out that humans did not have the right to modify the natural environment, but that they did so anyway.[53] In fact, one ecotourist remarked that the NEP statements merely explored which environmental ideology a person subscribed to, and that they were based on pseudo-cultural biases prevalent in the Western world.[54]

Ecotourists had a degree of environmental knowledge about Belize, but this was mostly confined to an awareness of the fragility of coral reefs. This reminds us that tourists were having a 'getting-away-from-it-all' experience; they expressed a desire to forget about environmental problems in their pursuit of enjoyment. Ecotourist knowledge about the coral reefs came from two main sources: guidebooks or background reading and tour guides in Belize.[55] Most associated Belize with being able to snorkel or dive on the second-largest barrier reef in the world.[56] Experienced divers tended to demonstrate a wider knowledge of reef ecology and of the activities that should and should not be allowed on coral reefs. For example, one interviewee was concerned at the amount of damage caused by trainee and newly qualified divers who, because of their inability to control their buoyancy, frequently crash into coral or grab on to it to steady themselves.[57]

In general, levels of environmental awareness were limited to very broad notions of reef fragility and the acknowledgement that marine life should not be touched on a snorkel or dive trip. Nevertheless, some ecotourists were even unaware of this. One diver commented that he could not understand why some other tourists had been upset with him for picking up a starfish; he wondered just how fragile such a creature could be.[58] This issue was causing concern for some tour guides and diving instructors. Some tour guides remarked that, despite being told not to touch the fish, some tourists still went ahead and did it.[59] It was clear that ecotourists tended to over-report their adherence to environmental behaviours in an attempt to be perceived as engaging in socially desirable behaviours (Scott and Willits, 1994, pp248–250). However, some tour guides do not inform their clients that they should not touch the coral or the fish; in fact, the more environmentally aware guides were concerned that their less vigilant colleagues ran the risk of destroying the basis of their common livelihood.[60]

Most of the ecotourists said that they thought it was important for individuals to behave in an environmentally conscious way, and in many ways they perceived their trip as their contribution to conservation in Belize. This idea of self-limiting consumption appeared to be popular with them.[61] However, despite this they also argued frequently that individual efforts, while necessary for marine conservation, were not sufficient on their own, and that government and private-sector regulations were necessary. For example, one couple remarked that if ecotourists were ignorant of the environmental sensitivity of the reef, then it was up to the tour guides and government to provide information and control behaviour.[62] Ecotourists were concerned that the coral reef and marine life should be conserved, but in many ways this was motivated by a desire to maintain the reef's beauty rather than by a belief in conservation for its intrinsic value.[63] Some remarked that they would visit Belize again to see the reef before it was destroyed, or before the country became too popular with tourists and over-crowded.[64] Reef conservation was clearly constructed and justified in terms of self-satisfaction: saving the reef is important in order to ensure that future generations of ecotourists will be able to gaze upon it.

Self-denial as Self-indulgence

The idea of self-denial in ecotourism, to ensure that vacationing has minimal negative impacts, is evident in the forms of travel that ecotourists choose. In choosing independent or physically strenuous holidays, ecotourists deny themselves the comforts of luxury travel as part of a journey of self-discovery and self-development. However, these 'rugged' holidays are still highly organized, supervised by tour companies either at home or in the host country, and so tourists are insulated from the more uncomfortable realities of life and travel in developing societies. The people who visit Belize are particularly interested in unstructured travel. It was noticeable that a number of those interviewed had previous experience of travelling in developing countries. It was clear that they had formerly been backpackers and were keen to continue in the same spirit. Their choice of destination and form of travel also reflected the fact that the majority were middle- to high-income earners, and they had chosen backpacker-style trips that offered a greater degree of comfort. One interviewee stated that he had previously travelled to Southern Africa, and that he liked this kind of travel because it was all about discovery and self-discovery.[65] Indeed, the use of extended periods of independent travel to take a break from everyday life and reflect on one's own self was a theme that recurred frequently in the interviews. A number of the volunteers on Calabash Caye were taking a year out before university, or taking a career break while they decided on future directions.[66] Some ecotourists interviewed on Ambergris Caye and Caye Caulker were taking an extended backpacker-style trip through Central America.[67]

Again, it can be seen that self-satisfaction is still the ecotourist's over-riding concern: the self-denying tourist is in fact the self-indulgent ecotourist. Rojek argues that satisfaction through leisure is elusive, because consumer culture confines the individual to a lifetime of false and unfulfilling desires and practices (Rojek, 1995, pp73–75). The ultimate commodified leisure escape is tourism; travel to exotic developing countries is portrayed as paradise gained, but such an ideal is never realized and so the individual is left with an unsatisfactory search for identity (Wearing and

Wearing, 1992, pp4–8). Ecotourism is an expression of consumer culture: like the choice of clothes, it is a signifier of social distinction, and the consumer (or ecotourist) responds to a market of signs rather than a market of goods (Rojek, 1995, pp75–86). Destinations fall in and out of fashion. The decision to travel is not an innate impulse, but is developed under the influence of the social environment. As such, it is a social 'position marker', like a second car or home, and indicates a person's social standing (Krippendorf, 1987, pp17–19).

For ecotourists, being environmentally aware is an important signifier of social position. For others, an independent holiday is all about retracing the steps that they had taken in their youth.[68] One couple said that, now they were both earning salaries, they were willing to pay a little bit more to be independent.[69] In some ways, those who visit Belize can be more adequately described as nature-based adventure tourists rather than ecotourists, because most of them go to Belize for watersports, such as diving, or for the experience of the trip itself. They expect to return home with a new set of travellers' tales about great moments or total disasters. It was clear that the idea of going somewhere off the beaten track appealed to them.[70] Many of them were keen to point out that they had simply bought a plane ticket and decided where to stay once they had arrived; they said that they liked to determine their own pace of travel and make their own decisions, rather than being dictated to by a package tour operator.[71] Of course, ecotourists are can only choose from a range of options offered by tour operators and hoteliers. For example, conservation volunteers on Calabash Caye pointed out that they liked to travel at their own pace and be independent,[72] but their days were clearly ordered with a set timetable of meals, diving and recreation.

For ecotourists, the need for status recognition is related to the desire to be seen to take an environmentally sustainable holiday that is in keeping with their environmental beliefs and practices as demonstrated in their home environment. This also relates to their willingness to take holidays that offer only low levels of physical comfort. Thus, these tourists are actually indulging themselves. Ecotours are usually rather expensive, reinforcing the notion of its use as a social position marker. It was noticeable that the tourists often wore T-shirts from previous holiday destinations; among the most common were Zimbabwe and Costa Rica, which are also off the beaten track but are still fairly well developed with access to transport, banking facilities and good international-standard hotels and ecolodges. Ecotourists and other tourists who define themselves as independent travellers tend to differentiate themselves from those who choose mass tourism by referring to themselves as travellers rather than tourists.

The interviewees presented themselves as people interested in the process of travel itself; their vacation experience was about self-improvement and self-recreation, and was a time to reflect on their own personality. Thus they maintained that their holiday-making was different from conventional forms of travel. One remarked on this idea of travel as a journey of self-discovery.[73] Travelling through a country rather than staying in a single resort was also perceived as a way of getting to know oneself, and testing one's own reactions to the problems and challenges that independent touring offers.[74]

This distinction between travellers and tourists was also apparent in the notion of self-denial. The combination of vacation time with learning experiences or character-building activities was common. Many ecotourists use their holiday in Belize to learn to scuba dive or to gain more diving experience.[75] Similarly, in the UK there has been increasing interest in actively volunteering for charities rather than passively donating money.[76]

Urry suggests that contemporary tourist practices are cultural, in that they comprise of signs, images, texts and discourses. In addition, he argues that identity is now formed through consumption and play rather than through employment (Urry, 1994, pp233–236). In this way, a holiday constitutes a positional good in which destinations are consumed because they are meant to convey superior status and taste (Urry, 1990, pp44–47). Munt suggests that ecotourism brings its own set of problems, arguing that 'ecotourist' is a misnomer and that independent, environmentally oriented travellers could be renamed 'egotourists'. For Munt, middle-class tourists from Western societies have increasingly aestheticized and fetishized developing countries as tourist destinations, and have glossed over the realities (Munt, 1994a; Munt,

1994b, pp49–60; Mowforth and Munt, 1998, pp125–187). He argues that egotourists search for a style of travel that is reflective of their own perception of themselves as having an alternative lifestyle, and which is capable of enhancing and maintaining their cultural capital (Munt, 1994a, pp105–108). For example, a number of ecotourists interviewed in Belize were concerned to point out that they were not 'the Cancun types', and they differentiated themselves on the social level through the consumption of a vacation in a very different kind of resort. One interviewee identified package tourists as 'dodgy people'.[77]

For the ecotourists interviewed in Belize, the self and the satisfaction of the self were the central determining factors in their vacation. In reflecting on their environmental impact they tended to examine the immediate and visible signs of their presence. This was indicated in interviews with divers who repeatedly chanted the slogan 'leave only bubbles', and then assured themselves and those around them that this rule governed their behaviour on a dive.[78] But ecotourists did not reflect on the environmental impact of the construction of hotels, the use of airlines, the manufacture of diving equipment, the consumption of imported goods or even something as visible as taking a motor-boat out to the reef, which polluted the water with petrol. Divers tend to desire a tactile experience, and so it is not uncommon for marine life (including endangered turtles and corals) to be touched, occasionally with the encouragement of the diving instructors. For example, on one diving expedition that I joined, the instructor found a loggerhead turtle and chased it through coral canyons, finally kicking it in the face in order to make it turn back towards me so that I could touch it. The issue of tourists touching and harassing marine life is a highly controversial and politicized issue in Belize. Clearly, ecotourists tend to reflect on their impact at an individual, small-scale and self-centred level, but they do not reflect on the wider implications of their presence in Belize.

Conservation volunteers in Belize definitely perceived their choice of a conservation diving holiday as a means to enhance the environment while experiencing the pleasures of leisure time away from the pressure of their home societies. Coral Cay Conservation provides conservation diving holidays, on which volunteers learn to scuba dive and undertake surveys of fish populations, with the aim of establishing fishing quotas and protected areas for Belize.[79] The volunteers saw their time on the island as a period of learning about themselves, as well as assisting conservation in a developing country. They also referred to the attraction of the very basic nature of their existence on Calabash Caye. This search for the novel, for something very different from life in industrialized societies, was reflected in remarks about enjoying the hardships of Belize. One conservation volunteer who called herself an ecotourist said that she chose Belize rather than a project in the Philippines because life was much rougher in Belize. She perceived the Philippines project as more luxurious because there were employees to do laundry and cleaning, whereas Belize 'seemed more hard-core, more self-sufficient, so I thought I would go the whole hog'.[80] However, the volunteers undertook their duties and regimented lifestyle with relish. It was clear that, rather like other independent travellers who are attracted by basic accommodation and food, the volunteers enjoyed the communal misery. The spirit of camaraderie was important; working together closely resulted in a strong group mentality.[81] This was encouraged by the organization's insistence on teamwork in all aspects of running the camp.[82]

Yet this self-denial is actually self-indulgence, since enjoyment was derived from the hardships. One interviewee stated that the problems he had faced while travelling, while unwelcome at the time, were what really made the vacation experience: he said that his flights had been disrupted, and that 'once I am home I would not change all the experiences for the world. It is the experience [that matters], and I would not miss it when I come to places like this.'[83] The importance of travellers' tales revolving around disasters and amusing incidents was clear, and this can be related to the need to intellectualize vacationing as character-building. Such tales are also good material for a curriculum vitae and can be used to impress peer groups at home. A number of conservation volunteers remarked that they had chosen a conservation holiday because it looks good on a curriculum vitae, or would assist them in gaining a place at university or employment when they returned home.

This is related to notions of novelty, since ecotourists expect to experience elsewhere what they cannot experience at home. The desire to see something new or different means that novelty-seeking has been identified as a key motive for travelling, and such novelty-seeking ecotourists are much more likely to prefer destinations that are perceived as different or unusual, impressive, adventuresome and exciting (Lee and Crompton, 1992, pp732–737). For example, one ecotourist mentioned that he looked at Belize on a map and thought it would be an exciting place, 'like you could get malaria there'.[84]

Conclusion

Ecotourists in Belize do not reflect on their own position in the ecotourist economy or their impact on the environment. Instead, rather like conventional tourists they are concerned with hedonistic pursuits, and as a result ecotourists in Belize are very similar to conventional tourists. Regardless of their nationality or which part of Belize they were visiting, they made remarkably similar comments about ecotourism, the environment and their preferred forms of travel. This was also the case with conservation volunteers. They believed that they did not cause environmental damage, but that they should still take some responsibility for the impact of ecotourism.

Changes in individual behaviour would not necessarily result in a more sustainable form of tourism. Individual ecotourists might be careful not to touch the coral or to be careful with their fin kicks if they are informed about the situation. However, very often they are not given environmental briefings. They expressed a concern about highly visible environmental degradation, such as litter, but, less visible damage has a much greater impact on the reef. Mangroves and seagrass have been removed to provide ecotourists with the appearance of a silver Caribbean beach outside their hotels, even though mangroves and seagrass are important nurseries for reef fish; without them, the number of fish for ecotourists to view on their trips declines. Ecotourists tend to assume that what they see in the resorts is authentic and natural. It is thus clear that ecotourists and the ecotourism industry are causing environmental change, and that a transformation in behaviour is ultimately beyond the control of individual ecotourists.

Rather than being self-denying, ecotourists in Belize engaged in the same self-indulgence as mass tourists; they merely approached it in a different manner. The hedonism witnessed in the resort areas in the evenings demonstrated that, while they were concerned to learn about the environment and undertake unstructured trips through developing countries, they still viewed their holiday as an opportunity to relax, let off steam and have a break from the constraints of their everyday existences in the industrialized states. It was clear that ecotourists, at an individual level, cannot be relied upon to minimize the social and economic impact of their own vacationing. Ecotourists will reduce their consumption of polystyrene cups if they are given the opportunity, or even adhere to the notion of 'leave only bubbles', but they have created a huge economic, environmental and social impact merely by arriving in a developing country. Ecotourists in Belize are part of a system that is structured by foreign companies in conjunction with local political and economic elites. Thus, on the one hand, they are powerless to minimize the impact they have on the country they visit; and, on the other hand, given the chance to reduce their impact, they would not anyway. In buying independent travel and ecotours from international travel companies, they want to believe that their holiday is working in the way the marketing literature said it would. However, in the face of visible impacts of their presence, ecotourists gloss over the negative aspects. Just like mass tourists, they are motivated by self-indulgence; for them, their travel acts as a marker of social position, which separates them from conventional tourists. Their self-denial of the luxuries of conventional travel is motivated by a need to demonstrate to themselves that they can cope with the hardships that they do not have to face in their comfortable lives at home. They want to believe that their vacationing does not have the same impact as that of the mass tourists from whom they like to distinguish themselves.

CHAPTER **3**

THE IMPACT SPIRAL IN
ECOTOURISM

The interaction between local people (hosts) and tourists (guests) is one of the vital relationships in any analysis of the politics of tourism. It embraces, at the most individual and personal level, all that can be beneficial, difficult or even exploitative about the operation of ecotourism in developing countries. The relationship in Belize indicates the intricate power relationships involved in this choice of development strategy. Concern about the cultural and social impacts of ecotourism has increased as ecotourism development has moved to new destinations outside the industrialized world. Although much of the literature on ecotourism claims that the environmental choices of individual ecotourists acts as a means of conservation, it is clear that ecotourism has an impact on host countries. Individual ecotourists are part of the process of ecotourism development, which brings economic, social, cultural, environmental and political transformations. This is because ecotourism relies on the same broader market structures as conventional tourism development. The question of profitability is central, because ecotourism is a blue-green strategy based on making conservation pay its way. This can directly undermine attempts to ensure that ecotourism is socially and politically acceptable, let alone beneficial. As a result it is critical to place any analysis of ecotourism within a broader discussion of conventional tourism and its reliance on neoliberal economics.

Ap suggests that, where there is an equal power relationship between hosts and guests, there is likely to be a positive perception of tourism development, because an equal relationship allows a genuine social exchange between hosts and guests. However, where the power relationship is unequal, it will result in a negative perception of tourists (Ap, 1992, pp677–682). Tourism development in the Caribbean has often been criticized for replicating the social and economic relationships of the old plantation economies (Brohman, 1996, pp55–59; Pattullo, 1996 pp61–69). Since tourists often come from the former colonial power, their presence, behaviour and desire to be served by local people replicates the colonial situation and stirs memories of unequal racial and class relationships. Within societies, tourism can reinforce existing social, economic and spatial inequalities; those with the ability to invest in tourism can take advantage of the new opportunities, while the poorest may not benefit (Weaver and Elliot, 1996, pp205–217). This has created a set of neocolonial structures in the developing world, which are not directly orchestrated by any single institution. Instead, like tourists, ecotourists create a spiral of impacts that affects the environment, economy, society and politics of the host country. This is driven by the need to accommodate the demands of individual travellers who are fed into a system of travel. Travel choices made by individual ecotourists are structured by international companies working in conjunction with local ecotourism businesses, parastatal agencies such as the Belize Tourism Board, and government agencies in the form of the ministries of tourism, finance and fisheries.

The responses of host communities to conventional tourism vary, but it often provokes a hostile reaction because of its disruptive effects on the social life of the area (Craik, 1995, pp89–93). The criticisms of conventional tourism relate equally to ecotourism, particularly because it relies on remote regions and communities. The impact of a relatively small number of visitors from the industrialized world can be enormous, and communities respond to such changes in a variety of ways. As Harrison suggests, it would be wrong to think of the culture of developing states as weak and in need of protection from outside influences. This view assigns local people a passive role, whereas locals often respond actively to tourism development (Harrison, 1992c, pp29–31; Abbott-Cone, 1995, pp314–327; Lea, 1993 pp710–715). This chapter will examine the interactions between hosts and guests in Belize. It will investigate the ways that these relationships indicate the broader politics of ecotourism and the social, environmental and economic impacts of the ecotourist presence in a developing country context.

Ecotourism as a Development Strategy

The interest in ecotourism as a development strategy is closely linked to a resurgence in neoliberal ideas about the causes of under-development and the policies needed to overcome those difficulties. The theoretical arguments about the nature of development and underdevelopment recur in debates about the ability of ecotourism to provide a new development strategy. As such, criticisms of ecotourism can be related to broader analyses of the effects of international economic and political systems on the developing world. In particular, ecotourism is responsible for similar kinds of impact spirals as other forms of capitalist development.

One of the main criticisms of tourism is that it reinforces the position of transnational corporations in relation to the state. Elson argues that the integration of developing states into the international economy takes place largely under the auspices of firms from the developed world. The most important characteristic of transnational corporations is the disproportionate role of a small number of large firms with ownership and control of knowledge, including marketing and financial systems (Elson, 1988, pp296–298). High rates of foreign ownership contribute to a loss of control by local businesses, and so it has been argued that tourism produces relationships based on dependency. In addition, the extent of transnational corporation involvement in tourism in developing countries often contributes to high levels of leakage of tourism earnings (Brohman, 1996, pp51–59; and Elson, 1988, pp302–306). Governments usually offer a number of incentives to entice investors and tour operators, such as tax-free concessions, exemption from land tax and the right to repatriate profits. This is often exacerbated by the fact that the tourism sector is highly dependent on imports to provide tourists with the level of service they expect (Opperman, 1993, pp535–556; and Pattullo, 1996, pp33–36). Leakages from tourism mean that, although tourism is perceived as a foreign-exchange earner, much of that foreign exchange is repatriated or is spent on imports to provide tourists with the food, drink and standards of accommodation they require.

It is clear that, while transnational corporations represent significant investment, the repatriation of profits to head offices in the developed world means that they constitute a mixed blessing for the South. For example, large international tour operators dominate the tourism business, so that sometimes one company will control every aspect of a tourist's visit, including the airline, the hotel and the travel agent. The tour operators play a crucial role and can exert significant pressure on host governments and businesses; they can pressurize locally owned hotels to increase their discount for block bookings, for example. Large foreign-owned hotels are often a precondition for creating confidence among airlines and tour operators in the mass tourism market (Sinclair, Alizadeh and Onunga, 1992, pp50–63; Pattullo, 1996, pp13–25). In many ways, this can be viewed as external dependency; these corporations increasingly dominate the tourism sector in developing countries, leaving little opportunity for local businesses to develop. Tourism is often regarded as an important generator of local employment; but, while it can create a variety of jobs, managerial positions are often reserved for personnel from overseas. Local people are often relegated to badly paid, unskilled or semi-skilled positions (Harrison, 1992b, pp13–18; Hall, 1994, pp112–120). Employment in the tourism industry is often gender-determined, with women acting as domestic workers, undertaking tasks they normally perform in the household. However, the employment of women in the tourism sector can also change employment patterns and contribute to breaking down traditional roles for women (Chant, 1992, pp93–100; Hall, 1994, pp112–120; Stonich, Sorensen and Hundt, 1995 pp21–24).

In contrast to mass or conventional tourism development, ecotourism is promoted as a business that will have only positive financial impacts. In theory, ecotourism reduces leakages and creates meaningful and fairly paid tourism-related employment. Ecotourism also aims to direct economic benefits to local people in ways that complement rather than overwhelm or replace traditional practices, such as farming and fishing. As a result, the local economy is supposed to become more diversified and better able to cope with changes or a reduction in ecotourism revenues (Wallace and Pierce, 1996, pp848–851). Apart from direct employment in ecotourism developments, local people are also expected to take advantage of the ecotourists' desire for local crafts. Healy suggests that the motivations for buying local crafts are varied, and range from hunting for souvenirs to seeking out authenticity or intrinsic beauty. As such, it is one of the least explored options for revenue capture (Healy, 1994, pp137–140; Stiles, 1994, pp106–111). However, ecotourism initiatives and other nature-based tourism developments do not necessarily lead to increased economic opportunities for local people. In some cases an expansion in ecotourism reduces the opportunity for local people to participate in its development, except as menial employees (Place, 1991 pp193–196). As remarked earlier, the profit motive is the main engine driving ecotourism; a study of ecotourism lodges in Amazonas (Brazil) found that profit was their primary motive, with conservation and community development as secondary considerations. While local people did benefit financially, this was limited because people from outside the region had the better-paid jobs (Moscardo, Morrison and Pearce, 1996, pp29–33).

Ecotourism developments also imply smaller and more specialist forms of accommodation. One of the criticisms of mass tourism is the effect that the building of accommodation for tourists has on the environment. Ecotourist accommodation is intended to be more in keeping with local culture and heritage; lodges tend to be sited in wilderness areas, and they tend to be smaller and locally owned, providing local employment and being spread over a wide area rather than clustered in one resort (Moscardo, Morrison and Pearce, 1996, pp29–33). The difficulties associated with conventional tourism definitely apply to ecotourism, because it forms one part of a global tourism business, and is also one of the fastest-growing sectors of the tourism industry (Cater, 1994, pp69–72). Ecotourism has become a significant marketing tool for tourism companies, as evidenced by the proliferation of advertisements for ecotours to an increasing number of destinations (Wight, 1994, pp41–44). The fact that ecotourism does not offer a significant challenge to existing economic, social and political structure in part explains its popularity. Ecotourism operators claim to be committed to environmentally responsible management as well as sustainable economic management (Bottrill, 1995 pp45–48; and Steele, 1995, pp29–44). This in turn has an enormous impact on host societies, which have to cope with the significant costs associated with tourism as a development strategy.

Tourism is often criticized for its negative social impact on developing countries. It is credited with introducing inappropriate Western values and encouraging local people to mimic the consumption patterns of the tourists. This is called 'the demonstration effect'. Harrison suggests that it is the cultural equivalent of the spread of market relationships and commodification (Harrison, 1992c, pp29–31; Lynn, 1992 pp371–377; Pattullo, 1996, pp84–90). Tourism is often associated with an increase in crime, prostitution and the supply of drugs (Stonich, Sorensen and Hundt, 1996, pp21–24; Pattullo, 1996 pp90–101). In addition, in order to attract tourists, local culture may be packaged and commodified to appeal to Western concepts of the exotic. In turn, the people in the tourist destination may then feel forced to adapt their lifestyles to ensure that tourists are not disappointed (McKercher, 1993, pp12–14; Hall, 1994, pp174–182).

In addition, the individual relationships between ecotourism industry workers and their clients is highly problematic. Difficulties are created when sets of very different cultures meet. Craik suggests that new forms of tourism such as ecotourism, adventure tourism and cultural tourism have become increasingly intrusive and dependent on the destination community, and this intrusion has resulted in the development of uneven power relationships between the destination and origin communities (Craik, 1995, pp87–89). Tourism can also contribute to the erosion of traditions in developing societies. For example, in The Gambia, local elders in Bakau have identified tourism as causing the collapse of a culture already under a great deal of strain from Westernizing influences (Brown, 1992, pp367–370). However, the analyses that point to the detrimental effect of ecotourism on indigenous cultures often fail to address whether local cultures respond positively to contact with visitors. It is important that local cultures should not be viewed as passive, suffering impacts only. Local cultures often prove to be highly resilient and capable of interacting with tourists so that both hosts and guests gain some valuable experiences (Abbott-Cone, 1995 pp314–327; Brown, 1992, pp361–370). It is clear that the outcome of host–guest interactions is more complex than a simple case of exploitation and domination. This chapter will analyse these complicated relationships.

Direct Impact Spiral

The environmental attitudes and behaviours of ecotourists are a central concern for tour guides and other interest groups involved in the ecotourism and conservation sectors in Belize. Mito Paz, the director of a local environmental non-governmental organization (NGO) called Green Reef, suggests that the ecotourists who come to Belize tend to be educated about the environment. However, he also argues that, even with proactive efforts at education, they still have direct and indirect impacts arising purely from their presence on the Cayes. The direct impacts of ecotourists include breaking the coral reef and touching marine life. However, the indirect impacts, which are not immediately visible, have a much greater effect on the wider environment in Belize. They range from the leakage of sewage from hotels that are not hooked up to the local sewage disposal system, to the increasing pressure from people arriving to look for work in the industry.[1] This section will concentrate on the spiral of direct impacts caused by the presence of ecotourists in the developing world.

Under the legislation that deals with the ecotourism industry in Belize, professional guides have to train to receive a licence from the Belize Tourism Industry Association, and the licence is renewed each year.[2] The Belize Tourism Board and the Belize Tourism Industry Association place a premium on training professional guides because they are frontline personnel who play a critical role in the ecotourist experience. While training for the licence, guides are expected to learn how to interpret the unfamiliar in Belize for foreign visitors so that it becomes familiar, how to provide information and how to make activities entertaining (Belize Institute of Management, 1996, pp1–33; Devres Inc, 1993, pp3–6; BTIA, 1990).

Nevertheless, the proportion of trained guides remains relatively low, leading to accusations that untrained guides are engaged in environmentally damaging activities and give ecotourists a negative impression of the industry in Belize.[3] In addition, some tour guides complained that the courses were disappointing in terms of their content, and there were concerns that guides who did not turn up for courses were still awarded the relevant licences.[4] As part of the attempts to increase professionalism in the ecotourism industry, the Belize Tourism Industry Association introduced a B$5000 (US$2500) fine for guides found operating without a licence.[5] In addition, it was stipulated that a person with a criminal record, especially one that relates to a drug conviction, could not be licensed as a tour guide. Yet it is clear in Belize that guides with criminal convictions, including drugs-related offences, are acting as licensed guides in the major ecotourist areas of the country.[6] Whether licensed and trained or not, all guides face complex problems in dealing with ecotourists. This is partly because ecotourists are not a captive audience, which means that the guides have to make the trips entertaining and interesting in order to ensure that their businesses are viable. Guides also have to be prepared to tackle difficult issues with their clients, such as ensuring that they are aware of the correct behaviour towards the environment, and especially wildlife in Belize.

A common complaint among tour guides is that ecotourists do not heed their environmental advice. At meetings of the Tour Guides Association in San Pedro, the issue of the correct briefings for visitors taking trips to the coral reefs constantly arises. One guide suggested that there are always arguments about the guides and tour shops that simply allow ecotourists into the water with no environmental briefing, and no support if they get into difficulties and have to hang on to coral heads. However, even when guides do provide environmental briefings and ask the ecotourists not to touch the reef, there is still a concern that ecotourists simply do not heed their advice. Tour guide Daniel Nunez stated that he gives an environmental briefing on the boats before snorkellers enter the water, and specifically asks the ecotourists not to touch or stand on the coral, and to signal for assistance rather than hang on to coral when they were tired. However, he finds that in general, despite a broad knowledge of the coral reef and an interest in local ecology, the ecotourists still do not listen to him. He suggests that they touch the coral because they are stubborn, believing that 'I have paid for this so I will do it'.[7]

Likewise, Miguel Alamia, Manager of the Hol Chan Marine Reserve says that, although most guides ask ecotourists not to touch the reef, they do get tired on trips and hold on to the coral heads to rest.[8] One scuba and snorkelling guide remarks that he has seen a lot of environmental change at Shark Ray Alley. The site is popular with ecotourists because nurse sharks and stingrays congregate there to be fed and swim with visitors. Diving guide Oscar Cruz says that the sheer numbers of visitors stirring up the sandy bottom as they swim, snorkel and dive causes pressure on the site, because the sand smothers the coral heads.[9] To combat some of these problems, Dave Vernon, a tour guide in Placencia, provided his snorkellers with life jackets to ensure that they stayed horizontal in the water. He found that without the life jackets, when the ecotourists needed to de-fog their mask or empty their snorkels they tended to move into a vertical position and the current easily carried them on to coral heads. Vernon had often witnessed snorkellers kicking corals with their fins because they were unaware that they were doing so much damage underwater.[10]

Those involved in the ecotourism industry also express concerns about ecotourists in Shark Ray Alley who attempt to ride the sharks or be pulled along by stingray tails. One worker says that she has often seen ecotourists holding on the sharks tails while having their photograph taken, and that the slapping, riding and feeding of the sharks and stingrays had made them uncharacteristically aggressive.[11] Clearly, this behaviour does not suggest that the visitors to Belize are more environmentally aware or are prepared to reflect on their impact on the environment and modify their behaviour accordingly. The pressure on two of the most popular sites on the coral reef, Shark Ray Alley and the Hol Chan Marine Reserve, has led to a debate about the best ways to manage the reef and the visitors. Alberto Patt, biologist at the Hol Chan Marine Reserve, says that

Hol Chan had been chosen because it was a beautiful spot. It had been heavily over-fished during the 1980s, and the marine reserve provided a chance for the area to benefit from conservation and tourism. The reserve received 35,000 visitors in 1997, raising questions about whether it was best to open new sites on the reef for visitors in order to spread the damage, or to allow heavier damage on a single site.[12] One diving-shop owner, Melanie Paz of Amigos Del Mar, says that she believes that Hol Chan Marine Reserve should be closed for two years, allowing the area to rejuvenate itself; the corals show signs of damage from visitors.[13] Likewise, tour guide Manuel Azueta suggests that the impact of ecotourism on the marine reserve has been so great that further reserves should be established to spread the volume of visitors and the damage they cause. He emphasized that as soon as Hol Chan Marine Reserve was established, it started to appear in ecotourist guidebooks. As a result, visitors came and asked specifically for trips to Hol Chan and were dissatisfied with the idea of paying to go somewhere else on the coral reef.[14] Ras Creek, whose trips are featured in the *Lonely Planet Guide to Belize*, argues that ecotourists came specifically to see sharks. He suggested that if they are not guaranteed a sighting (as at Shark Ray Alley), people will stop coming to Caye Caulker and Ambergris Caye.[15]

One tour guide recounts that as soon as ecotourists see manatees, or especially dolphins, they want to jump in to swim alongside them. This has provoked a debate about reintroducing 'swim with the manatees' trips. Belize has the largest number of the rare West Indian manatee in the world, and it is one of the best places to see them (Wildlife Preservation Trust International and the Wildlife Conservation Society, 1996, pp4–5). Currently, the manatee is a protected species and the Belize government does not allow tour operators to run trips that involve swimming with manatees. Instead, ecotourists are only allowed to view manatees in a boat with its engine turned off, so the animals can only be approached by using a pole to move through the eel-grass beds and mangrove swamps.[16] Initially, the guides in San Pedro and Caye Caulker decided to stop swimming with manatees, without any prompting from the conservation bodies, after discovering that the manatees had left the area. The guides lobbied the government and the Coastal Zone Management Plan to put regulations in place to prevent swimming with manatees.[17] One of the most vocal opponents of swimming with manatees is Chocolate, a manatee guide on Caye Caulker. He has continuously lobbied for the popular manatee spot of Swallow Caye to be declared a protected area that only allows a restricted number of guides and ecotourists.[18]

Nevertheless, some tour guides in San Pedro want to reintroduce swimming with the manatee because ecotourists are willing to pay much more for a tactile experience. Swimming trips can cost US$70, double the rate for watching trips. Clearly, for the tour guides and tour operators there is a strong financial incentive for reintroducing such trips.[19] Janet Gibson of the Coastal Zone Management Plan says that the controversy is the result of different guides being based in different areas. Some of the guides in favour of a reintroduction of swimming with manatees ply their trade in deep-water areas frequented by manatees surrounding Caye Caulker and Belize City. In deeper water, the manatees can easily escape from ecotourists if they feel stressed, and these guides would substantially increase their earnings if such trips were available. In contrast, Chocolate, who objects to swimming trips, runs tours to a shallow area of eel-grass beds around Swallow Caye. Swallow Caye is not suited to swimming with manatees because the water is not deep enough for the manatees to escape curious snorkellers. Likewise, he also draws in a major part of his income from promoting himself as a manatee-conservationist-cum-guide.[20]

In 1998, as a result of the debate surrounding manatee-based ecotourism and conservation, the Belize Coastal Zone Management Plan supported research into a Belize Manatee Recovery Plan that included a four-year schedule of activities including ecotourism activities surrounding the manatees.[21] One of the major areas for spotting manatees is Gales Point, and the Belize Manatee Action Plan agreed to support and monitor an ecotourism project there that allowed ecotourists to snorkel with manatees to gauge the effects of such interactions on the welfare of manatees. The Gales Point Ecotourism Project began in 1992 with advice and support from the US-based company, Community Conservation Consultants. In the same year, the Belize government declared

Gales Point a 'manatee special development area' to encourage conservation and ecotourism through the Gales Point Progressive Cooperative.[22] The highlight of the special development area is a trip to see the manatees (Ministry of Tourism and the Environment, 1994, pp34–37; Goff, 1995, pp211–212). The trips are carried out solely by the Gales Point Manatee Tour Operators Association, and the majority of visitors to the Gales Point area are US school and university groups on study programmes (Wildlife Preservation Trust International and the Wildlife Conservation Society, 1996, pp5–7; Coates, 1993, pp1–13; Ministry of Tourism and the Environment, 1994, pp34–37). Nicole Auil, a manatee expert at the Coastal Zone Management Plan, stated that the guides licensed to take ecotourists to swim with the manatees tours would have to pay a higher fee for their licence. The expectation was that the extra fees would be directly ploughed back into manatee conservation, and that since the guides made so much extra money from swimming with manatees they would not oppose an increase in the fees for the relevant licence.[23]

The debates over manatee trips indicate that host societies have to deal with a number of complex interactions between ecotourists and the environment. The difficulties raised by the ecotourist desire to get close to wildlife and touch marine life demonstrates that ecotourism brings peculiar problems in comparison with mass tourism development. In particular, tour operators feel under pressure to allow visitors to get close to marine life. The need to generate a profit has led to demands to provide visitors with what they want, even if it does have a negative environmental impact. In addition, a number of guides have indicated their disapproval of 'swim with the manatee' trips because they are interested in protecting the financial viability of their business.

The experiences of tour guides who take ecotourists to rainforested areas and archaeological sites indicate that there is a problem with touching and removing items from the natural environment. Ernesto Saqui of the H'men Herbal Centre says that he found that visitors wanted to touch the animals and plants in the Cockscomb Basin Jaguar Preserve. When he asked them not to remove them, the common response from ecotourists was that they were only removing a small part of the plant, and that such interference would not harm the environment. They also caught a dazzling blue 'morpho' butterfly and passed it among themselves, killing it in the process.[24] Saqui says that a number of groups who come to the Jaguar Preserve are on a holiday that is marketed in the US as an environmental and educational tour.

One guide who takes ecotourists to Mayan archaeological sites feels that he wages a constant battle to stop visitors from removing bits of pottery and stones from temples. He says that he often tells visitors that the removal of such artefacts will prevent archaeologists from understanding the history of Mayan society, but that such pleas are ineffective. Instead, he now follows a much more effective strategy of telling ecotourists that it is bad luck to remove artefacts, and that misfortune will befall anyone who does so.[25] Like the debates over the manatees, the pressures that tour guides face on Mayan ruins trips indicate that ecotourists display the same kind of behaviour as conventional tourists and cause very similar problems. The central issue for guides is that being too strict with visitors will have a negative impact on business and their ability to sustain their livelihoods. This is an especially difficult problem in developing countries like Belize, because there are few alternative sources of employment.

Despite the claims that ecotourists are more culturally and socially aware than their mass tourism counterparts, their engagement with sex and drug tourism has also led those who work in the industry to believe that ecotourists are not different from any other type of tourist. Ellen MacCrae, a well-known local environmentalist, argues that the visitors who come to Caye Caulker spend their days in the bars rather than spending money on trips. She is concerned that the image of Caye Caulker as a place to 'party and take drugs' is undermining efforts to make the area attractive to families. Her trips, primarily focused on bird watching, suffered from a decline in demand during the 1990s.[26] Similarly, one hotel manager suggests that she is tired of the attitude of Belize's ecotourists towards the heavily intertwined subjects of race and sex. She comments that they tend to come on holiday, buy up arts and crafts, and spend lots of money on food, drink and trips, often spending US$1500 in one go. They have a similar attitude towards sexual relationships, believing that Belizeans and other ecotourists could be bought for sex. She feels that they think they can come on holiday and engage in short-term sexual relationships with whomever they happen to like. One Belizean woman stated that on the islands where ecotourism was most developed, groups of Belizean men can earn a living by getting hotel rooms, meals and drinks in return for sex and company during the ecotourists' holidays.[27]

The engagement with drug culture in Belize has also caused some problems in ecotourist resort areas. Kent Sylvestre of the Tourism Police Unit argues that there is a small minority of ecotourists who come to Belize to smoke marijuana and take cocaine.[28] One scuba diving guide complained that he had to deal with ecotourists who brought drugs on trips to the reef, which could lead to him losing his guiding licence. At least one ecotourist taking a trip with him had decided to begin smoking marijuana without consulting him or the other trippers.[29] The ways in which ecotourists engage with the drug culture in Belize is one of the reasons that the Belize government set up the Tourism Police Unit; it was also intended to prevent crimes against visitors to Belize and to provide an atmosphere of safety. The tourism police are an integral part of the tourism industry. The unit is supposed to assist the regular police in patrolling the tourist areas of Belize City, which have been the site of muggings, drug dealing and thefts involving ecotourists. It soon became clear that the presence of the tourism police had led to a drop in the crime rate because regular patrols encourage criminals to move out of tourist areas. The crime prevention patrols were then extended to the prime ecotourist areas in Belize.[30] For example, in 1997 the unit undertook surveillance on Caye Caulker in order to uncover guides operating without a licence, which also resulted in nine people being arrested for trafficking drugs.[31]

Members of the Tourism Police Unit wear green T-shirts bearing the logos of the police and the Belize Tourism Board, rather than traditional uniforms. Kent Sylvestre suggests that the T-shirt looks distinctive and means that ecotourists can tell when the Tourism Police are coming from a distance; it also provides a more casual and approachable image. The highly visible nature of the unit also means that they are often used to provide information to ecotourists; their radio system is linked to the Belize Tourism Board office, meaning that they can call the office to get specific information for visitors.[32] However, as far as some local people are concerned the role of the tourism police is very controversial. Some guides and other sections of Belizean society believe that the unit polices locals rather than ecotourists. They specifically target popular bars to wait for and search local men, in particular those connected with drugs, and this has led to much local resentment. This is compounded by the perception that the regular police are aggressive, ineffective and corruptly involved in the drugs trade.[33] These difficulties have been compounded by the original belief that the tourism police were going to monitor and respond to the illegal activities of visitors, which has contrasted with their actual role in protecting ecotourists from harassment and crime. Despite the obvious benefits to visitors of having a unit dedicated to their wellbeing, the tourism police are not uncontroversial from a local point of view. These problems are rooted in the lack of local confidence in the regular police force, which fails to make locals and visitors alike feel secure and safe from harassment and crime. The resentment that has arisen of the tourism police is an illustration of the way in which the ecotourism industry and the government of Belize privilege the needs and desires of transient visitors over the security of their own populace.

Indirect Impact Spiral

Ecotourists also have indirect effects on the environment as well as social, political and economic relations in Belize. Since the wider effects of ecotourism are more difficult to gauge on short vacation trips, visitors are rarely able to reflect on longer-term environmental change. On their first visit, ecotourists tended to perceive a country as being 'the way it has always been'. It is clear that only those ecotourists who make repeat visits over a number of years become conscious of their impacts on Ambergris Caye and Caye Caulker.[34] For example, ecotourists use plastic or polystyrene cups, because wood and paper products are price-protected in Belize to offer protection to the indigenous timber industry. Consequently, more environmentally friendly paper cups are not available for ecotourist use.[35] On Ambergris Caye and Caye Caulker, polystyrene cups are disposed of in local dumpsites, where organic rubbish is burnt and the remainder is buried under layers of sand.[36]

Similarly, tourists are unaware of sewage disposal in the resorts. In 1994, the government of Belize identified the disposal of solid and liquid waste as one of the most important environmental problems it faced. The government suggested that the lack of proper waste management and inadequate water supply and sewage systems were negatively affecting the ecotourism industry and risked an outbreak of environmentally related diseases (GOB, 1994, ppi–iv; Department of Environment, 1998b). On Ambergris Caye most hotels and private homes are not hooked into the modern sewage disposal system because it is too costly. The government decided to build a desalination plant on the island to provide fresh water for washing and drinking, but the water from the plant is extremely expensive, and residents and hotels are unwilling to pay.[37] In addition, although new sewage ponds have been constructed on the island, most businesses preferred to rely on their existing septic tank system. The residents faced water bills of B$800 (US$400) per month, and withdrew.

Other homes and businesses sport pipes that imply the presence of a septic tank, but which in fact rely on 'soak-outs', which allow sewage to drain directly into the groundwater and out into the sea.[38] Janet Gibson of the Coastal Zone Management Plan suggests that the septic tanks themselves are ineffective and leak into the ground; because the land is composed of porous limestone, raw sewage is seeping onto the reef and destroying it. Likewise, Caye Caulker had no sewage management system at all, meaning that faecal matter was contaminating the reef and groundwater supplies.[39] The Department of Environment compliance monitoring/site visit report for San Pedro describes several PVC pipes used to dispose of effluent and wastewater. The pipes discharged into a nearby lagoon, creating a noxious smell of raw sewage. The report recommended that each resident and business should either agree to join the sewage and water supply scheme, or construct an above-ground septic tank, and that there should be an ongoing public awareness campaign about the disposal of liquid and solid waste (Department of Environment, 1998b). To compound matters, the government does not insist that all homes and businesses join the sewage system and receive water from the desalination plant. In fact, the issue of desalination plants is in itself controversial. The plants distil fresh water from seawater, thereby creating a large amount of brine, which is discharged directly into the sea. Corals are extremely sensitive to changes in levels of salinity, and so this process was damaging one of the prime natural resources in Belize (Department of Environment, 1998a; Belize Fisheries Department/ Mundo Maya/BTB, 1995, p15).

Ecotourism also creates environmental disruption through other forms of less visible and more indirect economic and social change in the destination country. The development of ecotourism also means an increase in the number of hotels, restaurants and other ecotourism-related businesses. An increase in the number of ecotourists creates knock-on effects, such as the need for more staff in hotels, restaurants, bars and on trips, more potable water and more electricity. Ken Leslie runs Blackbird Caye Resort, which provides accommodation for the Oceanic Society's dolphin research programme alongside other ecotourists. Leslie suggests that, as the groups get bigger, the resort will need more cabanas, boats, water, electricity and staff to cope with them. He has decided to build a new, larger resort on neighbouring Calabash Caye,[40] next to a queen conch hatchery and an important Morelets crocodile-nesting site.[41]

McCalla suggests that developers tend to make adequate provision for guest welfare, but that the common failure is weak environmental management during the phase of hotel operation. For example, dredging to provide ecotourists with sandy beaches and the dumping of construction waste destroy aquatic habitats and wildlife. The replacement of mangroves with concrete walls and coastal roads has destroyed coastal ecosystems that rely on a symbiotic relationship between mangrove swamps and coral reefs. Equally, the conversion or drainage of coastal wetlands into building land has radically changed the aquatic ecosystem (McCalla, 1995a, pp61–63; Maxwell Stamp Plc, 1991, pp19–26). Individual ecotourists are unaware of this type of indirect effect arising from their presence in the country, because by the time they arrive in Belize the services have already been put in place.

The environment in Belize has already been transformed to an extent by ecotourist use. This is, in a sense, inevitable; the environment must be modified in order to build accommodation and provide food for the shifting ecotourist populace. However, the interesting issue is that ecotourists think that such environmental changes are part of the natural ecology of their chosen destination. Despite the obvious remodelling of the environment to suit ecotourist needs, such as removing eel-grass to create perfect silver Caribbean beaches, the visitors to Belize still refer to it as unspoilt and underdeveloped.[42] This is partly because Belize promotes itself as an unspoilt and pristine ecotourist destination, and partly because of the obvious contrast between the levels of development in the industrialized world from which the ecotourists hail, and the levels of development in the developing countries in which they take their vacations. Although ecotourists are the ultimate cause of ecological transformation in these areas of Belize, they are individually powerless. In this way the ecotourism industry in Belize conforms to Beck's notion of the risk society (see Chapter 1). The spiral of impacts is a process that the individual ecotourist cannot control; he or she can only make choices about consumption of goods and services from the range already on offer, and these may be provided by Belizeans, foreign nationals or transnational corporations. This means that their power as a consumer is curtailed by the very businesses that decide in advance whether local people will benefit.

The Case of Coral Cay Conservation

The controversy over the role and activities of Coral Cay Conservation in Belize indicates the direct and indirect problems associated with a development policy based on notions of green capitalism. Alongside educational groups, another vital part of the growth of ecotourism is the increasing number of organizations offering conservation holidays in the South for Northern volunteers. In some ways, one could say that these organizations adhere to an extreme form of ecotourism, which aims to assist or enhance conservation objectives in developing countries. One such organization is Coral Cay Conservation, a UK charity, which offers conservation-oriented diving holidays that aim to protect coral reefs around the world. From 1993 to 1998, Coral Cay Conservation had an operation based in Belize, firstly on South Water Caye and then on Calabash Caye, where they worked in conjunction with the Marine Research Centre at University College of Belize (UCB). This section is primarily concerned with the conservation volunteers and interactions between Coral Cay Conservation and the university. It will examine how the volunteers perceived their conservation role in Belize, and investigate the political conflict that surrounded the decision to place volunteers on Calabash Caye.

Coral Cay Conservation was established in 1986 and its President is the internationally famous conservationist, Professor David Bellamy. In Belize, the Marine Research Centre at the university was attempting to establish itself as an international centre of excellence in the field of marine research, specifically reef ecology. As part of this, they entered into an agreement with Coral Cay Conservation allowing volunteers to build a research station that would eventually become university property and to undertake reef surveys, in return for being allowed to remain on the university-owned Calabash Caye. It was agreed that the volunteers would systematically explore and survey the forests, lagoons and reefs throughout the 350km area of Turneffe Atoll. This was also intended to intersect with the broader aim of the Belize government to develop a national strategy and management plan for sustainable development and protection of the Turneffe Atoll. The atoll is environmentally and economically important as a local fishing ground and a key tourist attraction.

In its promotional literature, Coral Cay Conservation claims to provide 'resources to help sustain livelihoods and alleviate poverty through protection, restoration and management of coral reefs and tropical forests'.[43] The expeditions cost from UK£715 (US$1073) for two weeks, to UK£2805 (US$4208) for 12 weeks, plus the costs of return flights from the UK. Although it is a registered charity, Coral Cay Conservation has to operate as a commercial organization within the growing ecotourism sector. It must be financially viable, and so it conforms to blue-green notions of using the environment as a profit-making resource. It advertises itself as an alternative holiday-making experience, and it exhorted potential volunteers to join expeditions over the millennium period when regular survey work was to be combined with festive celebrations.[44] The volunteers are selected through a brief application and interview process to assess their suitability for expedition life.[45]

However, the alternative perceptions of the role of Coral Cay Conservation and their volunteers held by the UCB and other Belizean environmental and ecotourism organizations are politically significant, and differ significantly from that of the organization itself and its volunteers. Coral Cay was heavily criticized within Belize and by other global environmental organizations. It was not thought to be performing a vital conservation service or the other services mentioned in its promotional literature.[46] It became clear that the UCB and Coral Cay Conservation had divergent goals and interests. As a result, the two organizations were constantly locked into a conflict over which organization held jurisdiction over decision making.

The conflict on Calabash Caye hit the national headlines in September and October 1997. It was reported in a locally respected national newspaper, *Amandala*, that Calabash Caye was being run as a tourist resort by Coral Cay, who were accused of being environmental terrorists rather than conservationists. The newspaper also alleged that, as a result of the atmosphere on the island, UCB clients from international research stations and other overseas universities were being subjected to abuse and poor standards of hygiene. Problems included the systematic destruction of mattresses through their use for sunbathing, cockroach infestation due to poor hygiene standards, contamination of the groundwater supply by a composting toilet that was cleaned out in an incorrect manner, and wild drinking parties involving the British Army when staying as guests of Coral Cay.[47] In 1997, a government health inspector closed down the volunteer camp because of infestations and generally unsanitary conditions. It was re-opened after three months of fumigation, the construction of a new kitchen and an agreement on the part of Coral Cay to pay for a full-time cook. Behind the newspaper headlines lay four years of disputes between Coral Cay, UCB and its previous hosts on the ecotourist island of South Water Caye. The conflict was effectively hidden from volunteers by Coral

Cay Conservation before they arrived in Belize, but once on the island it became very much part of their everyday lives. Firstly, UCB wanted to establish an internationally renowned centre for marine research. This was at odds with the perception of the volunteers and of the expedition leaders from Coral that this was a conservation holiday. University staff complained that the island needed to be made a 'dry station' with no alcohol allowed, a response to excessive drinking on the part of the volunteers and their expedition leaders. This request would have brought Calabash Caye into line with other research stations in Belize.[48]

The financial position of Coral Cay was also questioned by the host organizations. Coral Cay was widely thought to make a great deal of profit from the volunteers, and it did not plough the money back into conservation or local development in Belize. Critics have accused the British Coral Cay office of of retaining the volunteers' fees. They also argued that Coral Cay did not employ Belizeans, and that the university had not received the level of investment it had expected when it first signed the agreement. Despite Coral Cay's claims that it was investing in local development and conservation, it was reported that it had invested only B$345,000 (US$172,500) in these activities, compared with the university's contribution of B$783,000 (US$391,500). A further grievance was that, while Coral Cay sent 25 volunteers every two weeks to Belize, the university was allowed to send just one client for dive training every two weeks, with a minimum of 28 days' notice.[49] Far from encouraging local participation in the development of a marine research station, Coral Cay dominated the operation. Other tour operators felt that Coral Cay Conservation was in direct competition with them for customers. Coral Cay was able to keep its costs low by making use of its status as a charity; and, as we have already noted, it did not pay tax. Other tour operators were angry that they had to compete with an organisation that was, in effect, subsidized. Such disputes frequently arise when volunteer organizations operate in the developing world. By bringing in its own volunteers, who paid to be in Belize, Coral Cay left little space for local employees. This was nowhere more apparent than in Coral Cay's insistence that due to insurance rules only Coral Cay volunteers could drive the diving boats. There was also much Belizean resentment at Coral Cay's reluctance to pay a local cook to provide meals for the volunteers.

At the outset of discussions with Coral Cay, the UCB had been advised, by tour operators in Belize and other organizations that had dealt with Coral Cay, not to sign the deal. It seemed that the organization had already achieved a degree of notoriety on South Water Caye; the local landholder and resort owner, Tony Rath, had refused to allow it to continue its operations on that island. There had been complaints from ecotourist resorts that the excessive drinking and behaviour of the volunteers had affected their business.[50]

The director of Coral Cay, Jonathon Ridley, has said that he feels frustrated that he has never been thanked for bringing volunteers to Belize and producing data for the Belize Fisheries Department. He has also commented that a Coral Cay project in the Philippines had been much more successful; the atmosphere had been very different, and the directors had been entertained each time they visited the country. Ridley believed that no-one in Belize understood what the organization did; his critics thought that his volunteers merely collected inconsequential data. He blamed the conflict between the university and Coral Cay on Belizean naivety, jealousy and lack of trust.[51] When asked about the allegations of drug-use among the volunteers, Ridley replied that Coral Cay would ask drug users to leave, because the organization could not be seen to be condoning such activities.[52] Nevertheless, accusations of sexual impropriety, drug-taking and excessive drinking were often directed at Coral Cay.

The UCB eventually decided not to renew the contract, and instead turned to Programme for Belize for support in expanding their ecotourism and research activities to include marine ecology. After being refused permission to set up operations in Belize, Coral Cay moved on to the Bay Islands in Honduras amid the devastation caused by Hurricane Mitch, again promising local participation and development for conservation.[53]

Conservation volunteer movements are a significant force in the development of ecotourism in the South, but their presence is often fraught with local conflicts, which intersect with broader struggles over environment, development, resource exploitation and the global expansion of Northern-based ecotourism in the South. The example of Calabash Caye shows that ecotourism, and its leading edge of volunteer movements, can often replicate the problems associated with mass tourism, albeit on a smaller scale. The criticisms of mass tourism, such as recreating colonial patterns of behaviour and exploitation, failing to make significant investment in local economies, social exclusion of local people and environmental damage, were all levelled at Coral Cay Conservation. The case of Calabash Caye demonstrates the ways in which developing societies have been increasingly incorporated into global networks. In particular, it demonstrates the local-level conflict associated with charities that have not placed adequate emphasis on securing local agreement and investigating what kinds of conservation efforts might best suit the host country. In the realm of environmental politics and conservation efforts, developing states and individual institutions have been modified and even undermined by global networks.

Conclusion

It is clear that the choices made by individual ecotourists create spirals of impacts that affect social, political, cultural, economic and environmental conditions in the host country. The effects of an environmental holiday in Belize reverberate through the host country; they are closely interwoven and mutually reinforcing. As regards the example of Coral Cay, the effects ranged from disputes with the university to the leakage of ecotourism earnings through the purchase of imported food for the conservation volunteers. It is immensely difficult to extract and separate the impacts of ecotourists from the wider conditions of the ecotourism industry, and even the broader social, economic, political and environmental processes in Belize. In effect, individual visitors to Belize enter a system of ecotourism that is already organized and structured by local ecotourism businesses, which are in turn allied to the global tourism industry. The relationship between tour guides and ecotourists clearly illustrates this. The interaction between host and guest indicates the ways in which transformations in Belize are created and sustained by the need to accommodate the needs of travellers. Guides are placed in a very difficult position; their liveli-hoods depend on serving the desires of ecotourists, but they are also able to observe at first hand the environmental changes caused. There are significant pressures on Belizean coral reefs, Mayan archaeological sites and rainforested areas caused by ecotourists who want to see the sights.

CHAPTER 4

EXOTIC IMAGES: MARKETING THE NATION STATE

Ecotourism is part of a broader blue-green perspective, which posits that the environment has an economic value. In order to ensure that ecotourism is a financially viable means of conserving the environment and bringing development benefits, it has to compete in a global market. It is important for Belize to carve out a niche in the global tourism business, and to do this it must create an image that communicates how Belize differs from competing tourism and ecotourism destinations. In the process of creating this image, governments, tour operators, non-governmental organizations (NGOs) and other related organizations conjure up a peculiar idea of nationhood that is viewed through a prism designed for an external audience.

This packaging is one of the most important aspects of ecotourism. The conceptualizing of nationhood, including cultural, social, economic, political and environmental processes, is generally undertaken for domestic purposes by governments and other national interest groups. However, in the case of ecotourism, numerous national and international agencies are involved in defining, projecting and exporting a particular image of nationhood that is primarily intended to appeal to visitors rather than residents. As a result, certain themes such as pristine environments, friendly locals and a stable political situation tend to be key, while domestic conceptions of nationhood often emphasize hard-won independence from colonial powers and a high degree of self-reliance.[1] In trying to attract ecotourists from the industrialized states, developing countries must present themselves as exotic destinations promising pristine environments untainted by Western-style development. Likewise, they emphasize personal safety by playing down or actively suppressing information about crime, terrorism and political instability. Local cultures can also be repackaged to appear welcoming and pre-industrial, or worse, primitive, following a simpler, non-Western way of life. This marketing to an external audience has important impacts on domestic politics and concepts of nation, society and culture; it can even ensure that local people feel obliged to behave in a particular ways to suit foreign tastes.

This chapter will examine how the nation of Belize is presented and sold to an external audience. It will firstly examine the broad themes of imagined communities. It will then assess the environmental image of Belize, paying particular attention to the case of the Cangrejo Caye Dolphin Park. Thirdly, it will investigate the ways in which society and moral values are projected for the external visitors, and analyse how the government of Belize and the ecotourism industry reacted to the arrival of a cruise ship carrying gay tourists. Lastly, it will examine images of safety, stability and low political risk by analysing the development of a regional tourism identity by the El Mundo Maya marketing strategy; it will also consider how Belize presented itself on the international stage after Hurricane Mitch devastated parts of the region.

Exotic Imagery and the Nation State

Governments, the private sector and NGOs all assist in the creation and promotion of a specific identity for consumption by an external audience, notably tourists from the developed world. This can assist governments in the process of nation building and identity formation, and the images that are conjured up can be used for internal political advantage. Lanfant (1995) argues that tourism marketing shapes the image of a place, and the identity of a society is described according to seductive attributes and crystallized in a publicity image in which the indigenous population is insidiously induced to recognize itself. The state can then exploit a tourist image that flatters national identity and praises the nation state in order to reinforce national cohesion. For those involved in tourism, the projection of a state as a tourist destination creates an idea of the state itself, which can in turn be fed back in to the domestic political order (Lanfant, 1995; McCrone, Morris and Kelly, 1995, pp12–17).

The era of globalization is conceptualized as one in which national boundaries are blurred, fluid or even irrelevant, but tourism continues to rely on relatively fixed and static national borders and identities. This is because it uses notions of nationhood and distinct national cultures in order to attract tourists to the destination. However, alongside this fixing of national identity for marketing purposes, tourism also relies on using regional and sub-regional identities to develop the industry and increase profits. The regional, cultural and political identities used by the tourism industry also serve to define images of what it is to be Caribbean, Central American, African or Latin American. Likewise, sub-regional or sub-national identities are often used by the tourism industry. Bali uses its geographical features (it is an island) and its distinct Balinese culture to market itself as separate from Indonesia (Harrison, 1992c). Similarly, the Masaai in Kenya and in the Zulus of South Africa are used to sell their respective countries to an external audience (see Sindiga, 1999; Hitchcock, King and Parnwell, 1993).

In tourism, cultures and societies become commodities to be consumed by an external audience. McCrone, Morris and Kelly argue that the commercialization of culture is an ideological framing of history, nature and tradition (1995, pp8–12). The role that tourism can play in transforming collective and individual values is inherent in ideas of commodification, which imply that what were once cultural displays of living traditions or a cultural text of lived authenticity become a cultural product, which meets the needs of commercial tourism. Tourism can redefine social realities; when advertising creates images of a place, these create expectations on the part of the visitor, which in turn lead the destination to adapt to such expectations. The destination then becomes caught in a tourist gaze from which it cannot escape without abandoning its status as a destination. Such representations of cultures have vital implications for collective and individual identities within the destination country (Hall, 1994, pp178–182; Urry, 1990).

Hall suggests that tourism promotion has developed because of the perceived need to promote a destination and establish a distinct destination and image in the global marketplace (Hall, 1994, pp39–43). The promotion of a developing country also serves to enhance state security and bolster the acceptance of state boundaries and areas of authority, because tourists need to be assured of a country's safety. Jackson (1990) argues that juridical statehood (that is, international acceptance of defined political boundaries) is very important to numerous developing countries, while the importance of achieving empirical statehood, which depends on domestic political legitimacy, is not acknowledged (Jackson, 1990; Jackson and Rosberg, 1986; Clapham, 1996). Politically, tourism enhances images of state sovereignty and government control over the local populace. The state can exercise its sovereignty through tourism because it has exclusive legal control over human behaviour within its borders. For example, the state determines who may enter its territory, what documentation is required to do so, and where visitors may travel once inside the country. Normal travel flows are an international badge of respectability, adding to the notion of national legitimacy. The most obvious example of how this works is when the citizens of one country are banned from travelling to another. Travel bans, such as that enforced on US citizens who wish to travel to Cuba, signal disapproval of that state. Similarly, a number of governments did not allow their national carriers to fly into South Africa during the apartheid years. As Matthews and Richter suggest, all international travel is dependent on the willingness of the nation states involved to allow it (Matthews and Richter, 1991, pp128–130; Hall, 1994, pp32–37 and pp59–62; Hall, 1992, pp119–120).

Equally, foreign tourism can be used by governments and associated elites in their attempts to acquire international respectability for authoritarian and/or illegitimate regimes (Hall, 1994, pp79–83). This was most starkly represented by the tourism campaigns undertaken by South Africa under apartheid, and by the 'Rhodesia is Super' campaign during the 1970s when Rhodesia was an international pariah state. The current development and promotion of tourism in Myanmar (Burma) forms part of the State Law and Order Restoration Council (SLORC)'s attempts to gain international acceptance amid charges of human rights abuses, suppression of popular and democratic political movements and oppression of ethnic minorities. These tourism campaigns have aimed to enhance international acceptance of the state and its boundaries, while claiming that the state enjoys popular domestic support and has secured political legitimacy on the international stage. Once tourists arrive they become part of this demonstration of political stability and internal legitimacy. They are kept away from the areas where the worst political oppression occurs, and are shown only political showcases (Hall, 1994, pp83–87). In addition, such governments can point to the visitors as an indication that theirs is a safe country, which allows free movement within its borders.

Political ideologies are heavily involved in debates about tourism. Although tourism is commonly viewed as an economic process that is primarily the concern of individual private companies, it can be used to reinforce belief systems and political ideologies that suit the host and destination countries as well as the global businesses involved in the sector (Hall, 1994, pp59–62). For example, developing country governments are often keen to determine the appropriate mix of public–private ownership in tourism, which in turn reflects their own ideologies of development. Furthermore, governments are quick to couch public sector tourism development in terms of a pro-business rhetoric and policy. This leads on to political questions about who will benefit from public sector tourism development (Matthews and Richter, 1991, pp123–125). In addition, political ideology influences each country's foreign policy outlook, including policies related to tourism. In China, the government tries to ensure that tourists travel in a 'glass bubble' in order to minimize interaction between locals and international visitors. This policy is driven by a fear of importing undesirable values, and ideological and moral pollution

(Hall, 1994, p79). Politicians, diplomats, lending agencies and consultants have all proclaimed tourism to be an engine of growth, and its images of power and prosperity are claimed to have the power to launch Caribbean peoples into development and modernism and out of poverty (Pattullo, 1996, pp2–5). Harrison argues that tourism is where the modern and the traditional stand in stark contrast to one another; the most obvious effect of tourism is on the physical landscape, with the appearance of new buildings and amenities. These institutions often make reference to the colonial past in developing countries. In the Caribbean, it is common to see old plantation houses now in use as hotels and tourist attractions (Harrison, 1992c, pp19–22).

Tourist decision making is partially about weighing up risks and benefits, and so the perception of terrorism or high crime rates will increase the perceived cost of a destination. This means that tourists will more readily choose a destination that they perceive to be safe. One of the main difficulties with such perceptions of risk is that political instability and terrorism in one country can seem to imply an unstable region, thereby deterring tourists from perfectly safe destinations that border countries experiencing significant political upheaval (Sonmez, 1998, pp429–431). If there is any political instability, large foreign-owned tour operators tend to immediately cancel their arrangements with the host country. Short-term damage can be done by minor political incidents such as isolated terrorist attacks or even demonstrations (Pattullo, 1996, pp28–31). Poirier argues that it is difficult to separate political and economic risk, but that political risk and instability may mean different things to potential international investors. For example, instability does not translate into political and economic risk for multinational corporations involved in oil extraction in Angola (Poirier, 1997, pp675–686). It is important to distinguish between the two.

Political instability and civil strife are generally detrimental to tourism development. Political problems have severely inhibited the development of tourism in Sudan, Yemen, Eritrea and Ethiopia. In contrast, their Red Sea neighbour, Egypt, has experienced a boom in tourism, focusing on inland and marine attractions (Hawkins and Roberts, 1994, pp503–505). There are some tourists who seek out sites of political strife and warfare; Central and Latin

America are popular destinations with such people. For example, the Zapatista uprising in Chiapas State in Mexico attracted tourists who specifically wanted to gaze on the social and political conflict associated with the rebellion (Sonmez, 1998; Cothran and Cole-Cothran, 1998, pp484–493; Holloway and Pelaez, 1998; Herran, 2000). Similarly, although negative images can take a long time to overcome, once a destination has a new and positive image, people may want to go there and observe the situation that they have read about or seen on television. This was certainly the case with Zimbabwe after it had ended its liberation war and white minority rule in 1980 (Hall and O'Sullivan, 1996, pp116–120).

While tourism can be frustrated by crime rates, it can also use historical crimes as attractions; murder sites are an example (Tarlow and Muesham, 1996, pp11–15). For example, the Strawberry Fields Memorial in Central Park, New York, marks the spot on which John Lennon was shot in 1981. However, crime usually impacts negatively on tourism development because high crime rates deter most tourists. The Caribbean and Central America have suffered from a perception that they are crime-ridden and unsafe for visitors. Such perceptions are often created by the media; one bad article about a country can significantly affect tourist arrivals, bringing with it associated problems of reduced earnings (Lynn, 1992, pp371–377; Bach, 1996). The problem is that tourism itself can attract criminal organizations, because it encourages conditions in which developing world poverty meets Western-style wealth. The behaviour and lifestyle of tourists can attract criminal elements, leading to crimes such as muggings and robbery. The lifestyle of tourists in hotel compounds, restaurants, gift shops and bars often contrasts starkly with the economic stress and poverty in parts of the host country (Norton, 1994, pp237–239; Pattullo, 1996, pp90–101; Stonich, Sorensen and Hundt, 1995, pp21–24; Bloom, 1996).

Tourists and tourism infrastructure are favourite targets for organizations involved in domestic or regional political strife. Norton argues that tourism is targeted by terrorist organizations because it delivers a high-profile international incident that will have an enormous economic impact on governments and local and international businesses. With its points of emphasis around airports, bus terminals, sea ports and railway lines, the travel industry remains the target of choice for many organizations because it is uniquely vulnerable to attack (Norton, 1994, pp237–239). Terrorism is a symbolic act and can be analysed like other forms of communication. Aided by mass communication, terrorists are able to publicize their objectives to a larger audience than they would otherwise be able to access; and when nationals of other countries are involved, news coverage is guaranteed. This was demonstrated in The Philippines in 2000, when an international group of scuba divers was kidnapped at the popular diving resort of Sipadan and held hostage. The case captured global attention and went on to involve international heads of state, including Colonel Gaddafi of Libya who brokered agreements for the release of the hostages.[1] Terrorist acts also increase the public perception of the dangers associated with travel to a particular destination (Sonmez, 1998, pp418–426; Sonmez and Graefe, 1998). The relationship between tourism and terrorism is critical; the visibility of tourists in the developing world ensures that they are ready-made targets. While the risk of actual attack is relatively small, it is the perception of risk that really counts and affects travel decisions (Hall, 1994, pp92–107; Hall and O'Sullivan, 1996). For example, during the early 1990s the United Arab Emirates, Israel and Turkey all recorded a drop in visitor numbers because of the Gulf War in 1991 and associated terrorism incidents in the region (Sonmez and Graefe, 1998, pp136–138; Hall and O'Sullivan, 1996).

Finally, environmental instability can also affect tourism because, while natural disasters can trigger sympathy and understanding, they also deter potential visitors (Sonmez, 1998, pp443–450). The Caribbean and Central America are in the hurricane belt, and the threat of severe storms, as well as fears about the damage they can do to infrastructure, reduces visitor numbers. The negative impact on visitor numbers has significant economic implications for the host countries. For example, after Hurricane Gilbert, Jamaica lost one-third of its tourism earnings for the following year (Pattullo, 1996, pp28–31). Likewise, threats of disease deter some tourists from visiting certain destinations. Stonich suggests that in the Bay Islands of Honduras, all untreated sources of drinking water have become contaminated with sewage,

including the purified bottled water that is shipped from a processing plant in San Pedro Sula. In addition, anecdotal evidence shows
that local people are more frequently ill from diarrhoeal diseases
than in the past. The current conditions created by tourism development in the Bay Islands escalated the incidence of water-borne
diseases including cholera, dysentery and hepatitis, as well as facil-
itating the spread of malaria and dengue fever (Stonich, 1998,
pp44–46). Clearly, the risk of serious disease reduces the number
of tourists. The risk of disease is also often related to disasters,
such as water contamination after floods and hurricanes.

Ecotourism Marketing and Nation Building in Belize

Ecotourism is a relatively recent development in Belize, and really
began with the expansion of facilities during the 1980s. The
ecotourism industry in Belize has three key attractions: coral reefs,
rainforests and Mayan ruins. Belize is particularly popular as a
diving destination; many visitors come specifically to dive on the
second-largest barrier reef in the world. Belize was once dependent
on primary commodities, but tourism is now its single largest
foreign exchange earner, and the Belize Tourism Board (BTB)
estimated that in 1994 ecotourism earned the country B$150
million (US$75 million).[2] The expansion of ecotourism has signifi-
cantly changed the economies of areas such as Caye Caulker and
San Pedro, which had been largely dependent on fishing.[3] This
section will examine how Belize markets itself as an ecotourism
destination. In particular, it will examine how its environment,
political life and culture are used to project an image of nationhood to an external audience.

Belize is marketed to the outside world as a place of stereotyped Caribbean beauty, with a safe and stable atmosphere that
allows tourists to seek pleasure, relaxation and adventure.
Ecotourism operators use images that operate on three levels to
appeal to potential travellers. First, ecotourism operators use green
terms to describe their companies; they present themselves as assisting developed-country tourists to explore developing countries,
which are presented as having limitless resources that are simply

waiting to be discovered by travellers. Second, ecotourism operators utilize the language of sustainable development to legitimize
their travel package. For example, national parks are presented as
pristine wildernesses; who established them and why, and how such
reserves affect local people, are not discussed. Third, companies
rely on the underlying themes of nature, nostalgia and earthly
paradise. Developing countries are presented as unspoilt, but in
reality tourists never experience nature in the raw because unpleas-
ant realities are firmly separated from the ecotourist experience
(Dann, 1996b, pp240–249).

The environmental image of Belize is vital in creating an identity
that will enable it to sell its particular brand of ecotourism.
Development strategies based on ecotourism are very much part of
the debate about comparative advantage, which advocates that each
state should concentrate on exporting the goods that it is naturally
best at producing (Amsden, 1990, pp5–32; Porter, 1990).
Developing countries are considered to have a comparative advantage in tourism in the form of sunshine, beaches and other natural
and cultural attractions. Belize promotes ecotourism because it can
effectively compete with other potential destinations in this sector.[4]
Ecotourism, in particular, is dependent on representations that
present the environment as something that is available to be discovered and enjoyed by the tourist. This encompasses notions of the
exotic, the unspoilt and the 'other'. The imagery involved in
ecotourism is intended to appeal to environmentally conscious
individuals who are interested in learning more about the destination. Tourists from industrialized societies increasingly want to
experience what they perceive to be 'untouched' environments. As a
result, their holidays can become quests for sights and experiences to
be photographed (Urry, 1992, pp3–24). This use of the environment
as a marketing tool demonstrates that the green label definitely sells
products (Wight, 1994, pp41–44; Boo, 1990, pp1–4).

Tourism, including ecotourism, has been an important part of
the debate on market-led development strategies. The government
has been actively involved in promoting the tourism industry; a
tourism consultation document produced by the government states
that tourism was officially declared a priority industry in 1984,
and that the government and private sector have effectively worked

together to develop the tourism industry (GOB, 1995; Hall, 1994, pp112–120; Matthews and Richter, 1991, pp123–125; Harrison, 1992b, pp8–11). Small-scale eco-cultural tourism is cited as the preferred option for conservation and development in the 1994–1998 Government Development Plan for Belize (McField, Wells and Gibson, 1996, pp97–104). Ecotourism is thought to be the answer to economic and environmental problems. For example, *Destination Belize* (the official magazine of the Belize Tourism Industry Association) carries articles about the commitment to ecotourism, arguing that environmental responsibility makes excellent business sense which will be rewarded with higher profits.[5] It is clear that neoliberal notions of development, such as foreign exchange earnings, are being presented as entirely compatible with environmental conservation. Ecotourism has long been a central part of the debate about the opportunities for green capitalism.

In 1994, the then Minister of Tourism and the Environment, Henry Young, stated that for too long the derogatory expression 'banana republics' had been used to describe countries such as Belize that were seen as having too much jungle and too little development. Young argued that image of the corrupt and civil-war-stricken banana republic was rapidly being replaced. The new image presented a more positive perception of Central American states as places of rainforests teeming with biodiversity, filled with ancient cultures and offering a perfect place for visitors with an interest in the natural healing remedies used by the peoples living in the rainforest. Thus Northern ecotourists seek Southern countries precisely because of their lack of Western-style development, which was precisely the reason why they had once been shunned (Young, 1994, pp4–6).

The desires and expectations of potential visitors play a central role in the ways that Belize is packaged and marketed to the outside world. Culture, environment and politics are made to perform roles for the entertainment of the ecotourist. For example, the exotic island fantasies of potential clients persuaded one resort developer to change the name of one of Belize's coral islands. Mike Fairweather stated that he had begun to develop an ecotourism resort complete with basic accommodation and composting toilets. The island he was developing was originally called Cockroach

Caye, and he was understandably concerned that a name that conjured up images of one of the most universally reviled insects would put off potential clients. Consequently, he changed the name to Seahawk Caye to give it a more visitor-friendly image.[6] This is one example of how names have been changed to make them more visitor-friendly and ensure that Belize is able to accommodate the holiday fantasies of visitors.

The ecotourists' search for the new, exciting and exotic has been played upon in promotional materials about Belize. For example, in *Destination Belize* ecotourists are exhorted to experience a daring adventure:

> *Belize is truly where Indiana Jones meets Jacques Cousteau. From north to south, east to west, Belize will spark the daring spirit of wanderlust within you... every day is a new adventure.*[7]

The reference to two well-known Western characters (one fictional, one not) is clearly aimed at whetting the appetite for adventure of potential visitors to Belize. Jacques Cousteau (1910–1997) famously explored the Blue Hole, a prime dive site which is part of the Belize barrier reef, and his name is utilized by a number of tour operators who wish to appeal to Western tastes influenced by years of watching Cousteau's programmes about marine life on television.[8]

The BTB presents Belize as a pristine marine environment that is perfect for scuba diving and snorkelling. The BTB and private operators in the Belize tourism industry regularly attend international diving conventions and vacation exhibitions in the US and Europe. Belize was marketed as an ideal destination at the world's largest diving convention, the Dive Equipment Manufacturers Association (DEMA), held in the US, and at the World Travel Mart in London.[9] Tour operators are also interested in demonstrating the environmental sustainability of their pro-business strategies. For example, one resort developer points out that his resort is being built according to ecotourism guidelines, making use of solar power and collecting rainwater from roofs.[10] Similarly, diving operators use their environmental credentials as part of their marketing strategies; Peter Hughes Diving advertises its environmental consciousness on its website. The site provides information on permanent mooring sites intended to reduce damage to coral by boat anchors, and features its acceptance of the 'Responsible Diver of the Year Award' from *Skin Diver Magazine* (a widely read publication among divers in the US).[11]

The BTB's own promotional literature uses the slogan 'Friendly and Unspoilt' alongside photographs of the country's key attractions, its jaguars, Mayan ruins, rainforests, marine life and the Blue Hole.[12] A number of coastal resorts market themselves using images of the Caribbean designed to appeal to Western ecotourists keen to relax on silver sand and in turquoise water. The Manta Resort on the relatively underdeveloped Glovers Reef Atoll claims to have 'white sands, warm waters, pristine diving... no phones, no TV, no hassles'.[13] Blackbird Caye resort claims to be an ecotourist paradise offering adventure and a chance to relax. The resort's promotional literature described it as 4000 acres of remote, unspoilt tropical jungle, a virgin paradise where ecotrails allowed visitors to explore the breathtaking beauty of the island.[14] The notion of a pristine paradise, a fantasy island where the ecotourist can return to some kind of non-Western pre-modern primitiveness, is commonplace in ecotourism adverts. *Sport Diver Magazine* exhorted its readers to visit and revisit Belize because it was 'a little country filled with big surprises around every corner'.[15] In tour operator brochures Belize is described as a place where 'denizens of the deep glide gracefully through pristine waters. Belize is natural and unspoilt. It's like a real-life Jurassic Park... travel back in time; visit villages as they were years ago; talk with villagers whose ancestors inhabited these lands before Christ was born'.[16] The reference to the Hollywood blockbuster *Jurassic Park* is intended to spark the imagination of potential visitors, encouraging them to perceive Belize as a primeval rainforest area devoid of Western-style urbanization and development.

The image of a pristine environment in which ecotourists from the North can get back in touch with nature is evident in high-profile political debates about the development of a dolphin park. The question of whether such a park would damage the image of Belize as an ecotourist paradise, and therefore adversely affect business, was also a key theme. The debates surrounding the creation of Cangrejo Caye Dolphin Park indicated the importance of projecting the correct image of Belize as an environmentally friendly destination. Cangrejo Caye was part of a redevelopment programme for Ambergris Caye that included shrimp farming by Nova Shrimp Ltd and the construction of an airstrip and a new pier, all of which was to be developed under the auspices of the North Ambergris Caye Development Corporation (NACDC).[17] The proposed park was highly controversial because of the way it was planned and because of the tourism message it sent out to an external audience. Cangrejo Caye was to be developed by a Mexican company, Dolphin International, and it offered visitors an opportunity to swim with semi-captive dolphins, along the lines of the very successful and lucrative Dolphin Park in Xcaret in Mexico. The residents of Ambergris Caye were first informed of the plans for the park when an advert encouraging visitors appeared in *Destination Belize 1997* before the resort was even built. The advert made use of the green credentials of ecotourism businesses in Belize by declaring that visitors could 'swim with the dolphins! Enjoy the ecological adventure on this incredible island.'[18]

The Dolphin Park was announced without local consultation, and fears that it would amount to a rather bizarre zoo experience drew negative criticisms from the conservation and ecotourism sectors in Belize. As a result, Dolphin International embarked on a public relations campaign. This included drawing in local business people to act as promoters for Dolphin International, and the campaign ensured that donations to local charities received favourable coverage in the local press. For example, when the company sponsored the San Pedro football team, it was renamed the Dolphins in honour of its new backers.[19] On a similar theme, Dolphin International donated 200 gallons of paint to the San Pedro Town Board to cover up gang-related graffiti and for disbursement to poor families who could not afford to paint their homes.[20] This donation was partly motivated by the need to ensure that Ambergris Caye and its main town, San Pedro, conformed to the image of a Caribbean paradise. Homes had to be repainted in pastel shades and the demonstrable record of gang- and drug-related activity contained in the graffiti was to be expunged. In addition, Dolphin International, which also used the name Cangrejo Caye Educational

Experience Ltd, invited a number of Belizean 'movers and shakers' for a free weekend at its dolphin resort at Xcaret in Mexico.[21] This was to persuade prominent people in Belize that it was prudent to back the park, given the financial successes of the parent company in Mexico.

Some local tour guides and those involved in conservation opposed the park. They saw it as unwelcome competition and as contrary to the spirit of ecotourism in Belize. Ellen Macrae of the Siwa Ban Foundation expressed concerns that the Cangrejo Caye project would blacklist Belize in environmental terms by creating the impression that the country was not committed to genuine ecotourism.[22] Tour operators Daniel and Elodia Nunez openly opposed the park because they disagreed with the idea of keeping wild animals in a captive environment to satiate ecotourist desires. They stated that they believed that the dolphins at Xcaret were slowly dying, partly because dolphins liked to swim freely over large distances in order to feed. They argued that keeping them in pens would be cruel and detrimental to the environment since the dolphins would 'eat out' such a small area.[23] Those who opposed the park likened it to a zoo rather than the kind of environmentally conscious ecotourism project that would attract overseas visitors. According to Daniel and Elodia Nunez, in 1998 the park was forced by local opposition to accept demands for a full environmental impact assessment (EIA) before construction was begun.[24] The Belize Ecotourism Association (BETA) expressed concerns that the EIA was necessary to ensure that the dolphins would be well protected in the resort and not subject to harassment by human visitors.[25] Those who opposed the park formed a lobby group, which drafted the Lamanai Declaration in 1997. This document detailed major environmental abuses in Belize, including the proposed Cangrejo Caye project alongside logging in Southern Belize, live rock exports from coral reefs, the corrupt allocation of lobster fishing permits and the impact of cruise ships crashing into the reef. This strong pro-conservation lobby was identified by Victoria Collins, editor of the *San Pedro Sun*, as a major factor in preventing the construction of Cangrejo Caye.[26] Opponents of the development were keen to speculate that the owners had failed to pay off the right officials in the opposition People's United Party (PUP), which was tipped to win the next election.[27] Indeed, after the PUP had won the general election of 1998, the urban planning officer for Ambergris Caye, Al Westby, remarked that the investors from Dolphin International had been invited back to Belize for further discussions about the future development of Cangrejo Caye.[28]

The environmental image of Belize was also perceived to be threatened by a series of environmental abuses by dive ships. The 'live-aboard' dive ships advertise their on-board photographic processing facilities. The difficulty with this is that the disposal of toxic E6 chemicals used in the processing causes environmental problems. In addition, one of the main problems with live-aboard dive ships and other boats used by the ecotourism industry is that they run aground on the reef and drag their anchors across the corals. The environmental impact of boats on the reef ranges from the running aground of relatively small crafts used by ecotourists, such as *hobie* cats, to large live-aboard dive ships dragging their anchors. In more high-profile cases, the *Belize Aggressor*, the *Fantome* and the *Rembrandt Van Rijn* were accused of dragging their anchors on reef. These boats take scuba divers to places where there were no mooring buoys, and they are supposed to find sandy patches between the corals in which drop their anchors.[29] One of the difficulties with proving reef damage from dive ships is that underwater video evidence is required, and this is almost impossible to obtain.

The most infamous incidents involved the *Fantome* and the *Rembrandt Van Rijn* in Glovers Reef and Half Moon Caye respectively, both marine protected areas.[30] Fortunately for the Belize Audubon Society, which had launched a case against the *Rembrandt*, a client on board the ship had an underwater video camera and filmed the reef being damaged by the ship's anchor.[31] The companies that owned the vessels were offered an option to compensate for the damage they had caused by paying a one-off fine of B$75,000 (US$37,500). The alternative option was to have their licences revoked until they had complied with all the conditions set out in an environmental compliance monitoring report, and until appropriate mooring buoys had been placed on the reefs. Windjammer Barefoot Cruises, the owners of the *Fantome*, apologised for the damage and assisted the Ministry of Tourism and

Environment in charting the reef. Windjammer also hired local divers to search for appropriate places for mooring buoys to ensure that such incidents were not repeated.[32] However, the local press reported that there was a perception that the owners had not been sufficiently punished because of their high-profile connections in Belize. It was also reported that the *Fantome* had a prior history of environmental breaches and had already been fined by the Mexican government for damage to the reef off their coast.[33] The cases of these ships raised questions about how such incidents could damage the environmental reputation of Belize and, by extension, could have knock-on effects on the ecotourism industry. Critics were not only concerned about the environmental impact, but also about how it might dissuade potential ecotourists from choosing to visit Belize. This in turn would have a negative economic impact on the ecotourism industry and definitely reduce profitability.

The need to project an appropriate image onto the international stage also has a cultural dimension. The fierce debates in the Belizean press surrounding the decision to allow a cruise ship with gay clients to dock in Belize in February 1998 indicated the importance of controlling the image of the nation state that is presented to an external audience. The decision split tour operators into two groups. One believed the decision would hamper their attempts to market Belize to potential clients in the US and Europe, who might be deterred from visiting Belize if they thought it was a country with open attitudes towards homosexuality. The other perceived the cruise ship as a business opportunity. The MS *Leeward* was owned by US-based Atlantis Events, which provides holidays specifically for gay men. It had already been turned away by numerous other Caribbean nations; the Cayman Islands Minister of Tourism said that they could not count on the tourists aboard the ship to uphold standards of appropriate behaviour expected of visitors to the Caymans.[34] However, underlying the numerous refusals to allow the ship to dock in various Caribbean reports was not only homophobia, but also a fear that it would send the wrong message to potential visitors and external investors. Once the cruiser had been allowed to dock in Belize, newspapers printed a number of letters from people who were not resident in Belize, complaining about the decision. One letter came from the Chief Executive

Officer of BaBear Productions, a US-based company that promotes Caribbean destinations to travel agents. In his letter, he stated: 'Tourism is the biggest money earner in the Caribbean and are you willing to sacrifice that? I get the impression that you as a country have no standard of appropriate behaviour; if that is so I regrettably cannot promote your island.'[35] (Belize is not an island.) Likewise, potential honeymooners to Belize wrote to the local press to express their anger at the decision. One wrote: 'I assure you that we will cancel our plans to visit your beautiful country if we feel we might have to witness the same debauchery and sleaze we are trying to escape.'[36]

The story dominated the local press throughout January 1998. Belizean newspapers carried front page headlines such as '$$$ from Sodom', 'Anal idiocy' and 'From bay men to gay men'. Much of the discourse revolved around religious belief. However, even the religious or moral objections to the cruiser were intimately bound up with ideas about how the nation should promote itself, and concern over the growing economic interests involved in the cruise ship industry. For example, the president of the Baptist Association, Lloyd W Stanford, wrote an open letter to the minister Henry Young arguing that the decision to welcome the cruise ship gave explicit national approval to the gay rights movement.[37] Opponents of the cruiser also referred to the economic implications. For example, numerous letters referred to the importance of the tourism dollar to Belize, yet argued that the financial position of the country could not be so bad that it had to accept money from 'immoral' sources.[38]

In contrast, other groups argued for tolerance. However, once again there was a discussion about how Belize should be promoted to outsiders and the financial aspect of allowing the cruise ship to dock. The local anti-gay demonstrations when the cruise ship docked prompted news reports in which passengers from the cruiser complained that Belizean society was backwards and ignorant.[39] Yet CNN aired a report about Belize as the destination for the MS *Leeward* once it had been turned away from Grand Cayman. Belize was presented as a country with a more enlightened attitude purely because it had allowed the ship to dock (ignoring the local outcry).[40] In addition, tour operators argued that the financial benefits would be immense from allowing the cruiser to dock for six hours. For example, Wendy de la Fuente of Caye Caulker argued that 900 tourists landing in the country would result in so much money being spent that the figures could not be matched by a whole month of regular business.[41] The Belize National Tour Operators' Association stated its full support for the decision, arguing that cruise ship passengers brought excellent revenue and were of great benefit to tour operators and other service industry representatives. In fact they argued that Belize should become more involved in the international cruise ship industry, as it was one of the fastest-growing sectors in the global tourism business.[42]

In 1999–2000 the Belize Tourism Board began to promote the country as a prime cruise destination, encouraging the construction of infrastructure to cope with the passengers and a tourism village to sell souvenirs and crafts in Belize City.[43] The arrival of cruise ships in Belize has promoted debates in the environmental and tourism sectors about what this means for the future development. A report into the state of the coastal zone indicated that the decision to launch Belize as a major cruise ship docking point was highly controversial; conflicting with the government's publicly stated policy of promoting small-scale ecotourism. Cruise ships definitely represent a part of the mass tourism sector (McField, Wells and Gibson, 1996, pp97–99). Nevertheless, the debates about the religious, economic and political implications of the decision to allow the cruise ship to dock revealed the extent to which the image of a country as a tourist destination had a significant influence on the way in which the local citizenry view national government policy making.

As well as creating the correct national image to compete in the global tourism market, Belize has become involved in presenting itself as part of a broader regional identity to attract potential ecotourists. On a regional level, Belize is part of the Mundo Maya marketing strategy. Mundo Maya is an organization that covers states that include Mayan sites, namely Mexico, Belize, Guatemala, Honduras and El Salvador (Chant, 1992, pp85–88). Mundo Maya markets tourism routes through the region covering archaeological sites such as Chichen Itza (Mexico), Tikal (Guatemala), Caracol

(Belize) and Copan (Honduras).[44] The agreement between the countries involved in Mundo Maya is intended to facilitate the flow of tourists (and therefore the revenue derived from tourism) so that they can travel more freely through the region. One aspect of this is that the Mundo Maya organization has lobbied for cooperative agreements between regional airlines that would, for example, allow Mexican airlines to enter Belize to drop off and pick up passengers en route to a fellow Mundo Maya country.[45]

The creation of a single regional identity for tourism marketing purposes is not unproblematic. One of the difficulties associated with such regional plans is that some partners stand to gain more than others. For example, Belizean government officials refused to accede to a request from the Mexican government that the Belize barrier reef be renamed and marketed as the Maya Reef or El Gran Arrecife Maya. The Belize barrier reef is part of a much larger reef system that stretches to Honduras in the south and Mexico in the north. While the reef is marketed as part of the Mundo Maya experience, the Belize government was concerned that Mexico had already degraded many of its reefs (especially around Cancun) and so the Mexican tourism industry would benefit disproportionately from claiming that the Maya Reef was in Mexico. In effect the Mexican tourism industry would make financial gains from giving the impression that less environmentally damaged reefs in Belize were within Mexican borders.[46] On a cultural level, Mundo Maya places Belize firmly within the Central American region for ecotourism marketing purposes. However, the Latin culture of Central America contrasts sharply with the image of Belize as a Caribbean destination. This dual identification provides a potent mixture of cultures and sights for ecotourists to see, but presents problems for Belize when the state agrees to participate in a marketing strategy based on a uniform regional culture.

The identification of Belize with Central America has also raised questions about how Belize fits in to the perception that there is large-scale political violence in the wider region. As a result, Belize has also tried to distinguish itself from the political upheaval associated with Central America. Certain aspects of law enforcement have been advertised and emphasized in order to create an image of safety and stability. Some countries modify the way in which their history and culture is presented in order to appeal to Western tastes. This can work against the interests of the host state or even reinforce the state's definition of the nation's identity to the detriment of minority groups. On another level, coercive measures may be used against local populations in order to make the destination appear more appealing to Western tourists (Matthews and Richter, 1991, pp125–128; Stonich, Sorensen and Hundt, 1995, pp21–24). Images of safety and security are vitally important in helping to determine travel decisions. For example, one brochure from UK-based Reef and Rainforest Tours draws attention to the relative stability of Belize and its distinct culture, which sets it apart from its neighbouring countries. The brochure states that 'Belize is an oasis of peace in the often-volatile region of Central America. Indeed, it sometimes seems more like a Caribbean than a Central American country.'[47] This is in contrast to Belize's identification with the rest of Central America under the Mundo Maya banner.

The Belize government's tourism consultation document points to the difficulties involved in negative media coverage, and indicates that the BTB and Belize Tourism Industry Association (BTIA) should approach media houses to discuss the media management of incidents that are detrimental to the image of Belize as a safe tourism destination (GOB, 1994). Similarly, local newspapers in tourist areas have been under pressure from the government and tour operators to reduce the amount of reports related to crime or poor practice by hotels and tour operators. The concern was that visitors would read negative reports in the local papers and be deterred from returning to Belize or recommending the country to other potential visitors.[48] Through tourism the state can present itself as an ally to external business interests while remaining committed to providing local employment. In Belize, the government and the US-based Strategic Financial Advisers examined the development of a tourist centre in Belize City, which was promoted as a means to enhance the local economy.[49] In this way tourism assists in legitimizing the position of the state in relation to external and domestic interest groups

Since Belize competes with other potential destinations around the globe that offer reefs, rainforest and ruins, the need to ensure that potential visitors can feel safe and secure in their choice of destination was very apparent in the aftermath of Hurricane Mitch. Belize lies in the hurricane belt of the Caribbean and, in general, visitor numbers are lower in October and November due to the risk of hurricanes. In November 1998 the worst-ever hurricane hit the region, resulting in floods and mudslides, the deaths of over 11,000 people and homelessness for a further million. Rainfall, rather than strong wind, was the main source of damage. However, it would be inaccurate to suggest that the devastation of Central America by Hurricane Mitch was entirely the result of some freak natural event. Rather, the impact of Mitch was caused by a potent mix of an extreme and unusual weather event coupled with social, political and economic problems that had dogged the region for centuries. Deforestation in the region had left hillsides denuded of vegetation that would have prevented the catastrophic mudslides that buried villages and killed thousands. The unequal distribution of land in Central America was as much to blame for the death toll as the storm itself. In addition, the flooding and infrastructural damage raised the spectre of a major outbreak of infectious diseases such as malaria and cholera.[50] Hurricane Mitch caused damage that will take decades to overcome. In Nicaragua and Honduras the banana crops were destroyed, putting thousands of people out of work.[51] Likewise, the floods and mudslides swept away the bridges and roads that were needed to transport crops for local consumption and for export.[52]

The ways in which the disaster was reported in the international media created the impression that Central America had suffered a total collapse, and was heading for greater political instability because infrastructure, food supplies, health and educational achievements had been completely wiped out. Institutions ranging from the Inter-American Development Bank to the Red Cross pledged support for the region. For example, the US government pledged US$70 million for disaster relief in Central America. A small portion of the aid went to Belize, such as US$50,000 from the Inter-American Development Bank to assist in management of displaced people.[53] Some people were pleased with the immense media interest in the storm because it commanded the total and undistracted attention of an international audience. This created the myth of Hurricane Mitch as a devastator of the entire region with no regard for the local differences. For example, the international media reported the wind speeds of the eye of the hurricane while it was still out at sea (when wind speeds are at their highest) and it was those figures that stuck in the public mind. The mudslides and floods that hit Honduras and Nicaragua were further used to inflate the myth of Mitch as a superstorm that flattened every country in the region.[54] For example, it was reported in the Belizean and international press that up to 2000 people were feared dead after being engulfed by mud at the Castias Volcano in Nicaragua. Bodies were burnt in order to stop the spread of diseases such as malaria and gangrene, so funerals and mourning had become a luxury for most families.[55] Likewise, the image of a totally devastated region was built by the globally recognized story of Laura Isobel Arriola de Guity, who spent six days at sea after being swept along by flood waters.[56]

However, after a few days the Honduran government faced international embarrassment as it was revealed that the fatality figures had been inflated to ensure that Honduras was given maximum aid, loans and debt relief to assist it in rebuilding after the hurricane.[57] While the death toll remained enormous and development in the region had indeed been set back by decades, it was significant that the Honduran government exaggerated the disastrous consequences of the hurricane. The government and the international media worked together to create an image of a region in a state of collapse due to a natural disaster that could not have been prevented. Other commentators questioned why the death toll was so high and pointed to deforestation and the land distribution system in Central America as the culprits. The reservation of large areas of productive land by a few wealthy landowners in Honduras meant that the majority of poor people were forced to live in areas that were unsuited to subsistence agriculture. These social, economic and political factors all combined to create a disaster that was internationally reported as 'natural'. For example, the Belize media attributed some of the Belize's good fortune to the fact that its society is less socially and economically polarized than its Central American neighbours. This meant it had a good hurricane evacuation plan and its lands were less eroded because people had not been forced to cultivate poor land due to an unequal and unfair land distribution system.[58]

While the worst-hit countries were Honduras, Nicaragua and El Salvador, Belize sustained minimal damage. Hurricane Mitch was predicted to hit Belize on October 27 1998, but it suddenly turned southwards and hammered itself out on the Bay Islands and coastal areas of Honduras instead. The high waves smashed boat piers on the main ecotourism islands and winds caused minor damage to some buildings. After the threat of Hurricane Mitch had passed, most tour operators and hotels in Belize were back in operation.[59] In fact, Belizean organizations were offering advice and support to their Central American neighbours in the wake of the hurricane. For example, the Mennonite community in Belize built concrete houses in Honduras and the Belize Defence Force assisted in distributing aid packages. The Toledo Maya Cultural Council and the Kekchi Council of Belize also sent aid to their neighbours in Guatemala and Honduras.[60]

The problem for Belize was the perception that it had suffered a similar fate to the rest of the region. This was compounded by the fact that the Belize government executed a vital hurricane evacuation plan.[61] The evacuation of Belize City and the main ecotourism islands meant that there were no personnel to answer telephone calls from concerned travel agents and potential visitors. Jeffrey Avilez of the Belize Tourism Industry Association remarked that because the telephone lines were not working for a week after the storms hit Belize, this contributed to the perception that Belize had been 'wiped off the map'.[62] As a result, the main effect of Hurricane Mitch for Belize was the creation of a perception of significant risk among travel agents and potential ecotourists who were watching the pictures of the devastation in Central America on their television sets at home.

As a consequence of this public image, the agencies involved in promoting ecotourism in Belize had to mount a major public relations campaign. The aim was to persuade foreign travel agents and their clients that while there was deep sympathy for the suffering all around their borders, Belize had been exceptionally fortunate and was left virtually unscathed. Valerie Woods of the Belize Tourism Board stated that the Minister of Tourism and the

Environment travelled to New York to give interviews to CNN and that she went to issue statements and press releases to the major news organizations. Nevertheless, the pictures of Hurricane Mitch and its effects that were shown on CNN and the BBC did not distinguish between Belize and the rest of Central America. The image of Belize as part of Central America had been cultivated over the 1980s and 1990s and prior to that the country had really only identified itself in terms of ties to the former colonial power (the UK) and as part of the Caribbean region. In the wake of Hurricane Mitch, it was important for Belize to try to shake off its Central American image.[63]

The real disaster for Belize was an economic one. The perception that Belize had been devastated resulted in cancellations and a drop in the numbers of people visiting the country. There was some reluctance on the part of tourism suppliers that had dealt with Belize in the past to accept that the country was not devastated. As a result, a number of tours were cancelled due to fears about disease and safety in Belize and the wider region.[64] The owner of Kitty's Place in Placencia had numerous enquiries regarding the state of the resort in the aftermath of the disaster, so she took a photograph of the beach to send to potential clients via email. The picture was intended to reassure ecotourists and spread the news that the country was not experiencing the same kinds of problems as the rest of the region.[65]

In fact, for Belize there were some small environmental benefits from the storms that came in the wake of Hurricane Mitch. One was that some of the main ecotourism islands found they had suddenly acquired a beach. On Ambergris Caye, the storm surges in the sea carried sand onto the island and built a stereotypically silver Caribbean beach. In the following ecotourism season the new beach proved to be highly popular with visitors. Prior to the hurricane, areas on the island had either dredged the seabed to create beaches or persevered with unattractive sea walls. Likewise, the existing beach at a major ecotourism area, Placencia, became steeper and was more visually pleasing to ecotourists.[66] Mitch became an added attraction for visitors in the following season. It was clear that a number of bars in ecotourist areas had responded to the disaster by devising new cocktails with names like 'The

Mitch' and 'Mitch the Bitch'. In addition, a number of tour operators claimed that the surge in colder water brought by the storms
had arrested the development of coral bleaching and scraped off
the algal growth that can prove lethal to coral heads. While the
exact cause of coral bleaching is unknown, the phenomenon tends
to be associated with a rise in sea temperatures. However, the
storms also threw a great deal of sand onto the coral reefs, smoth-
ering a number of coral heads in the process.[67] This is the kind of
environmental damage that a first-time visitor to Belize might not
notice, but which experienced scuba divers and snorkellers would
find immediately apparent (Salvat, 1992; Hawkins and Roberts,
1994). Overall it was clear that Hurricane Mitch brought significant problems to Belize even though it did not hit the country.
Since ecotourism, like all tourism business, is highly dependent on
global image and the sophisticated marketing of that image,
anything that harms it can be highly detrimental and economically
disastrous.

Conclusion

It is clear that a development strategy based on ecotourism requires
the state, private sector and NGOs to formulate and project a
particular national image. This image is used to attract potential
visitors and investors that are primarily based in the industrialized
states. As a result, developing countries like Belize tend to emphasize their comparative advantage over the North. Numerous images
of the nation state and of national identity are used to draw in an
external audience. Belize highlights its pristine natural environments ranging from coral reefs to rainforests. Likewise, the
agencies involved in marketing Belize, such as the Belize Tourism
Board, rely on the history and archaeological heritage of the
country to sell it to Northern ecotourists. The Mayan ruins of
Caracol, Lamanai and Lubantuun along with present-day Mayan
culture are commodified and packaged to make them appeal to
holiday-makers. Since feelings of safety and security are vital
factors in the decision-making processes of potential visitors, Belize
also markets itself as a haven of stability in an otherwise turbulent
region. This contrasts with its cultural identification with Central

America through the Mundo Maya project, and with its claims to a common Caribbean heritage. What the debates about Cangrejo Caye and the cruise ship with gay clients demonstrate is that conservation and tourism agencies are very concerned to make sure that they are presenting the correct image of Belize to attract the relevant audience. The image of a nation that is presented to potential ecotourists does differ from domestic conceptions of nationhood. However, the ways that nationality, ethnic identity and political position are commodified and sold to ecotourists can also feed back into the domestic political order. In particular, Mayan heritage is used to attract visitors but current Mayan practices are presented only in so far as they constitute attractive festivals and colourful culture for outsiders. The suppression of Mayan interests and the ways that the central state has attempted to ignore Mayan political organizations is not part of the ecotourist package. The political elite, to enhance its own political legitimacy and economic status, uses the image of nationhood that is painted for ecotourism. The ways in which the ecotourism industry in Belize benefits some political and cultural groupings over others is the central focus of the next chapter.

CHAPTER 5

ECOTOURISM AND INDIGENOUS COMMUNITIES

One of the benefits of ecotourism as compared with conventional tourism is that it is meant to be socially and culturally aware. In general, ecotourism operations claim to be socially inclusive and ensure genuine participation for local people. The community-based form of ecotourism takes this idea of participation much further. Instead of merely joining a scheme run by private operators or government agencies, local people organize and manage their own ecotourism businesses to ensure that they are able to gain control over the economic and social benefits. In addition, community-based ecotourism is meant to ensure that communities are able to negotiate and mitigate potential negative impacts. Its emphasis on viewing people as part of an ecosystem indicates a mix of red-green communitarianism and deep green ideologies. In these ways community-based ecotourism seems to be at odds with blue-green policies of defining the environment as a resource. However, even ecotourism that is run by indigenous communities has business principles as the central focus, and so it retains an underlying rationale that is primarily blue-green. It still depends on the idea that ecotourism is an expression of green capitalism that does not require any kind of fundamental reorientation of the global or local economy. Instead, like other forms of ecotourism, the community-based variety essentially means a slight reshaping of the existing system. As such, while it claims to be capable of providing all sorts of developmental benefits to indigenous communities, in the end it is part of a wider system that actually frustrates their development and their capacity to engage in genuine participation in local, national and global political and economic processes. In this way, community-based ecotourism cannot be separated from broader national and global political factors that impinge on its everyday management.

Supporters of ecotourism use the relationship between indigenous communities and ecotourism development to point to its ability to provide development alongside environmental care. Ecotourism is promoted as a means of ensuring that conservation is financially viable through the development of revenue generating schemes. This emphasis on ensuring that the environment pays its way through ecotourism development is also related to a wider debate about community conservation. Ecotourism, it seems, is promoted as a means of negotiating complex conflicts within and between communities in fragile landscapes or near protected areas. The advantages of community-based natural resource management have been promoted by agencies as diverse as governments, local communities, global non-governmental organizations (NGOs) and the World Bank. In response to this broader debate about community-based natural resource management and the revenue-generating capacity of ecotourism, a number of local communities have decided to establish their own ecotourist facilities. Such ventures are intended to ensure that the host communities retain all the revenues from ecotourism and that local people have complete control over the pace and direction of ecotourism development, including choosing the ways in which they interact with ecotourists. This chapter will examine the development of ecotourism operations by Mayan indigenous communities in Belize. This chapter will also analyse the wider political difficulties associated with ecotourism in the region, notably the social and economic impact of paving the Southern highway, unsustainable logging practices, the politics surrounding the sudden death of Mayan leader Julian Cho, and the politics of establishing a trans-border conservation area with neighbouring Guatemala.

Community-based Ecotourism

The motto of the World Tourism Organization is 'Tourism: Passport to Peace', which indicates a wider commitment to the idea that it increases understanding through cultural exchange. However, critics of tourism development have pointed to its obvious shortcomings in the South, and the operation of tourism has certainly failed to match the slogan (Hall, 1994, pp89–91). Critics suggest that one of the major problems associated with tourism development in the South is that it exacerbates existing economic and social divisions in the host communities and creates new ones. In particular, enclave tourism has tended to create spatial inequalities through the establishment of all-inclusive resorts. These resorts cater solely for tourists, and the conditions in the resorts contrast starkly with the living standards of the local communities (Brohman, 1996, pp55–59; Dieke, 1993).

In fact the difficulties associated with rapid tourism development have led to local protests against the industry. Krippendorf suggests that the mass migrations involved in tourism have prompted responses among local populations about the negative effects of such development. The negative effect of tourism has meant that local people increasingly demand the opportunity to participate in tourism development (Krippendorf, 1987, ppxvi–xvii). For example, Lea points out that in 1987 a militant group of youths, workers, professionals and other concerned local people formed Jagrut Goencaranchi Fauz (JGF) to protest at the rapid and unwelcome tourism development in Goa, India. This was the start of a successful campaign of disruption that directly and adversely affected the Goan tourism industry (Lea, 1993, pp707–710; and Lynn, 1992, pp371–377). Likewise, Wallace and Pierce argue that in Amazonas, Brazil, it has been difficult to secure local acceptance of the negative effects of tourism precisely because the opportunity to provide benefits to nearby residents has been lost. For example, rainforest lodges have been built on private lands far away from the state capital Manaus and protected areas. In addition, there has been little cooperation between private tour operators and the staff of the state conservation agency IBAMA (Wallace and Pierce, 1996, pp843–846). Nevertheless, tourism development has been promoted as a key means of providing revenue for conservation in developing countries. In fact tourists, and especially ecotourists, have played an expanding role in the establishment and management of protected areas. For example, revenues from gate fees can be directly channelled back into conservation, and ecotourists may have the political and economic clout to pressurize local authorities into increasing support for the conservation of protected areas, and even for greater local community involvement in the industry (Lindberg, Enriquez and Sproule, 1996, pp547–551).

The development of community-managed tourism in the developing world is a response to criticisms of the socially and economically divisive effects of mass tourism. In many ways, the critiques of national parks and their history of excluding marginalized local people presaged the development of community-based tourism. This was partly because tourism, like national parks, involves managed development, conservation and issues raised by increasing visitor use (Bramwell and Lane, 1993). In the developing world, there is an added layer to the politics of tourism because of memories of colonial control. For example, Akama, Lant and Wesley argue that Kenyan conservation and tourism schemes have replicated the colonial system of separating people and the environment. As a result, local people may be excluded from national parks, and can be fined or arrested for trespassing and hunting in areas that they have historically used. These exclusive areas are then developed with relatively open access for international tourists. Consequently, local people are often drawn into conflict with wildlife and with competing users of the conservation area, in this case tourists (Akama, Lant and Wesley, 1996, pp338–345; and Place, 1991, pp186–189). Social or community tourism can be defined as tourism that resulted from participation by economically or otherwise disadvantaged people. Social tourism involves the extension of the benefits of the industry to economically marginal groups (Hall, 1994, pp43–47; Bottrill, 1995, pp45–48). Community-based ecotourism has arisen from debates about the impact of the tourism industry and it is intended to maximize the participation of local people in decision making from a very early stage. In particular, local communities are expected to play a major role in deciding on the direction and rate of ecotourism development in their area. Securing this community participation is often dependent on a commitment to sharing the benefits of ecotourism development. This means that the costs of setting aside local environments for conservation are offset by the direct provision of revenue and other non-material benefits to communities. These benefits should be an additional form of support for local economic activities, so that they complement rather than overwhelm traditional local practices (Wallace and Pierce, 1996, pp846–860). The handing over of conservation and ecotourism operations to sub-state entities such as local communities requires the development of dynamic and enthusiastic institutional arrangements. Only a few ecotourism schemes have such robust institutions ready to manage complex businesses for community development, and it is not suited to every situation (Steele, 1995, pp34–36; see also Duffy, 2000b).

The growing interest in the potential benefits of community conservation and community-based ecotourism has also raised concerns about the ways in which local people and their ways of life are customized, packaged and sold for consumption by foreign ecotourists. The most obvious example of this is when traditional rituals and festivals are re-enacted for the ecotourists' benefit. Hall suggests that this is commodification, which occurs when cultures and societies involved in tourism are treated as commodities to be consumed. In addition, the tourist intrusion has brought social and cultural change that is more in line with commercial values (Hall, 1994, p130–133; Pattullo, 1996, pp84–90). However, critics of this position argue that this theory exaggerates local susceptibility to tourist lifestyles. Harrison points out that, while tourism has been accused of degrading the meaning of local rituals, they may not lose their impact and importance for the local people performing them. For example, in Bali, the performance of Balinese rituals for tourist consumption has been used as a means of reasserting national identity in response to the increasing threat of assimilation into Indonesian culture (Harrison, 1992c, pp19–22; see also Hitchcock, King and Parnwell, 1993).

In addition, while community-based ecotourism implies a high degree of public participation, critics have pointed out that communities very rarely have the right or opportunity to say no to government-inspired schemes. In this way, community-based ecotourism can in fact end up serving the interests of local and global elites because the political nature of decision-making processes can often cut out communities and their interests. As a result, in many community schemes, a form of tokenism in public participation has developed (Hall, 1994, pp167–171). Such minimal participation then allows tour companies to package communities as tourism attractions, presenting local people as smiling and welcoming faces for international visitors. Yet aspects of indigenous society and politics are kept far away from the tourist gaze so that, for example, indigenous groups which assert land claims in tourist areas are branded as troublemakers by central government and the private tourism industry. Tourism development can provoke a struggle for the control of time and space in which the dominant group attempts to legitimate its understanding of the appropriate use of space and time, while the subordinate group resists this control. (Hall, 1994, pp182–200).

In turn, ecotourism development is also related to notions of community conservation and draws on blue-green and deep green ideologies of environmental protection. The commitment to community development through ecotourism incorporates blue-green ideas of environmental economics, where natural resources are viewed as a means of generating revenue. One of the central premises of neoliberal economic strategies is the promotion of new growth sectors such as tourism and other non-traditional exports. In essence, the emphasis on tourism is designed to increase economic diversification, reducing reliance on traditional exports, such as bananas in the case of Belize (Brohman, 1996, pp51–55; Stonich, Sorensen and Hundt, 1995, pp6–9; Pattullo, 1996, pp11–13). In addition, it also fits with ideas of privatizing the environment: part of the rationale is to devolve management and decision-making capabilities to non-state and sub-state entities, such as local community organizations. For supporters of such conservation initiatives, communities are conceptualized as key actors in ensuring that ecotourism initiatives are socially as well as environmentally sustainable. However, community conservation with ecotourism as the key also forms part of deep green ideas about local control over the environment and devolution of responsibility to the micro level. This ideology sees people as being part of the environment rather than dominating it. This chapter analyses the ways in which community-based ecotourism has been developed in Belize, and the political environments in which it operates. It will show how the broader politics of Belize and the relationships between indigenous Mayans and the central government have a critical bearing on the workings of community-based ecotourism.

The Politics of Community Conservation

Southern Belize is the particularly well known for community-based ecotourism ventures, related to wider conservation schemes which are reliant on the idea of local participation and management. There are a number of these initiatives in Belize that centre on conserving resources as diverse as bird life in Crooked Tree, howler monkeys in the community baboon sanctuary, jaguars in the Cockscomb Basin Preserve, manatees at Gales Point and Mayan ruins in the El Pilar Archaeological Reserve. These schemes are informed by the debates about community-based natural resource management (hereafter referred to as community conservation). Supporters of community-based ecotourism development suggest that protected areas with genuine community participation in ecotourism can form the cornerstone of development plans at the local, national and regional levels (Place, 1991, pp196–201). In addition, it is clear to supporters of community ecotourism that success is critically dependent on ensuring that the rights of indigenous peoples are not only respected but protected (Stiles, 1994, pp108–111). The development of community-based ecotourism is also part of a specialist niche in the broader tourism industry. For example, community ecotourism initiatives offer visitors alternative forms of accommodation, such as basic guesthouses that are locally owned and managed in a way that spreads the income around the whole community (Moscardo, Morrison and Pearce, 1996, pp29–33).

The first experiment in community-based conservation and ecotourism development in Southern Belize was the Cockscomb Basin Jaguar Preserve, which then became a model for further schemes that sought to learn from its successes and failures. The preserve was initially designated as a forest reserve in 1984, and it was later expanded and converted into a wildlife sanctuary. It was the world's first jaguar sanctuary, supported by the World Wide Fund For Nature and the car company Jaguar. In 2000 the European Union (EU) agreed a 1.28 million euros grant to support the co-management of the preserve and other protected areas by the Belize Audubon Society, in conjunction with local communities.[1] Like many other protected areas, the creation of the jaguar preserve required the relocation of local communities to a new site, the Maya Centre Village. The initial rationale was that Cockscomb would be a community-managed conservation area, and that the people of Maya Centre Village would directly benefit from the ecotourism revenues generated by the scheme. These revenues would then be used to compensate them for loss of access to areas that they had historically used for subsistence agriculture and hunting (Emmons et al, 1996). This was intended to ensure that the local communities did not have to live with all the costs of creating and enforcing protected areas without any of the benefits. The creation of Cockscomb meant that agriculture and hunting became illegal in the preserve, even though they were vital subsistence activities for local people. As a result, the establishment of the jaguar sanctuary led directly to a significant reduction in access to resources contained within the reserve, including locally important spiritual and religious sites. The preserve was managed by the Belize Audubon Society on a temporary basis to allow the community to develop institutional capacity so that it could eventually take over the running (Lindberg, Enriquez and Sproule, 1996, pp543–547; Boo, 1990, pp36–43; see also Place, 1991, pp193–196). This led to criticisms that the sanctuary merely replicated the traditional relationships between communities and state-run conservation agencies. Despite the promises that Cockscomb would constitute a significant departure in conservation policy, local communities have failed to gain substantial economic benefits or genuine participation in the management of the preserve. The experiences of Maya Centre Village have been important in further developments of locally owned and locally run ecotourism initiatives. In particular, the community ecotourism schemes in Toledo District have attempted to learn from the Cockscomb.

The Tourism Strategy for Belize (more commonly referred to as the Blackstone Report; Ministry of Tourism and the Environment/ Inter-American Development Bank, 1998) identified the development of community-based initiatives and micro enterprises as part of the key to a successful ecotourism industry. The report recommended that it was necessary to seek the initial agreement of all the stakeholders involved in community-based ecotourism, and that the benefits should be shared equally by all levels of society. This in turn would attract more ecotourists to Belize, thereby creating a successful industry. In particular, Toledo District was highlighted as a possible eco-cultural zone to attract international visitors, using a Mayan heritage trail as a marketing tool (op cit, pp1–10). The geographical remoteness of parts of Toledo District, its relative lack of development, its reliance on subsistence agriculture and the small scale of its revenue-generating ventures has led to a type of ecotourism, far removed from the culture of the Northern cayes. For example, Toledo District is not renowned for its scuba diving because the reefs are far from the shore, and the underwater visibility is poorer than the rest of Belize because so many rivers drain into the Gulf of Honduras. As a result, Toledo markets itself as a fly-fishing, kayaking, trekking and cultural tour destination.[2]

The ecotourism industry in Southern Belize ranges from up-market rainforest lodges to very basic accommodation in local communities. At the luxury end of the scale, the Fallen Stones Butterfly Ranch offers lodges overlooking the Maya Mountains and the Guatemalan border. The ranch is near the Mayan ruins of Lubaantuun, which have recently been developed with a grant from the EU.[3] However, the main source of revenue for Fallen Stones is the production of Blue Morpho butterflies for export to butterfly houses and botanical gardens across the world.[4] At the other end of the scale, Toledo has numerous community-based conservation and ecotourism initiatives that offer basic facilities to visitors. For

example, Will Maheia, Director of the Toledo Institute for
Development and Environment (TIDE), says that the organization
trains fishermen to act as fly-fishing and wildlife guides. TIDE
estimates that fly-fishing can earn a good tour guide US$200 per
day, an enormous contrast to the US$25 per day for commercial
fishing. Likewise, TIDE approaches local hunters to become
wildlife tour guides, since they know how to find pacas and jaguars,
which ecotourists are eager to pay to see, in the rainforests and
mangroves.[5] In fact, TIDE won an International Ecotourism
Society award for sustainable ecotourism development.[6] Clearly,
TIDE's strategy is dependent on the idea that ecotourism will
generate revenues for local people, and that the activities will be
environmentally and (critically) financially sustainable.

The identification of Toledo as a key part of the national
tourism plan was politically significant in the context of ethnic
divisions in Belize. The Mayan community lives mainly in the
Southern districts of Belize, and constitutes most of the population
in Toledo District. In ecotourism terms, Toledo is particularly
known for its Mayan village accommodation, where ecotourists
are encouraged to spend time in a Mayan village as part of a
cultural tour of indigenous peoples. This in turn has sparked
debates about the use of the word 'Maya' as a global brand name,
and the ways in which indigenous people are constructed, packaged
and sold as ecotourist attractions. This section will examine the
politics of ecotourism in Southern Belize and its place within the
broader context of controversies over paving the Southern
highway, illegal logging concessions, the death of Mayan leader
Julian Cho, and the creation of a trans-border conservation area
with neighbouring Guatemala.

The Toledo Ecotourism Association (TEA) was established to
ensure that communities retained revenues and other benefits from
ecotourism ventures. It was set up partly in response to experience
of other communities with ecotourism. Most villagers have little or
no experience of ecotourism and they lack the necessary capital and
training to ensure that ecotourism in their area is a commercial
success. However, with community-based ecotourism the objective
is to ensure that local people retain control. Villages involved in the
TEA share the revenue from all the activities surrounding

ecotourism, such as guiding, accommodation, provision of meals and entertainment. For example, in TEA villages such as Medina Bank, a different family provides for visitors each day, and they are directly paid for inviting ecotourists into their homes. In addition, members of the community have been sent on courses to enhance their hospitality skills and to discuss future options for developing ecotourism for the benefit of the community. The TEA programme is a communally managed project that provides separate guesthouses within Mayan villages. Participation in the TEA scheme clearly differentiates it from the other ecotourism initiatives in the district. Each participating village has an elected representative (*alcalde*) in the TEA project to ensure that the interests of all the communities are represented. In addition, it is run along very different lines to the home-stay programme that encourages visitors to stay with individual Mayan families.[7] The success of the TEA programme has won it international recognition for its sensitivity to community interests. In fact, the TEA guesthouse programme won the world prize for socially responsible tourism in 1996, presented at the International Tourism Exchange tradeshow in Berlin.[8] Laguna was the first village to complete its guesthouse in 1991, followed shortly after by other TEA villages such as San Pedro Columbia, Barranco, San Miguel and Santa Cruz. Laguna village hosted its first ecotourists in 1991, and from then on visitors were sent to the villages on a rota basis in order to spread the income.

The trips were specifically marketed to visitors who had an interest in Mayan and Garifuna culture, who were looking for a less-than-luxurious but rewarding experience, and who had the desire to see 'pristine natural environments' (Williams, 1993b, pp3–8). For example, some of the villages offered trips to nearby waterfalls, unexcavated Mayan ruins, horse-riding trails, medicinal plant trails in the rainforests and tours of herbal or botanical gardens in the villages. Furthermore, some of the participating villages had explored the development of eco-trails, incorporating two- or three-day hikes into the Maya Mountain Reserve with villagers acting as guides and porters.[9] Chet Schmidt (an adviser to the TEA) suggests that most of the ecotourists who are interested in the Maya village stays are upper-middle class, well educated, experienced in travelling in the developing world and concerned for care of the environment. In addition, he thinks that such visitors are willing to pay more for the TEA scheme than they would for similar trips because it is more socially responsible and culturally aware. One indicator of the types of traveller that the scheme appeals to is the fact that it was nominated for a sustainable tourism award by the up-market *Conde Nast Traveller* magazine.[10] The TEA programme also receives support from parts of the local hotel sector and assistance from other businesses on the grounds that it attracts ecotourists (and their spending power) to Southern Belize and especially Punta Gorda. For example, the US owners of Dem Dats Doin Farm in Toledo have passed on their knowledge about sustainable farming to the local communities participating in the TEA project.[11]

However, the ecotourist development of Mayan communities in Southern Belize has also attracted significant levels of criticism. Participating communities have experienced differential benefits according to their level of local organization, their ability to lobby within the TEA and their geographical position. For example, Medina Bank is situated on the Southern highway and has very good access to national bus networks, while San Pedro Columbia is served by a bus only a few times per week, and Barranco is normally only reachable by boat or by a lengthy and infrequent bus trip. Those ecotourists without their own transport are keener on villages with good transport links, particularly if they are working to a tight schedule.[12]

Gregory Ch'oc of the Kekchi Council for Belize has pointed out that ecotourism is not the solution to the problems facing Mayans in Central America. The Kekchi Council of Belize is more concerned to develop a variety of economic activities for Mayan communities, and ecotourism would be one opportunity among many others. In particular, there has been an attempt to develop sustainable forestry (focusing on tropical hardwoods) and organic farming of maize and cacao, because these require few initial resources. The Mayan communities of Southern Belize already have substantial experience in sustainable forestry and organic farming, and would not require much capital investment to cover start-up costs. They would also not have to wait long before seeing a return on the investment. Toledo is already nationally known for rainforest products such as cashew fruits and nuts, medicinal herbs and cacao. The Cacao Producers' Association is one of the major producers of Maya Gold organic chocolate, which is marketed in Europe as an ethical and environmentally friendly product.[13] Ecotourism development does not have these benefits: it can often take a number of years of investment and development before showing an economic return, and the question of genuine community participation is also problematic. For example, many of the villages in Toledo do not have the technical capacity to develop and manage bank accounts and deal with complex financial transactions. Similarly, the remoteness of some villages from banking facilities is also a barrier to communities being able to exercise full financial control over the economic benefits of ecotourism.[14]

One of the major obstacles to the full participation of Mayans in ecotourism in Toledo is the system of tour-guide licensing. Many of the people involved in the scheme are facing financial difficulties, because in this area tour guiding is a part-time activity. It is common for people in this district to have more than one job, so that guiding may undertaken one day per week, but the other six days will be devoted to cacao or maize production, or subsistence hunting and fishing. However, the Tour Guide Association rules stipulate that all guides must attend relevant courses and pay an annual fee to retain their licences. This is part of a broader process of professionalization of the Belizean ecotourism industry, considered by tourism policy makers to be vital for sustaining the industry. It was also a key part of their marketing strategy of presenting Belize as a safe place to visit, with high levels of professional service. For part-time guides, however, it is a significant barrier because they do not earn the same levels of revenue from ecotourism as guides on the cayes, and they cannot devote time to residential courses in Belize City if they are tied to subsistence agricultural systems.[15] In response to complaints, the Belize Tourism Board and the Ministry of Tourism agreed to a new category of guide, the village site guide, at a reduced licence fee of B$10 (US$5). Such guides do not have to attend formal training sessions in Belize City. However, this formal acknowledgement of the different circumstances for Mayan people led to complaints from members of the conventional tour-guiding sector. The other tour guides complained that their licences cost B$140 (US$70), and they had to attend courses in Belize City and prove they had no criminal convictions. They argued that the TEA guides were being privileged over other guides, and that a number of them had convictions for growing marijuana.[16] It was clear that despite winning global awards, ecotourism initiatives in Southern Belize were still facing problems and some opposition from other parts of the Belizean ecotourism industry.

In addition, Mayan organizations have raised objections to the ways in which Mayan culture has been packaged for ecotourist consumption. Mayan villages constitute a major cultural attraction for international visitors. Traditional Mayan crafts are particularly sought after by international ecotourists, and Mayan communities have actively responded by developing wood and stone carving, basket weaving and textile production. One of the difficulties with this is that Mayan crafts are then divorced from their cultural and religious context, and thereby lose a great deal of their significance. For example, ecotourists buy and use the brightly coloured woven bags (*cuxtal*) that are traditionally used by Mayan men when working in the fields (*milpas*). Likewise, the complex patterns that are woven into women's shawls (*huipiles*) tell a story of spiritual and historical significance; different colours in the shawls represent various spiritual forces and environmental elements. The *huipiles* that are crafted for international ecotourists end up as pieces of art or wall-hangings in homes in North America and Europe (Abbott-Conc, 1995; Benz, 1998; Toledo Maya Cultural Council and Toledo Alcaldes Association, 1997, p26). However, this is not to suggest that the production of local crafts benefits international visitors to the detriment of indigenous communities. For example, in the tourist and even the non-tourist towns and cities of the Yucatan Peninsula in Mexico, it is possible to buy *huipiles* made for Barbie dolls, which appeal to locals and international visitors alike.

One problem with crafts in Belize is that Mayan ceremonial baskets are often on sale to international visitors. The preparation of *jipijapa* and *bayal* plant fibres for the baskets requires a great deal of time and labour, and skilled craftspeople are needed to weave the baskets (Toledo Maya Cultural Council and Toledo

Alcaldes Association, 1997, p28). Consequently, the baskets are expensive compared with other souvenirs, and ecotourists complain that they are not worth the price because they are plain and unpainted. Of course, local people who attach a cultural and spiritual value to the baskets view this as an insult. However, there is an even greater problem than the feeling that the baskets are undervalued; according to Pio Saqui at the University College of Belize, it is not uncommon to find Mayan children who believe that the baskets are made purely for ecotourists and have no other significance beyond their material value. Traditionally, the baskets are special because they are used on particular occasions and have a spiritual dimension, but they are in danger of becoming mere trinkets that compete with other arts and crafts in the ecotourist markets.[17] Another example of this is the reinvigoration of traditional dances and spiritual rituals that villages had ceased to practise for a variety of reasons. Conejo Creek in the Sarstoon-Temash area has re-established its traditional deer dance with funding from the Kekchi Council of Belize. This funding allowed them to rent costumes from Mayan communities in Guatemala that still practised the dance. However, Mayan leaders have pointed out that these rituals and traditions should be revitalized to ensure that Mayan culture will continue, not simply for ecotourist consumption.[18]

Complaints about the use of the word 'Maya' as a brand name by local and international businesses were also a key part of local opposition to the development of a Canadian-owned dam. A company had taken the name Hydro Maya Limited; but despite using Maya as a brand name, the company had failed to consult local people about the construction of a hydroelectric dam at San Miguel in Toledo. The Toledo Maya Cultural Council, the Kekchi Council of Belize, the Toledo Alcaldes Association and the Toledo Maya Women's Council strongly denounced the government's decision to lease the land for the dam to the Canadian firm without allowing local people the opportunity to participate properly in the decision-making process.[19] Rather than benefiting from the use of the name, Mayan communities in Belize feel that their temples, rituals, way of life, history, culture and people are marketed to raise revenue for private businesses and government. Mayan communities have the highest rates of infant mortality, illiteracy, poverty and malnutrition in Belize.[20] This stands in stark contrast to the images of Mayan culture used by the government of Belize (and those of other Central American states) to attract ecotourists and the revenue that they bring with them; Mayans are shown as being untouched by modernity, living a simple, agrarian life, wearing traditional clothing and engaging in age-old spiritual rituals. Of course, the reality of life for Mayan communities is significantly more complex. Most Mayan people experience social, political and economic marginalization, and even exclusion.

This history of exclusion has meant that ecotourism in Toledo has provoked demands from Mayan organizations for the recognition of indigenous land rights. This has meant that community-based ecotourism has become intimately bound up with one of the most politicized issues in Central America. The Mayan communities in Toledo have consistently lobbied for the establishment of a Mayan homeland, which is related to calls for the development of a Mayan eco-park. The proposals for the eco-park include a controlled amount of ecotourism to ensure that it is self-financing. The proposal of a Mayan homeland arose with a map drawn by the Mayan communities showing the places where – according to Pio Coc, head of the Toledo Maya Cultural Council – they hunt, fish, farm, live, work, use the rivers, collect herbs and raise families. In effect, Mayan communities were asking for the area that they already inhabited to be designated as their homeland. The Mayan people occupy a government reservation in Toledo, which dates from the colonial period when Belize was under British control. Mayan people feel they have no ownership of their land, which could be taken away from them at any point.[21]

Calls for a Mayan homeland have been resisted by the central government because it would mean the de facto legal recognition of the rights of indigenous peoples to claim land and other political rights in the Central American region. The Toledo Maya Cultural Council was concerned that plans for the Mayan homeland were being frustrated because the central government in Belize believed that Mayans were asking for a state within a state. Chet Schmidt of the TEA has been one of the main proponents of the eco-park. He claims that the central government is resisting the eco-park because of old-fashioned anti-Mayan racism, and because the Mayans in the area have consistently opposed the government of Belize (regardless of which political party is in power). In addition, he suggests that a success in the economically impoverished region would highlight the political corruption that had swallowed up previous funds destined for development in the area. He also argues that there has been an active attempt to prevent ecotourism in Toledo because the north and west of the country already had a well-developed tourism infrastructure. The powerful interest groups in the established ecotourism areas (including tour operators, hotels and bars) wanted to retain control.[22]

In addition, some of the Mayan villages in Toledo are defined as non-Belizean and inhabited by illegal immigrants from Guatemala. The Mayan community is split between Mopan and Kekchi Maya, and there is some dispute over their nationality and origin. Mopans are generally accepted to have lived in Belize over a very long period, possibly since before the arrival of colonial settlers. It is unclear whether Kekchi are recent settlers fleeing from persecution in Guatemala, or whether they are the same as the Mopan, who have a recognized historical right to live in Belize.[23] The Kekchi have engaged in illegal migration from Guatemala to Belize over a very long period of time because it is viewed as a haven from persecution for Mayan people. However, the government of Belize has persistently refused to acknowledge the land rights of migrant communities in Southern Belize. This refusal is in spite of the constitutional commitment to acknowledge squatter's rights if they have worked the same piece of land for more than 30 years.[24] Migration from Guatemala to Belize is also a highly sensitive political issue because of the longstanding conflict with Guatemala over the site of the border, and because of decades of civil war and persecution of the Mayan majority by the Latino minority in Guatemala (Shoman, 1995, pp219–222). The Belizean government's questioning of the legitimacy of claims for a Mayan homeland is inextricable from the historical dispute between Belize and Guatemala, and is closely linked to the regional persecution of Mayans, which led to numerous waves of forced migration.

Ecotourism in Toledo is also problematic because broader development processes have brought new threats and opportunities to community conservation initiatives. Ecotourism is intimately linked with local, national and international politics. This is very apparent in the controversial Economic, Social and Technical Assistance Project (ESTAP), which is the major development plan for the district. In general, the local Mayan communities have protested against ESTAP, while other ethnic groups in Toledo have responded with mixed feelings. The centrepiece of ESTAP is a commitment to paving the Southern highway, financed by a loan from the Inter-American Development Bank (IDB). Supporters of ESTAP argue that it will develop local infrastructure and facilitate transport and trade through the region (ESTAP, 2000). Villagers have protested against ESTAP partially because of fears over land rights, although they do not have legal rights over the land that will be directly affected. The project has become more responsive to local needs in the face of resistance from local people to the idea of speculative interests coming into the area after the road has been paved. Local critics have good reasons to be concerned; there are already rumours that a deep-water port is being planned for Punta Gorda, aimed at attracting cruise ships on their way to Rio Dulce in Guatemala.[25] In addition, there are significant levels of local anxiety about a possible export processing zone that would allow internet gambling facilities to be set up in area near the Northern highway (near Belize City).[26] This has caused particular concern because leading politicians in Belize have been involved in supporting the idea of the internet casino in Toledo; they already control similar facilities in Northern Belize.

The main source of conflict is the plan to build a highway to join up with the Peten highway, which is a major transport artery in Guatemala. In 1998, at the start of his term as Prime Minister, Said Musa announced on a visit to Toledo that the only way for the Southern highway to be truly economical and deliver significant benefits to the district was for it to be extended into Guatemala.[27] However, this road is planned for an area that is a continuous stretch of rainforest crossing the border between Belize and Guatemala. The forest communities and environmentalists have protested that the road will destroy the rainforest. The Sarstoon-Temash area has been highlighted by the Belize Audubon Society as a possible site for rare bird conservation under the Convention on

Wetlands of International Importance, Especially as Waterfowl Habitat (RAMSAR). If Sarstoon-Temash were to get RAMSAR recognition it would immediately generate international support for establishing a protected area in the regions around the Belize–Guatemala border.[28] Mayan communities have pointed out that a road through to Guatemala would irrevocably change their way of life, and destroy a key resource on which they depend for subsistence. Mayan communities have claimed that paving the Southern highway will lead to land speculation, and since the land in the area is a government-owned reservation, local villages will have no real protection from private sector and government land speculators. In an attempt to mitigate this and prevent land specu-lation, there will be a two-mile corridor either side of the highway in which no new developments will be allowed.[29] Mayan commu-nity organizations remain concerned that the corridor will not be respected once the highway is paved.

K Mustafa Toure, the project manager for ESTAP, argues that while Mayan concerns are important, it would be inappropriate to skew the development of ESTAP to take account of their demands to the detriment of the other 45–50 per cent of local people who are drawn from the Garifuna, Creole, East Indian and Hispanic communities.[30] Likewise, when the *Toledo Development Corporation Bill* was introduced by Prime Minister Musa, it was made clear that, while it was important to listen to the land claims of Mayan communities in Belize, he would not be in favour of ethnic division of the country involving the creation of a Mayan homeland.[31] Clearly, the issue of developing Toledo is politically charged, with competing interest groups ranging from Mayan communities to the cruise ship industry claiming that they offer the appropriate pathway to development for the region. The competing claims on the land and resources of Toledo are at the heart of Mayan fears that their attempts at locally based development and conserva-tion will be undermined by policy processes over which they have no control. In addition, since ecotourism is primarily regarded as a business, its supporters fear that it will not be able to compete economically with other forms of development in the district.

One of the most controversial issues in Toledo is the logging of tropical hardwoods for export. The outcry over legal and illegal logging in the district is also intimately bound up with the death of the Mayan leader, Julian Cho. His death set interest groups in the area against each other, as they argued over whether it was accidental or whether he was murdered for his outspoken stance against logging companies. In the local press the issue of development in Toledo was debated, and links were made to broader questions of political corruption in the country. Rumour and counter-rumour were used to present the frustration of the eco-park as part of a political conspiracy aimed at preventing the region developing with any kind of genuine local participation. Opponents of the 'big development' plans in the area were convinced that political interests in the area were involved in the abuse of a Malaysian logging licence in the Columbia River Forest Reserve. For example, a national newspaper, *Amandala*, published an article suggesting that the concession to log the Columbia River Forest Reserve had unleashed furore among the local Mayans. The anger stemmed from the Mayan community's belief that the logging concession was detrimental to their way of life and unsustainable, and that there had been extensive abuses of the licence.[32] Likewise, the issue of logging was intimately linked to fears over paving the Southern highway, because there was a local perception that the road was to be upgraded to specifically benefit loggers rather than contributing to broad development in the district.[33]

Concerns were immediately raised about the way the licences were issued by the Ministry of Natural Resources. The logging question was also linked to broader allegations of political corruption surrounding the way that the licence was supported by Dito Juan, the then Minster of Lands and Natural Resources, who was also the local MP for Toledo.[34] Ting Jack Heng, a Belize-based Malaysian businessman, was granted two licences to log the Columbia River Forest Reserve on a sustained yield basis under the name of Atlantic Industries and Toledo Atlantic International. The companies were registered in Belize, but were financially backed by a larger Malaysian logging firm. The Toledo Maya Cultural Council responded to the announcement of the logging concession with an attempt to launch a lawsuit against the government of Belize and a petition to the Inter-American Commission on Human Rights to challenge the legality of the concession. This was tied to other

Mayan grievances over concessions that were given to AB Energy Incorporated, a US-based oil and gas exploration company that was granted rights to explore 750,000 acres of the district. The fact that the exploration sites were right next to Mayan settlements and environments that Mayans depend on for subsistence activities such as agriculture, plant collection and hunting caused a furore. The Maya Council asked the Supreme Court of Belize to cancel logging concessions in Mayan reservation lands on the grounds that logging was an infringement of their legitimate rights and that the licence to log had been granted in contravention of the constitution of Belize.[35]

In addition, the Maya Council and Toledo Ecotourism Association argued that the traditional Mayan system of selective logging, known as *teksen si*, was the only form of genuinely sustainable forestry for the district. *Teksen si* involves selective logging with minimal invasion by people and log trucks; timber is transported out of the rainforest on foot. *Teksen si* is a Mayan term for the leaf-cutter ant, and it refers to the way that the ant can carry more than its own body weight. Mayan organizations argued that this kind of ecoforestry coupled with the development of a Mayan eco-park would provide a central focus for fundraising from national and global conservation agencies. Indeed, they argued that if the Belize government gave its full support at an early stage, it too could benefit from the millions of dollars' worth of free advertising for Belize as an ecotourism destination. It was assumed that this advertising would appear in international news outlets, the travel media and (critically) numerous global conservation organizations.[36]

The conflict surrounding the logging licence eventually became such a key issue that the government of Belize could no longer ignore it. Once a new party had been elected to government in 1998, it had a greater capacity to tackle the problem than the previous government administration. In 1998 the licences were suspended and a review of the logging concession was ordered by Prime Minister Musa of the People's United Party. The review committee found that the licence had been issued in a clandestine manner, and that the Forest Department had exercised inadequate supervision, thereby allowing Atlantic Industries to engage in serious infractions of the licence. The review committee concluded that the operation of the licence had negatively impacted on the environmental and social wellbeing of communities in Toledo. It recommended the establishment of a transparent mechanism for issuing logging licences and the development of an independent monitoring unit for forest-based activities that included local Mayan leaders.[37]

Later that year the issue of logging hit the headlines again, with the controversy surrounding the death of Julian Cho, who was involved with the Toledo Ecotourism Association and the Toledo Maya Cultural Council. Both organizations had become increasingly engaged in lobbying for political recognition of the pressures facing Mayan people in Central America. Pio Coc of the Toledo Maya Cultural Council says that Cho was one of the greatest Mayan leaders and a real activist; the Mayan community has certainly suffered from his death.[38] In December 1998 Cho was found dead in a pool of blood at his home in Punta Gorda; he had died from a blow to the back of the head. On the night of his death Cho had been seen out with a friend in local drinking spots and another friend claimed to have escorted him home at 1am.[39]

His death immediately raised protests because there was a local perception that when Mayan people were killed there was never any proper police investigation, because they were denied real access to social justice in Belize. In letters and articles in the local newspapers Cho's family claimed that he had been murdered for his vocal stance on Mayan land rights, his support for the eco-park and his outspokenness in the campaign against logging by Atlantic Industries. In local newspapers such as *Amandala* Cho was initially presented as a hero of the Mayan people, and who had made personal sacrifices in order to fight for them. He actively lobbied against logging, was a part-time faculty member of the local chapter of the University College of Belize, and was chair of the Toledo Maya Cultural Council. He was widely known in the local community and perceived as a leader who was fighting against exploitation of the rainforest by international firms. Indeed, his supporters claimed that international capital did not respect national boundaries let alone the rights of Mayan people, and as a result Cho was campaigning for the future of Mayan people.[40]

The case was a high-profile story in the national newspapers for a number of weeks; latest developments were constantly reported. Two pathologists examined Cho's body: the first was a Belizean, who ruled that it was an accidental death. In response Cho's family brought in a second pathologist from the US, claiming that the evidence clearly pointed to murder.[41] However, after the police pathologist had finally ruled that Cho's death was an accident, his opponents placed stories and letters in the local press presenting Cho as an alcoholic who liked to fight in bars. His critics argued that his death was a consequence of his drinking and violent temper, rather than a result of an elaborate political conspiracy.[42] The way in which Cho's death was debated in the national press and among local people indicated how the incident inter-linked with broader political processes. It was clear that the issue of the Mayan eco-park could not be divorced from the death of Julian Cho, the Malaysian logging licence and wider concerns about corruption in Belize.

The politically charged atmosphere in Toledo has had a critical bearing on conservation and ecotourism policy-making processes. This is very apparent in the highly politicized debates over the creation of a trans-frontier peace park. It also indicates the ways that global networks comprised of international conservation organizations and local environmental lobby groups have an important impact on decision making by national government structures. Toledo is also the site for a planned trans-frontier conservation area that brings together territory from Guatemala and Belize under a single transnational management authority. The issue of the trans-frontier area, or peace park, has added another layer to the politics of ecotourism development in Belize. The peace park initiative would include two trans-frontier conservation areas: the first a terrestrial trans-border park to be shared between Belize and Guatemala intended to conserve rainforests, wildlife, plant life and archaeological ruins; and the second a marine-based conservation area in the Gulf of Honduras that would include the territorial waters of three states (Belize, Guatemala and Honduras).

NGOs have proved to be critical actors in negotiating in favour of trans-frontier cooperation in the realm of conservation. For example, the Toledo Ecotourism Association sent a representative to the Guatemalan side of the international border to discuss bringing tourists from Guatemala into the Mayan village guesthouse programme in Belize. It was hoped that this would have more potential than marketing home-stays in Northern Belize, where the majority of tourists come to scuba dive, snorkel and visit easily accessible Mayan ruins.[43] Likewise, the Toledo Maya Cultural Council has been involved in key negotiations to halt illegal logging in the rainforested areas that would eventually form part of the peace park. As part of its remit the council has been making links with Mayan communities on the Guatemalan side of the border to discuss sustainable development and assist with lobbying for the recognition of pre-Columbian Mayan land rights throughout Central America.[44]

However, international NGOs have caused some difficulties with local government agencies and locally based NGOs in Southern Belize. For example, the relationship between the local Toledo Institute of Development and Environment (TIDE) and the Belize representative for the US-based The Nature Conservancy (TNC) has raised concerns and suspicions about external dominance. TIDE derives some of its funding for its ecotourism and conservation projects from TNC.[45] However, some other interest groups in the area have pointed out that TIDE's development plans closely mirror the proposed ecotourism and development projects that were set out in a doctoral thesis by a TNC representative, Will Heyman. This has led to charges in the local press that TIDE provides a front for foreign interests who are keen to gain control of the Port Honduras tri-national marine park for themselves.[46] While these accusations are a little unfair in the case of TIDE, the criticisms of TNC come against a background of controversial interventions in tourism and conservation projects in Central America and a fear of US influence in the region after past experience of the Cold War. Consequently, the activities of a US conservation organization in the peace park raised historical fears of US political interference, and the inability to control foreign interests in land speculation in the region, especially with regard to ecotourism development (see Weinberg, 1991, for further discussion). The concerns raised by local people stemmed from their fears of external dominance and lack of control over NGO agendas that had been so prevalent in past projects that they had been involved in.

Another difficulty for agencies involved in peace parks is the rise of illegal migration in borderlands. The peace park implies a greater level of law enforcement through the increased presence of state agencies and NGOs with responsibility for conservation and ecotourism development in particular. The migrants from Guatemala rely on the border being a site beyond national control and far from the reach of law enforcement agencies. The proposed peace park will extend state control to the border regions as conservation agencies begin to patrol to enforce conservation laws and protect ecotourists as they visit remote regions of the country. These migrant communities are a key interest group in the peace parks, and yet they are often overlooked or even deliberately excluded from management plans and trans-frontier schemes. For example, the village of Graham Creek is entirely inhabited by illegal immigrants from Guatemala. The village is right beside the newly declared Sarstoon-Temash protected area, which will eventually become part of a trans-frontier initiative. The status of the inhabitants as illegal immigrants means that the Belizean communities in the area have deliberately excluded Graham Creek from management plans and discussions about conservation in the area.[47] Yet Graham Creek is one of the largest villages in Sarstoon-Temash and is an important stakeholder in the process of establishing a trans-frontier initiative. The residents of the village use the Sarstoon-Temash area, and their inclusion or exclusion in the management plans and discussions has a critical bearing on the future success of the park.

The peace park is also planned in an area that is a key resource for those interested in illegally harvesting flora and fauna for local use and international trade. There is a problem in Sarstoon-Temash with people from Sastun village, who cross the international border from Guatemala into Belize to collect orchids, log mahogany and harvest iguanas in the protected area. The orchids are used locally for medicinal purposes as a blood tonic, and there are concerns that they are also traded internationally. Belize is one of the few places where the extremely rare black orchid, which is prized by international collectors, can be found. Likewise, mahogany is also traded illegally. Iguanas are hunted for local consumption, but their status as a threatened species means that they are protected under

Belizean laws.[48] The problem is that the orchid, mahogany and iguana collectors simply disappear over the international border to avoid capture and prosecution. This is compounded by an understandable unwillingness among the local *alcades* (councillors and representatives) in Sastun to admit to the problem. The *alcaldes* fear reprisals from the illegal harvesters who are often heavily armed and have lucrative business interests to protect. Similarly, local people on the Belizean side of the Sarstoon-Temash area are afraid of the harvesters, whom they regard as particularly menacing and dangerous.[49]

Likewise, the Port Honduras area is used for the poaching of marine life, and of manatees in particular. Manatees are a protected species in Belize, but local communities have historically hunted them for meat, which is in heavy demand on the Guatemalan side of Port Honduras.[50] Will Maheia of TIDE estimated that, in the Port Honduras Marine Reserve alone, over 200 manatees had been killed between 1994 and 1999. The organizations involved in manatee conservation and management have found it especially difficult to prevent the illegal killing. This is because the meat attracts a very high price in Guatemala, and the area earmarked for the marine reserve is only 50 minutes by speedboat from Guatemalan territory. This meant that manatee hunters can enter Belizean waters, kill manatees, cut off the prime steaks and simply disappear back over the international border where Belizean authorities have no jurisdiction.[51] These criminal networks have a critical impact on the development of ecotourism initiatives in Southern Belize, and directly undermine schemes based on genuine community participation. The intimidation of villagers by smugglers and other criminal elements places an extra layer of pressure on an already-fragile community initiative. Since community-based ecotourism schemes rely on the natural environment to attract visitors and profits, any activity that damages the local ecology will also have a negative financial impact.

The plans for bi-national and tri-national peace parks have clearly raised important issues that centre on national and international security and even international legal arrangements. The security issue is compounded by the longstanding border dispute between the two countries. Since the Guatemalan government does not recognize Belize as a sovereign state, but considers it to be part of Guatemala, there is a question over the legality of trans-frontier initiatives and serious concerns about national security. Indeed, Belizean independence from the UK was delayed until 1980 not because of relations with the UK government, but because of fears about territorial disputes with Guatemala (Shoman, 1995, p206). The peace park in Southern Belize is controversial partially because of this border dispute with Guatemala. In the Sarstoon-Temash protected area, Guatemala defines the international border as the far side of the Temash riverbank, while Belize defines it as the deepest channel of the river. The ecologically significant Sarstoon-Temash river system is located in both Guatemala and Belize and it requires co-management so that the activities on each side of the international border are complementary.[52]

Despite improved relations there are still occasional border disputes that threaten to re-ignite conflict between the two countries. In 1999, Belizean Defence Force officers in the village of Arenal shot a Guatemalan civilian on the Western border. Arenal is split in two by the international border, but residents attend mass together, retain family and friendship ties and conduct trading together. However, the village's position on the international border makes it attractive to smugglers who traffic contraband goods such as drugs, immigrants and stolen items. The Guatemalan man who was shot by the Belizean military had allegedly attacked officers with a machete, but the incident strained the fragile relations between the two countries.[53] It came after a history of border incidents between the two countries; in 1999 the Guatemalan authorities had arrested Belizeans involved in illegal logging in a protected area in Guatemala.[54] The relationship between Guatemala and Belize was so tarnished in 1999 that senior ministers in the Guatemalan and Belizean governments began to consider turning to international arbitration to resolve the longstanding dispute.[55] These periodic disputes regarding the border have a direct impact on the development of ecotourism and the peace parks. Clearly, it is difficult to establish relationships based on cooperation and mutual trust so that conservation agencies are able to work together, when the governments of Belize and Guatemala are constantly engaged in disputes over control.

Political instability due to border disputes can reduce visitor numbers, and in Southern Belize, which attracts relatively few visitors, this could cause ecotourism initiatives to become unprofitable. Likewise, perceived or actual threats from criminal networks operating in border regions place community-based ecotourism ventures in jeopardy.

Conclusion

The question of genuine participation in ecotourism by indigenous communities is intimately linked with broader national and global political processes. The internationally recognized attempts by Mayan peoples to create and run their own ecotourism ventures have been simultaneously undermined and strengthened by the presence and operation of other interest groups in the region. The TEA guesthouse programme has had some successes in generating additional revenue for some Mayan villages, while others have not fared so well because of their relative inaccessibility. In addition, the international recognition associated with the tourism industry prize for socially responsible ecotourism provided global advertising for a very small scheme. However, ecotourism development for the benefit of Mayan communities is inextricably linked to the very processes that ensure these communities have remained relatively impoverished. For example, the potential for ecotourism development has been undermined by continued unsustainable and illegal logging practices in the Mayan forest reserves. In addition, the role of global environmental organizations such as TNC has not always been supportive of Mayan efforts. Global environmental organizations have their own agendas to fulfil, which may or may not intersect in a positive way with local needs. Globalized networks centred on interest groups as diverse as the conventional tourism industry, the road builders, international financial institutions and even dealers in illegal wildlife and timber products, have become a barrier to genuine participation by indigenous communities in development processes. Indeed, the debates that were sparked by Julian Cho's death indicate that Mayan communities have become highly politicized by the ways that the myriad of interest groups operate in Toledo. In the end, the calls for ecotourism as a pathway to environmental care with genuine locally controlled development cannot be divorced from or achieved without a recognition of the importance of Mayan claims to land and just treatment at the hands of central governments, private industry and the NGO sector.

CHAPTER **6**

ECOTOURISM AND THE POLITICS OF GLOBALIZATION

Ecotourism developments in Belize are intricately linked to processes of globalization, especially through networks of global capital. In general, analyses of tourism emphasize how it links developing countries to global capitalism through legitimate inter national business. Ecotourism in Belize is certainly derived from processes of globalization, such as the increase in international travel and the associated expansion of international travel agents, airlines and hotel chains. However, ecotourism in Belize and the wider Central American region is also interlinked with global capital in a peculiar way. The development of illicit networks that are involved in drug smuggling, money laundering, land specula-tion and illegal trafficking of Mayan archaeological artefacts also derive from processes of globalization. These global networks deal in legal and illegal sources of capital and they have a significant impact on the capacity of state agencies to enforce environmental legislation that is aimed at controlling the direction and form of ecotourism development.

The incorporation of developing states and societies into these global networks has had an important impact on notions of statehood in the South. Under globalization, state agencies have become unable to act as autonomous agencies that are capable of exercising sovereignty over their own territories. Instead, states in an era of globalization may be better regarded as arenas of complicated and often illicit transactions that are negotiated between global actors and local interest groups. In this way the state becomes an arena for those interest groups to compete and cooperate in their attempts to gain control over key resources. The state is then redefined as a source of power and wealth to groups with special interests to defend, and it becomes hollowed out by processes linked to globalization. In effect, visible international frontiers and structures of governance remain but are undermined and rendered useless. As these visible structures become less involved in the policy process, it is taken over by global networks allied to local elites. At issue, more basically still, is the clash between 'regulated' and 'unregulated' forms of globalization. On the one hand, there is the ideal of a globalized world in which common solutions can be negotiated and administered for common environmental problems, within an accountable and rule-governed global context. On the other hand, globalization means that the private interests of smugglers, money launderers and narcotics traders are capable of subverting or overwhelming any would-be structure of global or regional management of the environmental impacts of the ecotourism industry. This chapter will firstly explore the idea of a shadow state as developed by William Reno in his study of state collapse in Sierra Leone in order to illuminate how global networks undermine government policy making and enforcement in Belize. Secondly it will analyse the links between legitimate and illegitimate business and how they are related to global and local Belizean interest groups through an examination of land speculation, offshore banking and money laundering, and trafficking of Mayan archaeological artefacts, lobsters and drugs.

Shadow States, Ecotourism and Globalization

In general, the literature on tourism has focused on how processes of globalization that operate through legitimate private business have transformed parts of the developing world and captured it as part of a global world system. However, this chapter is concerned with a different kind of global network that incorporates developing societies. These are the illicit and transnational networks that are used by drug traffickers, money launderers and smugglers dealing in undersized lobsters and Mayan artefacts. It is essential to have an understanding of how these globalized networks undermine national governments. In particular, they frustrate and block attempts to ensure that the ecotourism industry is properly regulated so that it conforms to the international standards set by its advocates. This chapter will focus on the concept of shadow states to illuminate how illicit links between local and global elites have undermined attempts to provide a properly regulated ecotourism industry in which environmental legislation is properly enforced.

The concept of shadow states is derived from William Reno's work on Sierra Leone, and later work on Nigeria, the Democratic Republic of Congo and Liberia. There are obvious difficulties with drawing comparisons between developing states in sub-Saharan Africa and the Caribbean, but the specific history of Belize means that the similarities are sufficient to make an examination of the notion of a shadow state worthwhile. For example, Belize shares with much of sub-Saharan Africa a British colonial history that bequeathed a highly bureaucratic, British-style government apparatus. Equally, kinship and familial ties have a central role to play in Belizean society, politics and economics in a way that accords well with scholarship on patron–client networks in African societies. Finally, the drug trade in Central and South America displays some features similar to diamond trading. Where Belize definitely differs is in its international reputation as a holiday destination, because Sierra Leone has been the site of much violent conflict. In contrast, Belize has experienced political stability since independence in 1980, and the relative absence of large-scale political violence has allowed Belize to build up an ecotourism industry.

In his study of the organization of informal markets in sub-Saharan Africa, Reno formulated the concept of the 'shadow state'. In essence it is the study of the transformation of weak states to warlord politics through an understanding of how rulers control markets to enhance their own power (Reno, 1998, p15). Ultimately it is based on Jean-Francois Bayart's argument that any scholarly focus on the visible state does not provide a basis from which to analyse political authority; instead, Bayart's analysis examines what he terms *politique du ventre* (the politics of the belly), how political elites use informal and invisible networks to exercise political and economic power (Bayart, 1993; Reno, 1995, p5). In the postcolonial period, African rulers have been given unprecedented monopolistic access to resources, such as military hardware and diplomatic contacts, that can be mobilized to alter the power balance of domestic politics (Bayart, 1993, pp60–79). As a result the struggle for power has become inextricably linked to the personal struggle for wealth, and these processes are sustained by the personal links between local and global elites. This focus on the invisible state indicates that the state in Africa deviates from Western notions of statehood. Bayart argues that the African state is a rhizome rather than a root system, meaning that it operates through a cobweb pattern of personal networks and assures the centralization of power through agencies of family, alliance and friendship. This in turn is indissoluble from external dynamics that impact on the continent (Bayart, 1993, pp260–266).

Drawing on Bayart's understanding of African politics and statehood, Reno's investigation of warlord politics is also useful in providing an analysis of how the state in Belize has changed not only its form, but also its ways of operating and interacting with non-state interest groups. Reno's examination of the growth of informal markets indicated that they sprang up partially in response to the decay of central state authority, demonstrating attempts by political leaders and elites to exercise authority in realms outside institutional state boundaries, and that this breakdown of state–society dichotomies appears even in, or especially in, the weakest formal states (Reno, 1995, p5). In these circumstances, rulers and elites reject the broader project of creating a state that serves a collective good or even of creating institutions that are capable of developing independent perspectives and acting on behalf of interests distinct from the rulers'. In this situation external businesses take on more and more important economic roles inside the zone of the collapsed state (Reno, 1998, pp1–2).

Reno argues that shadow states are composed of high-ranking politicians and a few businessmen (local or foreign) without state office who exercise significant political authority through the private control of resources in informal and illicit markets. Such clandestine circuits sustain powerful political and economic networks, and can be used to manipulate policies designed to attract legitimate foreign investors who then serve to underwrite the emergent shadow state. The informal networks of exchange between these groups cross, and sometimes shadow, the boundaries of formal state responsibilities and powers. As a result of the survival and growth of a shadow state, the post-colonial institutional state is no longer the principal authority in Africa (Reno, 1995, p5). Instead the triumph of the informal networks, to the near exclusion of state bureaucracies, or the state collapse, leaves rulers able to pursue power through means that also secure their private interests. State rulers come to resemble mafias rather than governments, so that the collective interests of the people within the state boundaries become subordinated to the private and individual interests of the warlord ruler (Reno, 1998, p3; Bayart, Ellis and Hibou, 1999).

Reno's shadow state was created in the struggle to define and shape political power that was born with the founding of the colonial state. This shadow state grows outside the territorial boundaries of the colonial creation as new elites are added to the alliances between ruling elites, international business and local social groupings, and these new elites include creditor officials and foreign investors (Reno, 1995, pp23–26). Underdevelopment can be the product of internal social structures and class relations in developing societies. In particular, local elites often invite in foreign capital and exploit other classes in their own society (Blomstrom and Hettne, 1984, pp81–91; Tangri, 1999, pp7–13). Part of the shadow state is the rulers' need for sovereign control that stands outside and above the political order, and so extra-legal powers are the logical means of preserving a regime in crisis. The ruler struggles to define enemies and find enticements to attract friends, and these enticements, as well as some of the allies, can be found in the form of international capital (Reno, 1995, pp23–26). These non-state allies that are courted by warlords mean that the new types of African rulers are not only given access to important sources of wealth, but also to new forms of coercion. The economic and political liberalization witnessed in the 1990s further undermined weak state rulers' incentives to pursue conventional strategies for maximizing their power through generating economic growth, and hence state revenues. Instead, entrepreneurial opportunities became available though privatization to important opponents of the state rulers, and this contributes to the development of warlord politics and the continuing weakening of African states (Reno, 1998, pp4–5).

Turning to the case of Belize, the growth of a shadow state is important because it directly impinges on policy implementation. Since Belize markets itself as an ecotourism destination, the possible links between a shadow state and policy implementation are especially important in terms of environmental and ecotourist legislation. In addition, it intertwines with the blue-green basis of ecotourism. Since blue-greens view the environment in terms of its economic value and as a resource for businesses to utilize, the dependence of the shadow state on links between legitimate and illegitimate business means it has a key role to play in the ecotourism sector. In the case of Belize, the boundaries between legitimate and illegitimate business interests have become increasingly blurred. Ecotourism is part of a wider arena of legitimate business interests that intersects with illicit networks sustained by political corruption and global chains of traffickers.

The Shadow State in Belize

Ecotourism is directly affected by and is even intimately linked to the illicit networks that make up the shadow state in Belize. This raises peculiar problems for environmental management, particularly because the networks that constitute the shadow state are rarely discussed in official environmental policy documents or in lobbying by conservation-oriented NGOs. This is important because the shadow state has a critical bearing on how environmental policy decisions are made and enforced.

How the shadow state impacts on the rates and direction of ecotourism development can be explained through a broader discussion of corruption. Elites obtain control over lucrative resources by legal and illegal means, but one of the important

factors is the corrupt allocation of benefits in the ecotourism industry by public and private sector elites. Moran argues that
corruption is not necessarily a pathological phenomenon; rather, it
is integrated into a particular path of political and economic development (Moran, 1999, pp569–587). Corruption can be broadly
defined as behaviour that deviates from the formal rules of conduct
governing the actions of someone in a position of public authority
because of private motives such as wealth, status or power. The
primary economic effect of such corruption is an allocative one if,
as a result, the final user of the resource is someone other than the
person who should have had access to the resource. The relative
political power of the patron (the state or the private sector) drives
the allocation of benefits (Khan, 1996, pp12–21). A World Bank
policy research bulletin highlighted the potential for public sector
corruption to act as a barrier to development. The state's coercive
capabilities gives it the power to intervene in economic activities,
including the tourism industry, and also provides it with the power
to intervene arbitrarily. This power coupled with access to information that is not available to the general public provides public
officials with opportunities to promote their own interests (World
Bank, 1997c).

One area where the shadow state can flourish is in offshore
banking, and its development has been a significant economic and
political change for a number of small developing countries. In the
1980s, encouraged by the deregulation of the international banking
system and by successive UK Conservative governments that argued
it was a means of economic diversification, a few former British
colonies and dependencies began to flourish as offshore centres.
They provided the critical space for the growth of the offshore
sector by guaranteeing client confidentiality, a favourable regula-
tory environment and climate of political tolerance (unlike former
French and Dutch colonies) (Hampton and Levi, 1999, p651).

The conditions under which offshore banking flourishes also
provide an ideal environment for international illicit networks of
criminal organizations. Under these circumstances organized crime
often enjoys protection from all levels of government, because it
has invaded the structures of the state and taken advantage of its
power and resources (Morris, 1999, p630). In this way global

networks that often inextricably link legal and illegal businesses manage to incorporate developing states into the fabric of their organizations. Criminal organizations are well placed to take advantage of looser border controls and lower trade barriers. It is clear that they have been able to create highly effective and illegal financial and drug smuggling networks that advance their interests in the context of a world keen to reduce economic barriers (Gelbard, 1996a; Gelbard, 1996b). Advances in computer technology have facilitated electronic transfer systems that allow vast amounts of money to be transported around the globe in a matter of seconds (Grove, 1995; see also Bureau for International Narcotics and Law Enforcement Affairs, 1998d, pp1–2; Bureau for International Narcotics and Law Enforcement Affairs, 1998c). This means that key figures have access to the financial resources to underwrite the emergent shadow state.

The importance of international investment in Belize is enhanced by its status as a major offshore banking centre. The deregulation of international banking during the 1980s has been identified as one of the key determinants of the rise in offshore centres that are willing to accept deposits derived from illicit sources, and Belize is one such centre (Hampton, 1996, pp78–87). A legal framework that provides for total discretion about the source of the investment capital and the names of investors has assisted the involvement of legitimate and illegitimate sources of foreign investment in tourism developments. For example, Maria Vega (a local tour operator and member of the Belize Tourism Industry Association) says that an increasing number of absentee foreign investors ultimately own restaurants and bars in the tourist areas, and they are leased on long-term contracts of up to 30 years. In addition, Belize is the site of a number of 'holding companies' that are not required to disclose the identity of their investors or the origins of their funds.[1] This is also mentioned in US government documents regarding the drugs trade and money laundering activities in the Caribbean. For example, the International Narcotics Control Strategy report states that money laundering remains a potential threat in Belize, even though the 1996 *Money Laundering Prevention Act* criminalized it and imposed record-keeping requirements on banks for large foreign currency transactions.

The government of Belize has been building an offshore services sector since 1992, and the Central Bank of Belize has received numerous inquiries about offshore banking licences. However, patterns and changes in individual accounts are not seen by any Central Bank authorities unless specifically ordered, and no registry is kept on offshore trusts (Bureau for International Narcotics and Law Enforcement Affairs, 1998d). The involvement of external capital derived from legal and illegal sources is a key feature of Reno's shadow state. It is clear that there is extensive foreign investment and ownership in Belize, and that, rather like the shadow state of Sierra Leone, foreign investors are required either legally or through necessity to utilize local economic and political links. Equally, these local elites have found it necessary to attract foreign capital in order to underwrite their emergent shadow state.

The links between the development of Belize as an offshore centre, drug trafficking and foreign elites became the subject of intense international debate in July 1999 with the highly publicized story of Michael Ashcroft. His influence in developing Belize as a major player in the global offshore services sector was of particular interest to the UK press because of his position as Conservative Party Treasurer. The controversy surrounded his company, Belize Holdings Incorporated (BHI), and his role in writing the offshore legislation that turned Belize into a financial centre.[2] In 1994 a Foreign Office adviser, Rodney Gallagher, was contracted by the Belize government to write a report on regulating a burgeoning offshore sector. In the report Gallagher warned against allowing too much freedom to the sector, fearing its use by criminal organizations, particularly drug traffickers.[3] He also expressed disquiet at the special status given to BHI, which did not have to disclose information about its accounts and had a 30-year exemption from tax. In fact, under the 1996 *Offshore Banking and Money Laundering Prevention Act*, BHI was the only company to retain this special status.[4] This was attributed to the immense political and economic power held by Ashcroft, in his capacity as a Belizean citizen, the Belize Ambassador to the United Nations (affording him a diplomatic passport); he was resident in Florida for tax purposes, Treasurer to the British Conservative Party and a major funder of the People's United Party (PUP) in Belize. In addition, one interviewee pointed to the close relationship between Michael Ashcroft and a leading PUP politician, Glenn Godfrey. There was a clear perception that the level of control over politics and policy making that Ashcroft and Godfrey had meant they were able to write the offshore legislation that had made Belize a tax haven and a major offshore centre.[5] In fact, Belize Offshore Services is one of a group of companies owned by Glenn Godfrey.

It was reported in the local and international press that Michael Ashcroft was averse to interference by the Central Bank of Belize in the running of Belize Bank, a section of BHI. As part of his attempts to avoid such interference he sought permission to set up a separate bank in the Turks and Caicos Islands to take advantage of its lax regulations in its offshore sector. It was reported that Ashcroft had threatened the UK Conservative government in 1994 that, if he were not allowed to set up his own bank in the Turks and Caicos Islands, he would use his links to high-ranking politicians in the Commonwealth to cause trouble.[6] In addition, he paid for four Conservative MPs to visit the Turks and Caicos, Cuba, Panama and Belize, giving rise to speculation that those MPs then asked questions in the UK Parliament that provided support for Ashcroft's business interests.[7]

However, the press soon linked the rise of Belize as an offshore centre to the trans-shipment of drugs and money laundering in the wider Latin American region. The US Drugs Enforcement Agency (DEA) had already indicated that Belize was attracting money launderers to its secretive offshore services sector, and that it was a major player in the trans-shipment of cocaine. *The Times* then led with a front page story 'Drugs Agency has Ashcroft on its files', indicating that the DEA had four separate investigations on Ashcroft and his companies for possible money laundering and drug smuggling. However, the newspaper also added in the article that so far it had no evidence of actual wrongdoing or criminal activities.[8] Michael Ashcroft then issued a libel writ against *The Times* for defamation and damage to his business interests, but later dropped the case after direct discussions with Rupert Murdoch, owner of the parent company News International.[9] This meant that two of the most prominent supporters of the Conservative

Party in the UK were able to reach an amicable agreement and stave off a politically damaging libel case. The Ashcroft case is an example of the influence of foreign elites in developing countries and, according to Reno, these elites are an essential component that allows the expansion of the shadow state. Certainly, in the international and local media, the reporting of the case indicated a perception that powerful foreign elites were able to induce policy changes favourable to their interests by issuing threats and possibly engaging in illicit activities.

The sector where the shadow state is at its most pervasive and its most effective in Central America is in drug trafficking. The organizations and the networks involved in trafficking have not only incorporated the state apparatus, but also created a set of state agencies that protect and support their activities. While Colombian drug cartels of the 1980s and early 1990s were highly visible and posed a direct threat to the state, the nature of trafficking changed significantly in the late 1990s, and its focus has turned to Mexico. The new breed of traffickers is more discreet and has established a series of smaller-scale organizations that are interested in co-opting key personnel within the political and judicial systems. Traffickers are also more likely to work through legitimate small businesses and contract out manufacturing and transport to specialist groups.[10] Drugs may be only one part of a broader criminal business that includes legitimate operations on the one hand (such as tourism) and bank robberies, car theft, arms trafficking and kidnapping on the other (Morris, 1999, p630).

The US Department of State estimates at least US$85 billion in drug profits can be found within the banking system (Grove, 1995; Bureau for International Narcotics and Law Enforcement Affairs, 1998c; Bureau for International Narcotics and Law Enforcement Affairs, 1998d; Calvani, Guia and Lemahieu, 1997, pp659–672), and the tourism industry has proved to be a place where illegitimate business interests can converge with corrupt public sector managers, because the arrival of tourism is often associated with an increase in crime, prostitution and an expansion in the supply of drugs (Stonich, Sorensen and Hundt, 1995, pp21–24; Pattullo, 1996, pp90–101). Tourism development in Belize has been partially dependent on drug culture in the industrialized world on two levels: recreational drug taking by tourists, and funding of tourist developments by capital derived from dealing and smuggling. The demand and supply routes for drugs, particularly, cocaine, have had a significant impact on the direction and rates of development in the tourism industry in Belize.

The Caribbean and Central America are two regions that have been targeted as trafficking routes by drug cartels. Within the Central American/Caribbean region, Belize has not been immune to the development of this illegal international trade in narcotics. The US Department of State identified Belize as a significant drug transit country. Since Belize lies between the producing countries of South America and the consumer countries of Europe and North America, its position marks it out as an ideal route for smugglers. In addition, the unique geography of the Caribbean, and especially Belize, means that hundreds of islands provide points to drop off and pick up consignments of drugs. Belize's contiguous borders with Mexico and Guatemala, large tracts of forested land, unprotected coastline, numerous cayes, inland waterways, unpopulated rainforest and coastal areas and a rudimentary infrastructure for combating trafficking and abuse present the opportunity for significant trans-shipment of illicit narcotics.[11] In the local press, the increases in trafficking of so-called hard drugs has been partially blamed on drug cartels utilizing the old trafficking routes for marijuana through Belize to Mexico and ultimately through to the US in order to target its markets for cocaine and heroin.[12] In fact it was reported in the Belizean press that officers from the US Counter-Narcotics Cocaine Unit visited Customs at the port of Belize and the sniffer dogs were so overwhelmed by the smell of drugs that they suffered sensory overload and were unable to function.[13]

Belize has fallen foul of the internationally publicized 'war on drugs' and the high-profile country certification process. The Belizean government was criticized for failing to curb the use of Belize as an entrepôt state and this has affected relations between Belize and the US. The country certification process is an annual assessment of the 32 major drug producing and drug transit countries, where the countries are judged according to the steps they have taken to enforce the goals of the 1988 UN Convention

Against Illicit Traffic in Narcotic Drugs and Psychotropic Substances. Certification is used as a diplomatic tool by the US government to focus attention on producing and trafficking states rather than consumer states. There are three categories: full certification, de-certification and a grant of 'vital national interests' certification. Belize was de-certified by the US for failing to be active in the war on drugs. However, US government documents indicate that Belize was granted the position of vital national interests, which meant that US aid was not suspended and that the US would not vote against loans to Belize from the multilateral development banks.[14]

One of the striking features of the drugs trade is the way that growers, traffickers and dealers are increasingly paid in drugs rather than cash. This means that trans-shipment countries will be subject to an expansion in the availability of drugs and its attendant problems of narcotic abuse and rising crime (Calvani, Guia and Lemahieu, 1997, pp659–672). Belize certainly provides an example of this because the inter-relationship between drug trafficking, money laundering (through offshore banking and construction of hotels) and the ecotourism industry could only be sustained by the existence of a shadow state. The expansion of trafficking in Belize has impacted on the tourism industry. For example, it was reported that cocaine trafficking brought a new spurt of wealth to the local economy in Placencia where the local press noted the appearance of new speedboats and the beginnings of a construction boom.[15] Similarly, there was local speculation from critics of the involvement of foreign interests and possible criminal elements that entire resorts were bought with millions of dollars in cash, derived from the drug trade.[16] In 1999 James Kavanagh, a citizen of Colorado, was expelled from Belize and escorted out of the country by US marshals and DEA officers. He had been a resort owner in Cayo District, but had been found to be engaged in money laundering and the drug trade, using the resort as a legitimate business front for illegal activities.[17]

Likewise, in Belize City, the government built a tourism village to welcome visitors to the city and make it more attractive to ecotourists and the growing number of cruise ship passengers. The tourism village was designed to sell craft goods and souvenirs to foreign visitors.[18] However, the problem still remained that the majority of crafts on sale in Belize were imported from Mexico, Guatemala and El Salvador, rather than genuinely benefiting Belizean craft producers. For example, those living in the south of Belize City were unable to access markets for souvenirs with their wood carvings because ecotourists did not explore the city, but tended to remain in the coastal Fort George area.[19] The tourism village was highly controversial from its inception for other reasons. The government of Belize was heavily criticized for giving the contract to build the village to Mike Feinstein who retained majority ownership of the site. He had previously been involved in alleged drug smuggling and money laundering activities that had allowed him to buy entire private island resorts for cash.[20] So it was clear there was a direct link between legitimate ecotourism businesses and allegations of involvement in corrupt activities.

It is clear that authorities in Belize were, on the one hand, overwhelmed by the extent of trafficking, and on the other hand, that elements in the formal state apparatus were complicitous, leading to the state's incorporation into global trafficking networks. For example, the US Bureau for International Narcotics and Law Enforcement Affairs stated that the ability of the government of Belize to combat trafficking was severely undermined by deeply entrenched corruption, which reached into senior levels of government. In addition, it indicated that ministers in the government as well as police officers were complicitous in the drug trade (Bureau for International Narcotics and Law Enforcement, 1998d). The extent of trafficking in Belize is the direct result of complicity in the institutions that are intended to prevent smuggling. There is a perception in Belize that there are elements in the police force and Fisheries Department that are involved in the drug trade.[21] The US insists that local military and law enforcement agencies are involved in internal drug enforcement missions, and this increases the potential for corruption and human rights abuses. A number of interviewees remarked that they believed elements in the Fisheries Department, the Belize Defence Force and the police to be engaged in the drug trade. One interviewee, who was formerly involved with fisheries, explained how it was possible to intercept drug drops so that the relevant authorities would not know if a few bales of cocaine were not handed in, but were sold by the officers themselves. The ability to find and sell bales of cocaine that were washed up on the shores of Belize's cayes was locally referred to as winning the 'sea lotto'.[22] Likewise, other interviewees made reference to the experiences of people who worked for the Fisheries Department, and local members of the fishing cooperatives in San Pedro. They explained that they had often come across bodies and drugs floating in the waters around Bacalar Chico, a remote protected area that sits right on the border with Mexico.[23] This conforms to Reno's argument that a key feature of the shadow state is the creation of private armies to protect the illicit trading networks from which political and economic elites draw their strength. It also indicates that the stipulations regarding law enforcement and control of the drugs trade that are expected by Northern interests are subverted by the very nature of those North–South linkages. As a result any possibility of controlling the drugs trade in the manner favoured by US interests, in particular, is rendered impossible.

The Impact of the Shadow State on Ecotourism Policy

The shadow links that are ultimately responsible for decision making in Belize are evidence of a process that is more formalized than simple ad hoc or uncoordinated corruption. The links between the public and private sector, local elites and external capital constitute a shadow state, and this is nowhere more apparent than in the inability of the formal state apparatus to enforce environmental legislation in the ecotourism industry. The existence of shadow links between the private sector, the public sector and criminal elements means that enforcement of environmental legislation is problematic in Belize. Since Belize is promoted as an ecotourism destination, enforcement of regulations to ensure that tourism developments do not damage the environment is important. Belize has an extensive framework of environmental legislation, including the *Environmental Protection Act*. It has established a Department of the Environment whose stated aim is to prevent and control pollution.

Since one of the major attractions for ecotourists is Mayan culture and history, in which the shadow state impacts on the development of Mayan archaeological sites is especially significant. The routes and methods used by drug traffickers are also used to take culturally and financially valuable Mayan archaeological artefacts out of Belize and into North America, Western Europe, the Far East and elsewhere. There is legislation that governs the removal and treatment of archaeological artefacts, but the problem lies in a lack of enforcement. The *Ancient Monuments and Antiquities Act* stipulates that an ancient monument is anything over 100 years old. The minister in charge of the Department of Archaeology grants permits to enter, explore and excavate or remove specified antiquities. The minister is also empowered to grant a permit to any occupier or developer to demolish monuments for agricultural or industrial reasons (but such permits are rarely given out) (McCalla, 1995a, p47).

However, the Department of Archaeology has found it very difficult to prevent the illegal trafficking of Mayan artefacts. In order to tackle this, the department has embarked on a series of training workshops for the Customs and Immigration Department, the Belize Defence Force and the police. The participants were taught how to identify genuine Mayan artefacts in order to reduce illicit trafficking.[24] However, one of the greatest difficulties facing law enforcement officials is that representatives of legitimate organizations are often responsible for trafficking. In Central America in particular, academics from North American and European universities are given access to archaeological sites so that they can be excavated and explored. Since many of these sites are in remote regions that are far away from law enforcement agencies, it affords the opportunity to siphon off key artefacts.

For example, at a number of Mayan temple sites tour guides complained that original *stelae* (carved stones) were missing because they had been taken to museums in industrialized countries. The guides also suggested that some of the more valuable Mayan artefacts were spirited out of the country without ever being registered with the Department of Archaeology. Mayan temples are often in remote locations with no law enforcement officials on site to ensure that archaeologists adhere to legal or ethical standards.[25]

Missing *stelae* and other artefacts is common in Mayan sites such as Caracol in Belize and Tikal in Guatemala; the original carved stones have been replaced with fibreglass casts. Archaeologists often excused the removal of artefacts by claiming that Belizeans did not know how to look after them and that they would be properly investigated, studied and looked after once they were taken out of the country.[26]

However, archaeologists have also been engaged in illicit trafficking – sometimes unwittingly, but often they have been actively involved in what they know to be an illegal trade. For example, in 1998 seven US citizens were arrested and charged with possessing antiquities without a licence, attempting to export and conspiracy to export artefacts. They were found in possession of 50 ceramic pieces that dated back to AD150. The group was comprised of students, led by Professor Murray from Ohio, who had been on a study trip to investigate the flora and fauna of Southern Belize. Professor Murray pleaded that he had been visiting Belize every year for 15 years and had never been stopped by the Customs and Immigration service before. He claimed that he and his students had taken pieces out of the country on each trip.[27] The Department of Archaeology was dismayed since this meant that the study groups from the US had probably trafficked out hundreds of articles every year.[28]

In addition, a number of Mayan community leaders were concerned about how one village, Medina Bank, had been treated by a US-based university. The village had assisted archaeological teams in the initial excavations of a newly discovered Mayan temple in their reservation. However, later the university team had approached the Belize government to allow them to take over the area and move out the people who were cultivating crops there. The archaeologists asked that the Mayan villagers should be given an alternative area to grow their crops, but Mayan leaders suggested that the new land was not adequate because it was poor, stony soil and lacked sufficient water resources. Since the villagers practised subsistence rather than commercial agriculture, the effect on the community would be devastating. One Mayan leader called it 'an act of genocide against our people'.[29] In this case there was a clear perception that a shadow set of interest groups had assisted that university in getting the land signed over to archaeological exploration in a way that directly disadvantaged local Mayan communities. In fact he had secured agreement from the British High Commission to use UK forces based in Belize to build a field camp at the site for students and academics interested in excavating the site.[30]

The ways in which Medina Bank residents and local Mayan activists perceived their interactions with the archaeological digs indicated how global interest groups intersect with national elites in developing countries. Mayan activists felt that it was another example of how global interest groups can arrive with an agenda filled with good intentions about discovering ancient Mayan history and culture. However, the ways the operation was carried out directly disadvantaged Mayan groups living in the area. The Medina Bank case demonstrated how global networks are intertwined with local political and economic interest groups. These connections between local and global interest groups undermined the agendas of Mayan activists in favour of a Mayan homeland and greater appreciation of the economic, social and political problems that faced indigenous peoples in Central America.

The ways in which global and local networks intersect in Belize has also had a significant impact on the forms of environmental protection. For example, a common complaint among locally based tour guides and the conservation community was that while legislation was in place, it was rarely enforced. Godsman Ellis, president of the Belize Ecotourism Association, stated that policing was not carried out because of the country's limited financial resources and manpower, inadequate technological and administrative resources, and its open borders, and that very few cases of environmental violations had been brought before the courts despite the legislation that had been put in place (Ellis, 1995, pp305–307). One interviewee who was involved in marine conservation in Belize stated that, although environmental impact assessments were legally required for all new ecotourism developments, the government office responsible for monitoring such assessments was completely overwhelmed by requests for assessments because they were so poorly staffed.[31] In addition, when conservation authorities have tried to press for prosecutions for breaches of environmental legislation, they have faced opposition from powerful interest groups.

One of the major issues that environmental agencies face in Belize is the trade in crustaceans and shellfish. It has proved especially difficult to regulate the trade because of the operation of the shadow state in Belize. The shadow state assists local elites in illicitly trafficking crustaceans. A report into the state of the coastal zone indicated that in 1995 the annual export value of conch was B$2.3 million (US$1.2 million); for lobster it was B$17.6 million (US$8.8 million). Apart from lobster and conch, the report suggested that Belize has a major role to play in the trade in wild shrimp, the development of shrimp farms, the export of live rock (corals) and of fish for tropical aquariums (McField, Wells and Gibson, 1996, p114). Aquaculture (shrimp farms) has been a growth area for Belize, and members of the Fisheries Department have argued that shrimp farms will replace banana production as a major source of foreign exchange for Belize. As with other forms of big development, the main shrimp farms in Belize (Cher-ax and Laguna Madre) are ultimately owned by non-Belizean investors. Conservation organizations in Belize have been critical of the sale of undersized lobsters, the way in which lobster and queen conch fishing licences are handed out, and the development of aquaculture. This is partially because there is a perception that the Fisheries Department contains individual highly corrupt members of staff, and because the department has been at the centre of a number of high-profile staff purges that were widely regarded as politically motivated.[32]

The relationship between lobster fishing and ecotourism development is very close. On Ambergris Caye for example, numerous lobster fishermen went from working in the Fishermen's Cooperative straight into acting as tour guides, which earnt them more money. The members of the fishing cooperative went from earning B$10–12 (US$5–6) per pound of fish and B$30–40 (US$15–20) per pound for lobster to US$30–40 per day as guides. Likewise, families that had made money through selling lobster went on to invest it in hotels, resorts and restaurants.[33] There are two main markets for the lobster and conch meat: export to the US and the Far East, and ecotourists in local restaurants. Numerous restaurants in Belize offer lobster or conch ceviche. The meat is cut into small pieces making it impossible to tell if it came from an adult animal. In response, some environmental campaigners have started to ask ecotourists to eat such dishes that are made of only whole lobster tails so that it is easy to determine whether the animal was fully grown.[34] As with other forms of criminality, Belizean lobster fishers have placed the blame on Hondurans and Guatemalans crossing into Belizean territorial waters to take undersized lobster and then escaping law enforcement agencies by flitting back over the international border.[35]

The fears among the conservation community in Belize were expressed in the Lamanai Declaration, which specifically detailed lobster fishing as a major threat to the environment in Belize.[36] It was perceived that the decision-making process was not transparent. While there is legislation in place to prevent undersized lobster and conch being removed, such as closed seasons, these are rarely enforced and the Fisheries Department has been criticized for failing to send inspectors to restaurants to check that they are not using lobster out of season or using baby lobsters and conch.[37] The Conservation Compliance Unit of the Fisheries Department is responsible for monitoring fishing, but it has had its budget cut so that its enforcement and management capabilities are already overextended (McField, Wells and Gibson, 1996, pp118–120).

The question of lobster fisheries is also controversial because of how licences are granted by the state to local and global economic interests. For example, James Wang had already been involved in a scandal over sale of Belizean passports to Taiwanese business people as part of the economic citizenship programme. The decision to grant a lobster licence to Wang was regarded as an example of the shadow links between local and foreign elites. A&J Aquaculture, owned by James and Andrew Wang, was given a licence to fish for undersized lobsters by the then Minister of Agriculture and Fisheries, Chiste Garcia. The licence was issued because the company wanted to start up a lobster farm, but thus far it has proved impossible to raise lobsters in captivity from the larval stage. Consequently, the Wang brothers were allowed to catch juvenile lobsters to start off their farm. In contrast, the Department of the Environment claimed that this was in contravention of fisheries legislation, and was reported to be very unhappy with the decision.[38] One newspaper claimed that the decision to grant the licence to the Wang brothers came just three days after the Taiwanese Foreign Minister had approved a loan of US$20 million to the United Democratic Party (UDP) government for the Southern highway project.[39] Clearly, there was a local perception that Wang, who had a history of corrupt business activities, was being shown favouritism by elements within the state apparatus. The grant of a lobster licence amid such controversy indicated that shadow links between local politicians and global businesses were primarily responsible for decision making rather than an accountable and transparent government policy process.

The shadow links between local and global elites were also important in debates about the environmental impact of leisure vessels. One example of this was on Ambergris Caye, when there was a flurry of debate between the resident 'gringo' community, the local community and conservation officers over the fate of resort owners whose catamaran ran aground in the Hol Chan Marine Reserve, causing extensive damage to the coral reef. The incident occurred against a background of highly publicized environmental breaches by live-aboard dive ships owned by external investors. The most high-profile incidents involved the *Fantome* and the *Rembrandt Van Rijn* in the marine protected areas, Glovers Reef and Half Moon Caye (respectively).[40] The companies that owned the vessels were offered options to compensate for the damage they had caused or risk having their licences revoked, but the local press reported that there was a perception that the owners were not sufficiently punished because of their high-profile connections in Belize.[41] The catamaran incident also occurred against a history of local resentment against foreign land and property owners who had settled on Ambergris Caye. A Department of Environment report detailed how several foreign-owned resorts or hotels were not abiding by the legal requirements for the construction and management of piers. This was especially contentious because several residents had complained that, while the regulations state all piers must be open to the public, any Belizean who went to the pier would immediately be removed by the owners or managers of the establishment (Department of Environment, 1998b). In the case of the catamaran in San Pedro, those involved in the conservation community, such as Mito Paz, the director of

Green Reef, were highly critical of the catamaran incident and felt that the owners should be taken to court.[42] Those who opposed high levels of foreign ownership speculated that the catamaran ran aground because of the carelessness and general disrespect for the environment they associated with newcomers to the island.[43] In contrast, external investors in the ecotourism industry in San Pedro were concerned that the incident was being used by local opponents to criticize the gringo community as a whole. One member of the gringo community, who had assisted in pulling the catamaran off the reef, vigorously argued that it was an accident that could have happened to any boat.[44] In fact, the owners of the boat took the step of writing a public apology in the local *San Pedro Sun* in an attempt to quell rumours about negligence, and in it they stated that the engine had failed and the winds had died, and so the boat ran on to the reef before the anchor could be dropped.[45]

This criticism of foreign interests also extends to their Belizean partners. In order to own businesses and land in Belize, a Belizean must be involved. This has led to accusations that wealthy Belizeans have been engaged in leasing land from the government, developing resorts and then selling a share of the business on to a foreign investor. The Belizean partner then retains a share of the business and makes a profit, in line with government policy, but effectively allows foreign business interests to dominate key ecotourism resort areas. The creation of powerful networks of global capital in the form of foreign investors coupled with locally powerful and wealthy families has led to real difficulties in enforcing environmental legislation. For example, key Belizean families in prime ecotourism sites have been accused of degrading the local environment in the pursuit of ecotourism developments. Rival ecotourism developers and environmental activists have claimed that such activities have not been properly monitored or prevented because they are the 'big family' on the island.[46] Likewise, it was suggested that foreign developers were allowed to get away with building beach lodges and beach roads without any acknowledgement that their developments were going to run straight through a turtle reserve and a beach used by rare turtles as a nesting site.[47]

Despite the arguments between different interest groups in the tourist areas of Belize, it was clear that ultimately there was a perception among both sets of interest groups that a shadow decision-making process was underway that would determine the outcome regardless of the legislation. This indicated a perception that breaches of environmental legislation and wider problems with criminality among foreign and local elites were overlooked, tolerated or actively supported and encouraged by key members of state agencies because parts of the state apparatus had been co-opted by these powerful networks of elites.

It is also important to provide the political context in which the shadow state operates. Within Belize it is essential to acknowledge the deep divide between supporters of the People's United Party (PUP) and the UDP. This division permeates local politics, can be exploited by foreign elites in the ecotourism industry and plays a central role in determining the coverage of certain issues in the Belizean press. In terms of the ecotourism industry it is important because key figures in both parties are able to offer significant levels of patronage to their supporters. The stakes became higher in 1997, an election year in which the opposition PUP was expected to win (and did indeed achieve a landslide victory). Political opponents and economic competitors in Belize have pointed to the role of the current and former ministers of tourism and the environment as major players in the ecotourism industry. The former Minister of Tourism and the Environment, Glenn Godfrey (PUP), has been able to utilize contacts in his own constituency, which covers the two prime ecotourist areas of Caye Caulker and Ambergris Caye. In particular, the construction of a new airstrip and condominiums on Caye Caulker has been credited to Godfrey. Indeed, one interviewee suggested that conservation organizations in Belize were firm supporters of the PUP. Political opponents of this party were keen to point out that conservation non-governmental organizations (NGOs) might have turned a blind eye to his activities because they were PUP supporters.[48]

The shadow state has also affected organizations that engage in lobbying on conservation issues, especially when they have fallen foul of the deep political divide between the PUP and UDP. The Lamanai Room Declaration of 1997, which detailed major environmental abuses in Belize and was signed by numerous local conservation agencies, including the Belize Audubon Society and

Coastal Zone Management Project, was criticized for political bias by those who supported the then UDP government. Victoria Collins, editor of the *San Pedro Sun*, suggests that the Lamanai Room Declaration was perceived by UDP supporters as designed to strengthen the position of the PUP amid public speculation that an election was to be called. The Minister of Tourism and the Environment, Henry Young, accused the parties at Lamanai of trying to topple the UDP government.[49] Over the course of the UDP government, Young became a developer in Placencia, where large areas of ecologically important mangroves were cut to make way for ecotourism developments.[50] Political opponents of such developments speculated that local business elites and external investors were able to seek protection from prosecution for environmental breaches due to their links with politically prominent figures in Belize, and their links to the ruling UDP. It is clear that in accordance with Reno's model of the shadow state, local elites utilize informal networks to reward their clients. The ecotourism industry provides one example of the manner in which those elites can bestow political and economic favours upon their international and local supporters.

In promoting tourism as a development strategy, elites often aim to entice foreign investors and large international tour operators into the country to underwrite their own investments and patron–client networks. The involvement of foreign interests in the Belizean tourism industry has assisted the creation of a shadow state. The convergence of legal and illegal business interests with government interests is apparent in the development of coastal tourism. The dominance of foreign capital in the ecotourism industry is made possible by the compliance of and collaboration with local companies and the political and economic elite. This is especially the case in Belize, where there is a legal stipulation that international tour operators and investors must have a Belizean partner. In Belize a few key families own or are major figures in the operation of a number of ecotourism and transport-related businesses, and as a result ecotourists brought in by overseas operators can be funnelled through a series of businesses all owned by one family or elite group, which is ultimately reliant on international tour operators. Historically on Ambergris Caye three key families, Blake, Alamilla and Parham, who are also related through marriage, have been economically dominant. They held sway over the development of the island through gunrunning to the Santa Cruz Maya in Mexico during the middle of the 19th century, and later through the ownership of coconut and timber plantations and land (Godfrey, 1998, pp23–28). Furthermore, Gach Guerrero, secretary of the conservation organization Green Reef, is also owner of Amigo Travel and manager of Island Air, a member of the board of the Ambergris Caye Historical Society, an officer of the Belize Tourism Industry Association, and the 1997 and 1998 chairman of the International Sea and Air Festival.[51] Similarly, the Vega family on Caye Caulker own the tour operator Belize Odyssey and the Vega Inn, are involved in environmental and tourism consultancy and a fishing business, and members of the family sit on the BTIA, the Protected Areas National Council and the Coastal Zone Management Programme.[52] However, it is not unusual in a country with a relatively small population to find that certain individuals and families have a major role in the public and private sectors.

An examination of how land for ecotourist development is sold and resold in the coastal zone reveals the extent to which external capital is involved in the expansion of ecotourism in Belize. For example, large parcels of land on Ambergris Caye are owned by a US-based company, Sunset Coves. The role of Sunset Coves on Ambergris Caye was the subject of some debate in the local press, specifically the *San Pedro Sun*. Sunset Coves began as a San Pablo town board project, and the land was paid for by local islanders who were promised they would be full partners in its development. The scheme had support and assistance from the local MP (and former Minister of Tourism and the Environment), Glenn Godfrey.[53] However, Sunset Coves went into receivership in 1996 with unpaid debts of B$300,000 (US$150,000), and it was sold to Raymond Yusi of Western Caribbean Properties, based in California.[54]

This pattern of sale to external investors is very common in the ecotourism islands of Belize. A report into the state of the coastal zone indicated that leased national lands were often sold to external investors or subdivided in joint ventures and then sold on to the highest bidders who were primarily non-residents.[55] An examination of the tax and valuation rolls for Ambergris Caye revealed that there was a small number of US citizens, including Albert Dugan, Corrie McDermott, Gerry McDermott and Ian Ritchie, who owned or controlled the sales of large swathes of land on the island.[56] Ian Ritchie was formerly the owner of Southwinds Property, which facilitated the purchase of properties in Belize by external investors. He is also owner of a major resort (Captain Sharkey's) on Ambergris Caye and is beginning land speculation in Roatan in Honduras.[57] A Department of Environment compliance monitoring site report for San Pedro stated that:

> *Several foreigners who live or own hotels/resorts along the beach prohibit people from using or passing through the beach reserve... totally disregarding the 66-ft reserve as required by the National Lands Act... these people do not even own the beach and yet they lay claim to ownership by not allowing anyone to use the beach.*
> (Department of Environment, 1998b; also see Department of Environment, 1998a)

In their election manifesto for 1998–2003, *Set Belize Free*, the PUP claimed that the decline in ecotourism was due to corrupt practices that allowed 'unscrupulous foreigners to side-step Belizeans' and that the BTB had been 'plagued by mismanagement and corruption'.[58]

Caye Chapel (owned by a former miner from Kentucky) has proved to be a controversial tourist development that highlights the links between foreign investors, support from local political and economic elites and local perceptions of corrupt business practices. The island was completely re-landscaped and artificially expanded to provide an exclusive ecotourist resort. The development of the island included building a beach and a golf course, and dredging for sand to build the beach and to allow larger boats to dock at the island. In the process, the dredging stirred up the seabed, disturbed lobster fisheries and destroyed Caye Caulker fishing grounds.[59] This reconfiguration of the environment for ecotourism development had also led to an illicit trade in sand. The increasing phenomenon of sand pirates in Belize had raised concern among local conservationists. The sand pirates operated at night and removed sand from neighbouring islands; it was then used to build up artificial but aesthetically pleasing beaches on sand-free coral atolls.[60] This phenomenon has been created because of the ecotourist desire to have destinations that conform to their stereotyped image of a pristine Caribbean paradise of turquoise water, white sand and coconut palms. Ambergris Caye has suffered from the activities of sand pirates more than other islands, with tons of sand being removed over time. The sand is an important part of the wider ecosystem on the island, which supports coral reefs, mangroves and a variety of fauna, and so sand piracy has a significant negative impact on the environment.

Caye Chapel in particular has been perceived in Belize as an example of an environment being totally remastered in the pursuit of tourism development.[61] The alliances that form the shadow state in Belize ensure that the island can be overhauled to conform to the image of cayes presented to potential visitors. There was a great deal of local speculation about the way in which the owner of the island appeared to be able to dredge around the island and build a beach without proper permission. Those who opposed the development of Caye Chapel speculated that the owner was allowed to undertake such activities because he was protected by the highest political authorities in the country in return for free trips to the island, and that the owner had been careful to pay the relevant officials in order to avoid environmental regulations.[62] For example, one interviewee stated that Caye Chapel was a glaring example of what happened to the environment in Belize when a corrupt politician and a foreign millionaire cooperated, and that it was all about money and there was no one willing to stop it.[63] Caye Chapel will have its own airstrip and casino to allow gamblers to fly direct from Miami to the island. Critics of such ecotourist developments have complained that while the US and UK berate Belize for failing to tackle money laundering, drug trafficking and a possibly corrupt offshore sector, it is the citizens of those countries that are most likely to avail themselves of the facilities on offer in Belize.[64]

Conclusion

It is clear that Belize displays the broad features of a shadow state, as conceptualized by Reno. Even without any evidence of a shadow state, the perception of its existence among those in the ecotourism and conservation communities means that the relevant interest groups act in such a way as to assume its existence. Despite the obvious differences between the cases of Sierra Leone and Belize, the similarities are sufficient for useful comparisons to be drawn. Reno suggests that there are a set of shadow links between international capital and local elites that ultimately determine the direction of policy making. In Belize, despite an extensive framework of environmental legislation, the direction of ecotourism policy is determined by the informal links of the shadow state. The expansion of corrupt activities through ecotourism development means that enforcement of the environmental regulations on which ecotourism is founded is problematic. Government regulations designed to protect the environment are rendered ineffective when a junior arm of the state is opposed by more powerful interest groups that lie within and outside the state apparatus. The expansion of organized crime has resulted in the emergence of state facilitators and protectors of criminality and an institutional presence of massive drug producing, trafficking and money laundering entities. Consequently, these sets of interest groups are able to challenge elected governments for control of key state institutions, thereby ensuring that enforcement of legislation is impossible and effectively preventing domestic political accountability.

CONCLUSION

It is critical to place the debate over sustainable development in the South in its political context. Ecotourism is a clear example of blue-green environmental ideas about conservation, as opposed to red-green or deep green ideologies. This means that the commitment to ecotourism as a blue-green strategy ultimately leads to weak sustainability rather than strong sustainability. It is also an example of how interest groups, such as business operators, are able to claim green credentials. Ecotourism, like other forms of business involved in green capitalism places profit at the forefront of its operations. The establishment of ecotourism ventures is very clearly related to ideas of valuing the environment as an economic resource because it means that conservation has to be financially sustainable. The difficulty with this is that only environments and landscapes that are attractive to ecotourists will be conserved, regardless of their importance to a wider ecosystem. One example of this is that mangroves have tended to be overlooked by ecotourists in favour of coral reefs. Ecotourism, which uses visitor-valuation techniques, means that mangroves are less financially viable than coral reefs because visitors are less likely to want to see them. However, in environmental terms, mangroves are essential for reefs as a nursery for fish and a means of filtering out mud from rivers that would otherwise smother reefs.

It is clear that ecotourism creates a mixture of positive and negative impacts on host societies, and that it is far from the ideal of a culturally and environmentally sensitive form of travel. Ecotourism, like conventional tourism, presents developing countries with a series of challenges and it is not the cost-free strategy that its advocates suggest. Rather, it is a highly politicized strategy that does not offer a neutral path to sustainable development for the South. It does not require a radical or fundamental shift, but operates within existing social, economic and political structures. It is a policy that is easily implemented by governments, private businesses, local communities and non-governmental organizations (NGOs). Ecotourism can be defined as one part of a broader commitment to blue-green environmental ideologies, which is intimately linked with neoliberal economics. The difficulties that developing countries have experienced in following neoliberal development strategies are well documented; like other neoliberal policies, ecotourism creates a series of problems. Despite the claims that ecotourism is not open to the same kinds of criticisms as conventional tourism, it does in fact create a series of complex relationships between hosts and guests and it holds a number of problems for developing countries. It is clear from the case of Belize that ecotourism is not unproblematic, and has negative political, economic, cultural and environmental impacts on host countries.

The emphasis on the market value of environmental resources leads on to a political analysis of the nature of ecotourism. It is important to place ecotourism industry in its political context at all levels, ranging from individual ecotourists to tour operators, and from indigenous communities to global environmental organizations. The roles and behaviour of ecotourists are often overlooked in analyses of tourism, and are often reduced to sociological interpretations of individual leisure choices. However, the ways in which ecotourists interact with host societies and the kinds of behaviours they exhibit are politically important. The idea that ecotourism can benefit the environment and bring development through a reliance on self-reflexive travellers is questionable. Ecotourists, like other types of tourists, are primarily interested in themselves. It was clear that the main concern of travellers to Belize was how the holiday benefited them in a variety of ways, such as hedonistic pursuits, the capacity for self-reliance and organizational skills, and the building of character. In many ways they were engaged in a performance, portraying themselves as environmentally aware and culturally sensitive. In fact, it was clear that they were keen to impress their peer groups at home with tales of their self-denial and tenacity, and to display their genuine concern for the environmental welfare of the planet and the cultural wellbeing of the communities that they visited.

However, ecotourists still engaged in the hedonistic pursuits that are more closely identified with mass tourists, who are deemed to be culturally unaware and insensitive to the needs of host communities. The visitors in Belize are keen to drink, take drugs and have sexual contact with locals and other ecotourists, just like the tourists they wish to set themselves apart from. Like other tourists, the visitors in Belize want to see the key sights that tour operators advertise; reefs, rainforests and ruins remain the three big attractions that motivate them to choose Belize. The behaviours and attitudes of ecotourists in Belize also lead to resentments among local people, who regard them as a business opportunity on the one hand and as a threat to their culture and environment on the other. Ecotourists do not display features of self-reflexivity that might produce environmentally sustainable development. Since they are ecotourists, they are in a sense obliged to think of their vacation choices in the most positive way possible. This meant that ecotourists gloss over the really damaging aspects of their presence in Belize. Rather, they prefer to point to their role in generating foreign exchange for the national government and local businesses, and in providing household income to the poorest members of the host society through their craft-buying habits. Instead, the ways in which ecotourists interact with the host communities in Belize creates a variety of political, social and economic problems, over which the visitors ultimately have very little control. It is this structural context that is vitally important to an understanding of why ecotourism is a problematic form of development for the South.

The choices made by individual ecotourists create a spiral of impacts for host societies in the South. These impacts on political, economic, environmental and social conditions are intimately interlinked. The travel choices made by individuals in Northern industrialized states bring a series of transformations to the destination country that are beyond the control of the traveller no matter how keen on green consumerism they are. Once an ecotourist arrives in Belize their decisions about where to eat, stay and visit means that the ecotourism industry interacts with other political and economic interest groups in a way that is not under the control of any single person or institution. The relationships between visitors and tour guides indicate the ways in which transformations in Belize are powered and sustained by the need to accommodate the demands of individual travellers who want to enjoy their time away from home. The ecotourism industry in Belize is already organized as a business that is allied to the global tourism industry; it is reliant on airlines to bring visitors from the industrialized countries, and on tour operators to book itineraries with local companies and hotels. An individual traveller to Belize will use a conventional airline and travel agent before they even arrive. This reliance on a bigger global industry means that the environmental credentials of ecotourism are immediately questionable, since it is dependent on air travel which uses vast amounts of fossil fuels. On a more local level, the reefs, rainforests and ruins that the visitors come to look at have experienced significant impacts. Those pressures also bring new difficulties and opportunities for state agencies, environmental campaign organizations, tour operators and guides, as well as for local people who live in and around those attractions.

One of the impacts that is created by ecotourism is the creation of a highly politicized image of national identity. The image of a pristine paradise of silver beaches, turquoise water, palm trees, primeval rainforests, and welcoming and exotic locals is designed to attract overseas visitors. It marks out a destination according to its comparative advantage in relation to the other holiday locations in the South. The difficulty is that this peculiar national identity is created for consumption by an external audience of ecotourists and the tour operators that deal with them. The image emphasizes Belize's difference from Northern industrialized states, and relies on the idea that Belize lacks modernity and is devoid of development. This invention of national identity to ensure that ecotourism remains an economically viable industry has a direct impact on the domestic political order in Belize. In particular, the ways in which the various ethnic groups in Belize are presented as exotic, welcoming, primeval and mysterious have an effect on those communities. For example, images of Mayan customs, traditions and histories are used by national governments to attract visitors. In contrast, those same governments have criticized Mayan communities in Belize for their lack of Western-style development. Attempts by Mayan communities to engage in the development process (including ecotourism) in any meaningful way have been directly frustrated by their involvement in ecotourism. Likewise, attempts by Mayan organizations to lobby for their own political interests have been downplayed and blocked by central governments, partially because of the need to present Belize as a stable destination with little civil strife and an equitable social and economic system. It is clear that ecotourism, like any other kind of business or any other form of development, privileges certain interest groups over others, and can enhance the position of the existing political and economic elite. In this way ecotourism can contribute to a continuing process of marginalization for groups that are already subjected to social, economic and political exclusion.

The claims by advocates of ecotourism that it affords local communities a chance of genuine participation in the development process is also disputable. The internationally applauded attempts by indigenous Mayan communities to set up their own ecotourism schemes have brought their own opportunities and difficulties. The ecotourism ventures that are owned and run by Mayan communities are inextricably linked to wider political and economic processes. For example, the involvement of global environmental NGOs in ecotourism has not always been supportive. It is important to recognize that the varied interest groups engaged in ecotourism have competing political and economic agendas. These conflicts between the communities, NGOs, state agencies and private businesses are prolonged and intensified by globalization. In effect, the very political and economic structures within which ecotourism operates constitute a barrier to effective sustainable development for Mayan communities in Central America. The calls for sustainable development for Mayan communities cannot be divorced from the claims for a Mayan homeland and the need to be treated as equal partners in the development process at the local, national and global levels. Consequently the ecotourism industry in Southern Belize cannot be analysed in isolation from its relationship to international financial institutions, logging companies, environmental NGOs and even dealers in illegal goods such as wildlife and drugs.

The link between legal and illegal businesses is often ignored in analyses of ecotourism and tourism. Ecotourism is one component of a bigger arena of business that has both illict and legal sides. In many ways, the interlinking of the global drugs trade, money laundering and other illegitimate businesses has become a central part of globalized business strategies. The development of the shadow state in the South has been assisted by globalization, of which ecotourism is one example. The difficulty is that the existence of a shadow set of decision makers means that there is no real possibility of enforcing environmental legislation intended to protect ecosystems from visitors and other activities that may damage them. The expansion of organized crime, and its intimate relationship with legitimate ecotourism businesses, has produced a state that is willing to protect and assist criminal networks, and it also means that state agencies then become traffickers and money launderers themselves. Ecotourism has become one of the fastest-growing sectors of the global tourism industry, partially because of globalization. However, those involved in organized crime have likewise benefited from the permeable frontiers that have been created by globalization. Ecotourism and organized crime are two different sides of the same process: the global resurgence of the idea that neoliberal economics will provide development. Ecotourism forms a part of blue-green development strategies that will lead to business-oriented weak sustainability. Yet that same global neoliberal paradigm has also supported and assisted illicit interest groups with the ability to frustrate and undermine sustainable development.

NOTES

Introduction

1   I would like to thank the Economic and Social Research Council and its Global Environmental Change Programme for sponsoring this research while I was a Research Fellow at Edinburgh University, 1997–99 (grant number L320253245), and at Lancaster University, 1999–2000 (Grant number R000223013).

Chapter 2

1   Interview with Liam Huxley, San Pedro, 25.12.97.
2   Interview with Mindy Franklin, San Pedro, 1.12.97.
3   Interview with Dawn Harbicht, San Pedro, 2.12.97.
4   Personal communication, Heidi, Coral Caye Conservation (CCC) volunteer, Calabash Caye, 30.1.98.
5   Interview with Jan, Caye Caulker, 21.1.98.
6   Interview with Yvonne Vickers, San Pedro, 30.11.97; interview with Steve, CCC volunteer, Calabash Caye, 27.1.98; interview with David Snieder, Caye Caulker, 12.12.97; interview with Shawn Nunnemaker, Caye Caulker, 3.1.98.
7   Interview with Brie Thumm, San Pedro, 30.11.97; interview with Dan Smathers, San Pedro, 3.12.97; interview with Mindy Franklin, San Pedro, 1.12.97.
8   Interview with Lucy, CCC volunteer, Calabash Caye, 29.1.98; interview with Petra Barry, San Pedro, 4.12.97; interview with Brie Thumm, San Pedro, 30.11.97.
9   See for example interview with Beat Ziegler, San Pedro 30.11.97; interview with Christian and Ulrika, Caye Caulker, 20.1.98; interview with Mary Tacey, San Pedro, 23.12.97.
10 See for example interview with Pam Stratton, San Pedro, 5.12.97; interview with David Snieder, Caye Caulker, 12.12.97; interview with

Michael and Vasili, Caye Caulker, 12.12.97; and interview with Yolanda Kiszka and Erica Earnhard, San Pedro, 30.11.97.

11 Interview with Jillian Porter and Patrick Kelly, San Pedro, 31.1.98; interview with Megan, Caye Caulker, 11.1.98; interview with Yvonne Vickers, San Pedro, 30.11.97.

12 Interview with David Snieder, Caye Caulker, 12.12.97; interview with Fabrice Zottigen, San Pedro 27.12.97; interview with Shawn Nunnemaker, Caye Caulker, 3.1.98; interview with Jim, San Pedro 3.2.98.

13 Interview with Liam Huxley, San Pedro, 25.12.97.

14 Interview with Eddie D'Sa, San Pedro, 25.12.97; interview with Yvonne Vickers, San Pedro, 30.11.97; interview with Dave, Caye Caulker 3.1.98.

15 Interview with Mary Tacey, San Pedro, 23.12.97.

16 Interview with Steve, San Pedro , 3.2.98; interview with Yvonne Vickers, San Pedro, 30.11.97; interview with Shawn Nunnemaker, Caye Caulker, 3.1.98.

17 Interview with Dan Smathers, San Pedro 3.12.97; interview with Barbara Burke, San Pedro, 22.12.97; interview with Mito Paz, Director, Green Reef, San Pedro, 2.2.98. Mito Paz remarked that French angel fish and parrotfish were important to the tourist industry because they are brightly coloured and highly visible large fish, and ecotourists like to see them.

18 Interview with Melanie Paz, Owner, Amigos Del Mar Dive Shop, San Pedro, 1.2.98.

19 Interview with Jim, San Pedro, 3.2.98; interview with Barbara Burke, San Pedro, 22.12.97.

20 Interview with Mito Paz, Director, Green Reef, San Pedro, 2.2.98.

21 Interview with Fred, Caye Caulker, 15.12.97.

22 Interview with Shawn Nunnemaker, Caye Caulker, 3.1.98.

23 Interview with Dan Smathers, San Pedro 3.12.97; also see interview with Shawn Nunnemaker, Caye Caulker, 3.1.98; interview with Bob Goodman, San Pedro, 5.12.97; interview with Petra Barry, San Pedro, 4.12.97; interview with Peter Liska, San Pedro, 25.12.97.

24 Interview with Tony, Caye Caulker, 12.12.97.

25 Interview with Barbara Burke, San Pedro, 22.12.97.

26 Interview with Beat Ziegler, San Pedro, 30.11.97; also see interview with George MacKenzie and Katy Barratt, San Pedro, 2.12.97; interview with Chris, San Pedro, 28.12.97.

27 Interview with Pam Stratton, San Pedro, 5.12.97; interview with Mary Tacey, San Pedro, 23.12.97; interview with Michael and Vasili, Caye

Caulker, 12.12.97; interview with Lucy, CCC volunteer, Calabash Caye
29.1.98; interview with Heidi, CCC volunteer, Calabash Caye, 30.1.98.
28 Interview with Al and Marion, San Pedro, 5.12.97; interview with Mary
Tacey, San Pedro, 23.12.97.
29 Interview with Bob Goodman, San Pedro, 5.12.97.
30 Interview with Steve, San Pedro, 3.2.98; interview with Eddie D'Sa, San
Pedro, 25.12.97.
31 Interview with Mary Tacey, San Pedro, 23.12.97; interview with Bob
Goodman, San Pedro, 5.12.97; interview with Eddie D'Sa, San Pedro,
25.12.97; interview with Mindy Franklin, San Pedro, 1.12.97.
32 Interview with Brie Thumm, San Pedro, 30.11.97.
33 Interview with Shawn Nunnemaker, Caye Caulker, 3.1.98; interview
with Jan, Caye Caulker, 21.1.98; interview with Leia and George, Caye
Caulker, 2.1.98; personal communication, Craig and Elena Wall, San
Ignacio, 1.1.98; personal communication, Steve Dieter, Caye Caulker,
14.12.97.
34 Interview with Mindy Franklin, San Pedro, 1.12.97; also see interview
with George MacKenzie and Katy Barratt, San Pedro, 2.12.97; interview
with Simon, Caye Caulker, 19.1.98.
35 Interview with Brie Thumm, San Pedro, 30.11.97; also see interview
with Beat Ziegler, San Pedro, 30.11.97; interview with Theresa
Heckman, Caye Caulker, 21.1.98; interview with Mindy Franklin, San
Pedro, 1.12.97.
36 Interview with Barbara Burke, San Pedro, 22.12.97; interview with Dan
Smathers, San Pedro, 3.12.97; interview with Michael and Vasili, Caye
Caulker, 12.12.97.
37 Interview with Christian and Ulrika, Caye Caulker, 20.1.98.
38 Interview with Barbara Burke, San Pedro 22.12.97.
39 Interview with Dwight Neal, Director, Marine Research Centre, UCB,
Calabash Caye 24.1.98; interview with Karie Holtermann, Research
Coordinator, Marine Research Centre, UCB, Calabash Caye 12.1.98;
interview with Eden Garcia, Station Manager, Marine Research Centre,
UCB, Calabash Caye 12.1.98; also see Dr Leroy Taeger, *Amandala*
(1997), 'Exposing Coral Cay and Rio Bravo', September 7.
40 Interview with Ellen McCrae, CariSearch Ltd, Siwa-Ban Foundation and
Belize Tourism Industry Association, Caye Caulker, 3.1.98. The
problems associated with tourists taking drugs as a recreational activity
were also highlighted in an interview with Ken Sylvestre, Head of the
Tourism Police Unit, Belize City 9.1.98. One tourist mentioned his intention to take drugs as part of his vacation experience (interview with
Dave, Caye Caulker, 3.1.98) but recreational use of illegal substances

was widespread and not necessarily associated with a younger age group. This is more fully dealt with in Chapter 6.

41   Interview with Thomas Ack, Divemaster (Adventures in Watersports), San Pedro, 5.1.98; interview with Kent Sylvestre, Director, Tourism Police Unit, Belize City, 9.1.98; interview with Frenchie, Owner, Frenchie's Dive Shop, Caye Caulker, 11.1.98.

42   Interview with Tony, Caye Caulker, 12.12.97; interview with Theresa Heckman, Caye Caulker, 21.1.98.

43   Interview with Dave, Caye Caulker, 3.1.98.

44   Personal communication, Andy Palacio, (divemaster); personal communication, Tony (tour guide); personal communication, Joe (divemaster); personal communication, Divan Vasquez (hotel manager).

45   Personal communication, anonymous interviewee. This remark was made during an interview, but the woman concerned asked to remain anonymous.

46   Interview with Theresa Heckman, Caye Caulker, 21.1.98.

47   Personal communication, anonymous source.

48   Personal communication, anonymous source. Since the researcher was constantly arriving on islands as a woman travelling alone she also came to the immediate attention of such men, until it was explained she was there to work.

49   Interview with Tony, Caye Caulker, 12.12.97.

50   Interview with Peter Liska, San Pedro, 25.12.97.

51   Interview with Debbie Davis, Caye Caulker, 12.12.97; interview with Tony, Caye Caulker, 12.12.97; interview with Steve, San Pedro, 3.2.98; interview with George MacKenzie and Katy Barratt, San Pedro, 2.12.97.

52   Interview with Wink and Robyn, Flores, Guatemala, 31.12.97; interview with Lee, CCC Volunteer, Calabash Caye, 30.1.98; interview with Shawn Nunnemaker, Caye Caulker, 3.1.98; interview with Simon, Caye Caulker, 19.1.98; interview with Jim, San Pedro, 3.2.98.

53   Interview with Jim, San Pedro, 3.2.98; interview with Christian and Ulrika, Caye Caulker, 20.1.98; interview with Steve, CCC Volunteer, Calabash Caye, 27.1.98; interview with Fred, Caye Caulker, 15.12.97; interview with Yolanda Kizska and Erica Earnhard, San Pedro, 30.11.97.

54   Interview with John Colt, Caye Caulker 18.1.98; also see interview with Christian and Ulrika, Caye Caulker, 20.1.98.

55   For example, interview with Yvonne Vickers, San Pedro, 30.11.97; interview with Christian and Ulrika, Caye Caulker, 20.1.98; interview with Fabrice Zottigen, San Pedro, 27.12.97; interview with Pam Stratton, San Pedro, 5.12.97.

56 For example, interview with Fred, Caye Caulker, 15.12.97; interview with Bob Goodman, San Pedro, 5.12.97.
57 Interview with Petra Barry, San Pedro, 4.12.97; also see interview with Barbara Burke, San Pedro, 22.12.97; interview with Tony, Caye Caulker, 12.12.97; interview with Bob Goodman, San Pedro, 5.12.97.
58 Interview with Dan Smathers, San Pedro, 3.12.97.
59 Interview with Daniel Nunez, Owner, Tanisha Tours, San Pedro, 30.12.97; interview with Carlos Ayala, Carlos's Guided Eco-Tours, Caye Caulker, 20.1.98; interview with Ras Creek, Tour Guide, Caye Caulker, 21.1.98; personal communication, Derek Angele, Instructor, Gaz Coopers Dive Shop, San Pedro, 22.12.97; personal communication, Julie Seldon, Sales and Marketing, SunBreeze Hotel, San Pedro 5.12.97; personal communication, Andy Palacio, Divemaster, Gaz Coopers Dive Shop, San Pedro, 5.1.98.
60 Interview with Daniel Nunez, Owner, Tanisha Tours, San Pedro, 30.12.97; interview with Carlos Ayala, Carlos's Guided Eco-Tours, Caye Caulker, 20.1.98; interview with Ras Creek, Tour Guide, Caye Caulker, 21.1.98. The researcher was also encouraged to touch marine life (including a loggerhead turtle) on a few dives with certain instructors.
61 Interview with Beat Ziegler, San Pedro, 30.11.97; interview with Pam Stratton, San Pedro, 5.12.97; interview with Steve, CCC volunteer, Calabash Caye, 27.1.98; interview with Lee, CCC volunteer, Calabash Caye, 30.1.98; interview with Liam Huxley, San Pedro, 25.12.97; interview with Megan, Caye Caulker, 11.1.98.
62 Interview with Michael and Vasili, Caye Caulker, 12.12.97; see also interview with Megan, Caye Caulker, 11.1.98; interview with Dawn Harbicht, San Pedro, 2.12.97; interview with Liam Huxley, San Pedro, 25.12.97.
63 Interview with Tim McDonald, San Pedro, 8.12.97; interview with Jim, San Pedro, 3.2.98.
64 Interview with Peter Liska, San Pedro, 25.12.97; personal communication, David, Black Bird Caye Resort, 31.1.98.
65 Interview with Eddie D'Sa, San Pedro, 25.12.97.
66 Interview with Lee, CCC volunteer, Calabash Caye, 30.1.98; interview with Harriet, CCC volunteer, Calabash Caye, 29.1.98; interview with Heidi, CCC volunteer, Calabash Caye, 30.1.98.
67 Interview with Mike and Kerry, Caye Caulker, 12.12.97; interview with Simon, Caye Caulker, 19.1.98.
68 Interview with John Colt, Caye Caulker, 18.1.98; interview with Wink and Robyn, Flores, Guatemala, 31.12.97.

69   Interview with George MacKenzie and Katy Barratt, San Pedro, 2.12.97.

70   For example, see interview with Liam Huxley, San Pedro, 25.12.97.

71   Interview with Debbie Davis, Caye Caulker, 12.12.97; interview with Jan, Caye Caulker, 21.1.98; interview with Chandran and Martin, Caye Caulker, 4.1.98; interview with Pam Stratton, San Pedro, 5.12.97; interview with Steve, CCC Volunteer, Calabash Caye, 27.1.98.

72   Interview with Lee, CCC Volunteer, Calabash Caye, 30.1.98; interview with Steve, CCC Volunteer, Calabash Caye, 27.1.98.

73   Interview with Eddie D'Sa, San Pedro, 25.12.97; also see Munt, 1994a, pp114–116.

74   Interview with Wink and Robyn, Flores, Guatemala, 31.12.97; interview with Dave, Caye Caulker, 3.1.98.

75   Interview with Dan Smathers, San Pedro, 3.12.97; interview with Jim, San Pedro, 3.2.98; interview with Jan, Caye Caulker, 21.1.98; interview with Eddie D'Sa, San Pedro, 25.12.97.

76   *Guardian* (1998), 'Uphill struggle', April 22.

77   Interview with Yvonne Vickers, San Pedro 30.11.97; also see interview with Mary Tacey, San Pedro, 23.12.97; interview with Christian and Ulrika, Caye Caulker, 20.1.98; interview with Fabrice Zottigen, San Pedro, 27.12.97; also see Munt, 1994a, pp101–123.

78   Interview with Bob Goodman, San Pedro, 5.12.97. This is a modified version of the slogan 'leave only footprints', which is chanted by ecotourists.

79   Interview with Jonathon Ridley, Director, Coral Cay Conservation, Calabash Caye, 25.1.98. The case of Coral Cay Conservation is more fully discussed in Chapter 3.

80   Interview with Isobel, CCC volunteer, Calabash Caye, 30.1.98; interview with John Colt, Caye Caulker, 18.1.98.

81   Personal communication, Lee, CCC volunteer, Calabash Caye, 30.1.98.

82   Interview with Karie Holtermann, Research Coordinator, Marine Research Centre, UCB, Calabash Caye, 12.1.98; interview with Eden Garcia, Station Manager, Marine Research Centre, UCB, Calabash Caye, 12.1.98. The CCC expedition leader commented that he felt he had to be 'hard' to knock the volunteers into shape in order to keep the camp running efficiently; during the time that the researcher spent on Calabash Caye the expedition leader was a former policeman, and the diving instructor had formerly been in the Royal Air Force.

83   Interview with Dave, Caye Caulker, 3.1.98.

84   Interview with Leia and George, Caye Caulker, 2.1.98.

Chapter 3

1   Interview with Mito Paz, Director, Green Reef, San Pedro, 2.2.98.
2   Interview with Valerie Woods, Director of Tourism, Belize Tourism Board, Belize City, 26.11.96; *San Pedro Sun* (1997), 'National certification tour and travel guiding services training program', August 8; *Amandala* (1997), 'Success of the national certification tour guiding program', April 18.
3   Interview with Wende Bryan, Barracuda and Jaguar Inn and BTIA President (Placencia Chapter), Placencia, 11.1.99; Devres Inc, 1993, p3; *San Pedro Sun* (1997), 'Fishing guide con artist identified', June 13; *San Pedro Sun* (1997), 'National certification tour and travel guiding services training program', August 8; *Amandala* (1997), 'Tourist guide fined', February 23.
4   Anonymous interviewees.
5   Interview with Daniel Nunez, Tropical Tours, San Pedro, 30.12.97; *Amandala* (1997), 'Tourist guide fined', February 23.
6   Anonymous interviewees.
7   Interview with Daniel Nunez, Tropical Tours, San Pedro, 30.12.97; see also interview with Ras Creek, tour guide, Caye Caulker, 21.1.98; interview with Neno Rosado, tour guide, Caye Caulker, 12.12.97; interview with Frenchie, Frenchie's Dive Shop, Caye Caulker, 11.1.98; interview with Ricardo Alcala, Ricardo's Adventure Tours, Caye Caulker, 4.1.98.
8   Interview with Miguel Alamia, Manager of the Hol Chan Marine Reserve, San Pedro, 2.2.98; interview with Alberto Patt, biologist, Hol Chan Marine Reserve, San Pedro, 2.2.98; interview with Ricardo Alcala, Ricardo's Adventure Tours, Caye Caulker, 4.1.98.
9   Interview with Oscar Cruz, Belize Diving Services, Caye Caulker, 10.1.98.
10 Interview with Dave Vernon, Toadal Adventures, Placencia, 15.1.99.
11 Interview with Julie Seldon, Sales and Marketing, Sunbreeze Hotel, San Pedro, 5.12.97; interview with Tony Calderon, Park Ranger, Hol Chan Marine Reserve, San Pedro, 22.12.97.
12 Interview with Alberto Patt, biologist, Hol Chan Marine Reserve, San Pedro, 2.2.98.
13 Interview with Melanie Paz, Amigos Del Mar Diveshop, San Pedro, 1.2.98.
14 Interview with Manuel Azueta, Ruby's Tours, San Pedro, 3.2.98.
15 Interview with Ras Creek, tour guide, Caye Caulker, 21.1.98.
16 Interview with Chocolate, Tour Guide, Chocolate's Tours, Caye Caulker, 19.1.98; interview with Nicole Auil, Manatee Researcher, Coastal Zone

Management Plan, Belize City, 23.11.98; personal communication with Evan, Tour Guide, Monkey River, Stann Creek District, 13.1.99.

17 Interview with Nicole Auil, Manatee Researcher, Coastal Zone Management Plan, Belize City, 23.11.98; see also interview with Ricardo Alcala, Ricardo's Adventure Tours, Caye Caulker, 4.1.98.

18 Interview with Chocolate, Tour Guide, Chocolate's Tours, Caye Caulker, 19.1.98.

19 Interview with Sylvin Codd, Hustler Tours, San Pedro, 4.2.98; interview with Chocolate, Tour Guide, Chocolate's Tours, Caye Caulker, 19.1.98.

20 Interview with Janet Gibson, National Project Advisor, Coastal Zone Management Project, Belize City, 11.2.98; interview with Chocolate, Tour Guide, Chocolate's Tours, Caye Caulker, 19.1.98.

21 Interview with Nicole Auil, Manatee Researcher, Coastal Zone Management Plan, Belize City, 23.11.98; Amandala (1998), 'Manatee recovery plan', December 13.

22 Amandala (1998), 'Gales point manatee', May 10; Amandala (1998) 'Gales Point Wildlife Sanctuary', August 23.

23 Interview with Nicole Auil, Manatee Researcher, Coastal Zone Management Plan, Belize City, 23.11.98; Amandala (1998), 'Manatee recovery plan', December 13.

24 Interview with Ernesto Saqui, H'men Herbal Centre and Botanical Garden, Nu'uk Cheil Cottages and Restaurant, Maya Centre Village (Cockscomb Basin Jaguar Preserve), Stann Creek District, 16.1.99.

25 Interview with anonymous informant. The interviewee asked not to be named because of fears that the employer would look unfavourably on this behaviour towards clients.

26 Interview with Ellen Macrae, Carisearch Ltd, Siwa-Ban Foundation and BTIA, Caye Caulker, 3.1.98.

27 The women who talked about this preferred to remain anonymous. However, from personal observation and comments from others involved in the ecotourism industry and ecotourist themselves, it is feasible to suggest that this form of prostitution is heavily entrenched in parts of Belize.

28 Interview with Ken Sylvestre, Head of the Tourism Police Unit, Belize City, 9.1.98.

29 Interview with Frenchie, Frenchie's Dive Shop, Caye Caulker, 11.1.98.

30 Interview with Ken Sylvestre, Head of the Tourism Police Unit, Belize City, 9.1.98.

31 Amandala (1997), 'Tourism police unit on the beat', December 14.

32 Interview with Ken Sylvestre, Head of the Tourism Police Unit, Belize City, 9.1.98.

33 A number of interviewees (who preferred to remain anonymous because
    of fears for their safety) agreed that this was how they perceived the
    role of the tourism police unit and the regular police. This issue is dealt
    with more fully in Chapter 6. However, complaints have been raised
    more formally about local police units; see *Amandala* (1997), 'Police on
    Caye Caulker ineffective' (letter from Charles E Burner, US citizen),
    February 23.
34 For example, see interview with Jim, San Pedro, 3.2.98; also interview
    with John Colt, Caye Caulker, 18.1.98.
35 Interview with Malcolm Hitchcock, Fido's Bar, San Pedro, 5.12.97.
36 Personal communication, Gary Peacock, Fido's Restaurant, San Pedro,
    18.1.98; interview with Ellen McRae, Carisearch Ltd, Siwa-Ban
    Foundation and BTIA, Caye Caulker, 3.1.98.
37 Personal communication, Dwight Neal, Director of the Marine Research
    Centre, UCB, Calabash Caye, 24.1.98.
38 Interview with Mito Paz, Director, Green Reef, San Pedro, 2.2.98; inter-
    view with Victoria Collins, Editor of the *San Pedro Sun*, San Pedro,
    23.12.97; *Amandala* (1997), 'Belize/IDB sign solid waste management
    plan', March 16; *San Pedro Sun* (1997), 'The smell of progress', August
    18.
39 Interview with Janet Gibson, National Project Advisor, Coastal Zone
    Management Project, Belize City, 11.2.98.
40 Interview with Ken Leslie, Resort Developer, Calabash Caye, 28.1.98.
41 Interview with Karie Holtermann, Research Coordinator, Marine
    Research Centre, UCB, Calabash Caye, 12.1.98; interview with Eden
    Garcia, Station Manager of the Marine Research Centre, UCB, Calabash
    Caye, 12.1.98.
42 Interview with Mary Tacey, San Pedro, 23.12.97; interview with David
    Snieder, Caye Caulker, 12.12.97; interview with Debbie Davis, Caye
    Caulker, 12.12.97.
43 Coral Cay Conservation website, www.coralcay.org.
44 Interview with Jonathon Ridley, Director of Coral Cay Conservation,
    Calabash Caye, 25.1.98; also see the Coral Cay Conservation website
    (www.coralcay.org).
45 Interview with Alex Paige, Director of Coral Cay Conservation,
    Calabash Caye, 25.1.98.
46 www.coralcay.org.
47 Dr Leroy Taeger, *Amandala* (1997), 'Exposing Coral Cay and Rio
    Bravo', September 7; *Amandala* (1997), letter from Dr Taeger to Dr
    Barrow, September 21.

48 Interview with Eden Garcia, Station Manager, Marine Research Centre, UCB, Calabash Caye, 21.1.98; and interview with Karie Holtermann, Research Coordinator, Marine Research Centre, UCB, Calabash Caye, 21.1.98. This view was also held by a number of other University College of Belize staff who commented to the author (anonymously) that they held similar views of CCC.

49 Dr Leroy Taeger, *Amandala* (1997), 'Exposing Coral Cay and Rio Bravo', September 7; *Amandala* (1997), letter from Dr Taeger to Dr Barrow, September 21. The financial wealth of CCC, and the directors' salaries, are confirmed in a set of accounts placed at the Records Office, Companies House, London.

50 Dr Leroy Taeger, *Amandala* (1997), 'Exposing Coral Cay and Rio Bravo', September 7; *Amandala* (1997), letter from Dr Taeger to Dr Barrow, September 21. See also interview with James Sanchez, Boat Captain, Marine Research Centre, UCB, Calabash Caye, 29.1.98; interview with Eden Garcia, Station Manager, Marine Research Centre, UCB, Calabash Caye, 21.1.98; interview with Karie Holtermann, Research Coordinator, Marine Research Centre, UCB, Calabash Caye, 21.1.98.

51 Interview with Jonathon Ridley, Director of Coral Cay Conservation, Calabash Caye, 25.1.98.

52 Interview with Jonathon Ridley, Director of Coral Cay Conservation, Calabash Caye, 25.1.98.

53 Personal communication, Jonathon Kelsey, Researcher, Marine Research Centre, UCB, Belize City, 28.11.98; personal communication, Pio Saqui, Lecturer, Marine Research Centre, UCB, Belize City, 10.1.99.

Chapter 4

1 *Guardian* (2000), 'Tourists taken hostage in Malaysia', April 24; 'Gadafy pays to free island hostages', August 16; 'Travellers beware, it's up to you to avoid the terrorists', April 30.

2 Interview with Maria Vega, Vega Inn and BTIA, Caye Caulker, 21.1.98; *San Pedro Sun* (1997), 'Ecotourism to become the fastest growing segment in world tourism', October 31; *San Pedro Sun* (1997), 'Tourist arrivals increase second quarter', August 8; McField, Wells and Gibson (1996), p97.

3 Interview with Dwight Neal, Director, Marine Research Centre, University of Belize (UCB), 24.1.98, Calabash Caye; interview with Mito Paz, Director, Green Reef, San Pedro, 2.2.98; interview with James Azueta, Marine Protected Areas Coordinator, Fisheries Department, Belize City, 9.2.98; interview with Mike Fairweather, Resort Developer,

Calabash Caye, 13.1.98; *San Pedro Sun* (1997), 'Where have all the sardines gone?', May 30.

4   Interview with Maria Vega, Vega Inn and BTIA, Caye Caulker, 21.1.98; also see interview with Mike Fairweather, Resort Developer, Calabash Caye, 13.1.98.

5   See *Destination Belize* (1998), p66.

6   Interview with Mike Fairweather, resort developer, Calabash Caye, 13.1.98.

7   *Destination Belize* (1998), p29; also see *Sport Diver Magazine*, vol 6, p79.

8   See for example 'Dive Guide International: Belize Scuba Diving Live-Aboard' (www.diveguideint.com/p0875.html); 'Dive Belize, Adventures in Watersports (Ambergris Caye)' (www.adventureswatersports.com/diving.html).

9   *San Pedro Sun* (1997), 'Booths available at DEMA', December 5; *San Pedro Sun* (1997), 'Belize promoted in London', December 12; *San Pedro Sun* (1997), 'San Pedro delegation to attend "Dive Dallas Scuba and Travel show"', April 5; interview with Victoria Collins, Editor, *San Pedro Sun*, 22.12.97, San Pedro; also see Lynn (1992), pp371–373, for further discussion.

10   Interview with Ken Leslie, Resort Developer, Calabash Caye, 29.1.98; also see interview with Mike Fairweather, Resort Developer, Calabash Caye, 13.1.98; *Destination Belize* (1998), pp66–67.

11   Peter Hughes Diving (http://peterhughes.com/phdeco.html).

12   BTB promotional tourism pack, 1997.

13   Advert for Manta Resort in *Destination Belize* (1997), p51. This is a recurrent theme in adverts for live-aboard dive ships and resorts in Belize; see for example, advert for the *Rembrandt Van Rijn* Live-Aboard, Dive Guide International (www.diveguideint.com/p0875.html).

14   Blackbird Caye Resort brochure, 1996. The ownership of Blackbird Caye Resort changed hands in 1997 and it ceased to be marketed as an ecotourist resort; the new owners prefer to promote it as a diving resort.

15   *Sport Diver Magazine* (1998) vol 6, p79.

16   Reef and Rainforest World Wide Adventure Travel: Belize (www.reefrainfrst.com/belize.html).

17   *San Pedro Sun* (1997), 'Dolphin International receives lending commitment... meeting held with First Company', June 27; *San Pedro Sun* (1997), letter from William (Mike) Campbell, Dolphin International Development Ltd, July 4.

18   *Destination Belize* (1998); *San Pedro Sun* (1997), '*Destination Belize* features "Swim with the Dolphins"', August 22.

19 *San Pedro Sun* (1997), 'Dolphin International helps football club', Feburary 14; see also *San Pedro Sun* (1997), 'Dolphin International donates paint for beautification project', July 18; *San Pedro Sun* (1997), 'Dolphin International donates to the Reina De La Costa', August 8. For further discussion of different types of human–dolphin interaction, see D Perrine (1998), 'Divers and Dolphins', *Sport Diver Magazine*, vol 6, pp40–47.

20 *San Pedro Sun* (1997), 'Dolphin International donates paint for beautification project', July 18.

21 *San Pedro Sun* (1997), 'Cangrejo Caye Educational Experience Ltd applies for duty-free tax exemption', July 25.

22 Interview with Ellen McRae, CariSearch Ltd, Siwa-Ban Foundation and BTIA, Caye Caulker, 3.1.98.

23 Interview with Daniel and Elodia Nunez, Tour Operators, Tanisha Tours, San Pedro, 30.12.97; see also interview with Victoria Collins, Editor, *San Pedro Sun*, San Pedro, 22.12.97; interview with Janet Gibson, National Project Advisor, Coastal Zone Management Project, Belize City, 11.2.98. See also *San Pedro Sun* (1997), 'BETA concerned about Cangrejo Caye Project', August 8; and *San Pedro Sun* (1997), 'Private hearing on the proposed dolphin park', June 27.

24 Interview with Daniel and Elodia Nunez, Tour Operators, Tanisha Tours, San Pedro, 30.12.97; interview with Victoria Collins, Editor, *San Pedro Sun*, San Pedro, 22.12.97; *San Pedro Sun* (1997), 'Lamanai Room Declaration issued by BTIA, Audubon and others', August 22; *San Pedro Sun* (1997), 'Private hearing on the proposed dolphin park', June 27.

25 *San Pedro Sun* (1997), 'BETA concerned about Cangrejo Caye project', August 8.

26 Interview with Victoria Collins, Editor, *San Pedro Sun*, San Pedro, 22.12.97.

27 Anonymous interviewees.

28 Interview with Al Westby, Housing and Planning Department, San Pedro, 31.12.98.

29 Interview with Mito Paz, Director, Green Reef, San Pedro, 2.2.98; interview with Jonathon Ridley, Director of Coral Cay Conservation, Calabash Caye, 25.1.98.

30 *Amandala* (1997), 'Dive ship damages Belize barrier reef', July 13; *Amandala* (1997), *'Rembrandt Van Rijn*; Fantome offered "options"', August 7.

31 *Amandala* (1997), 'Dive ship damages Belize barrier reef', July 13.

32 *Amandala* (1997), 'Windjammer Ltd apologises for reef destruction', August 10.

33   *Amandala* (1997), 'Windjammer Ltd apologises for reef destruction', August 10; *San Pedro Sun* (1997), 'MTE sanctions reef crunching vessels', August 8.

34   *Amandala* (1998), 'Cayman Islands government denies access to charter cruise for gays', January 11.

35   *Amandala* (1998), 'Cannot promote Belize' (letter), February 1.

36   *Amandala* (1998), anonymous email, January 18; *Village Voice* (1998) 'Controversy surrounds cruise ship cargo', January 24.

37   *Amandala* (1998), 'Baptist community protests visit of homosexuals on cruise ship' (letter from Lloyd W Stanford, president of the Baptist association of Belize, to Henry Young), January 18; *Amandala* (1998), 'No gay parade in Belize' (letter from the Muslim community of Belize), January 18; *Amandala* (1998), 'Association of Evangelical Churches speaks out against the homosexual ship', January 18.

38   *Amandala* (1998), 'D-revelation speaks out' (letter from Louis M Wade, Director, D-Revelation), January 25; *Amandala* (1998), 'Fort Point was an armed camp on Sunday', February 8.

39   *Amandala* (1998), 'Belizeans are backward and ignorant, says homosexual visitor', February 8.

40   *Amandala* (1998), letter from Howard A Frankson, February.

41   *Amandala* (1998), 'Wendy de la Fuente says send homosexuals to Caye Caulker', January 18.

42   *Amandala* (1998), 'Tour operators welcome MS *Leeward*', January 11.

43   Interview with Deon Pascascio, Assistant Minister of Tourism, Belmopan, 22.1.99; *Amandala* (1998), 'Why the gays had to come', April 19.

44   Interview with Wiezsman Pat, Executive Secretary, Mundo Maya Organization, Belmopan, 27.11.98.

45   *San Pedro Sun* (1997), 'Minister says Mexican air routes through Belize are not a done deal', November 28.

46   *Amandala* (1997), 'Airlines in bed together: Tourism Minister Henry Young', May 18.

47   Reef and Rainforest Tours brochure, 1997.

48   Interview with Victoria Collins, Editor of the *San Pedro Sun*, San Pedro, 23.12.97.

49   *Amandala* (1997), 'Tourist centre proposed at Fort Point', October 19; *Amandala* (1997), 'EU funds Maya archaeological site development programme', October 26; *San Pedro Sun* (1997), 'BTIA meets with Mundo Maya and IDB', November 28. The impact of tourism as a provider of local employment was also mentioned in interviews with tourists and with representatives of interest groups involved in the tourism industry. For example, interview with Tony Calderon, Park

Ranger, Hol Chan Marine Reserve, San Pedro, 22.12.97; interview with
Mike Fairweather, Resort Developer, Calabash Caye, 15.1.98; interview
with Mito Paz, Green Reef, San Pedro, 2.2.98.

50 *Amandala* (1998), 'Fields of death', November 15; *Amandala* (1998),
'Netherlands gives US$25,000 for medicine', November 15; *Amandala*
(1998), 'Mitch took everything from her but life', November 15;
Amandala (1998), 'El Salvador hosts emergency meeting by PAHO
officials', November 29; *New York Times* (1998), 'International ship into
eye of storm leaves grief and suits', November 14.

51 *Amandala* (1998), 'Dole, Chiquita feel the effects of the hurricane',
November 8.

52 *Amandala* (1998), 'A tragedy without precedent: Mitch victims face
years of hardship', November 22.

53 *Amandala* (1998), 'US donates humanitarian aid to victims of Hurricane
Mitch', November 15; *Amandala* (1998), 'Belize receives funding after
Mitch', November 8; *Amandala* (1998), 'IDB to host meeting of
Emergency Consultative Group for Central America', November 15;
Amandala (1998), '$12 million for regional recovery fund', November
22; *Amandala* (1998), 'IDB President calls for solidarity with Central
America', November 15.

54 *Amandala* (1998), 'Mitch and myth', November 8; *Amandala* (1998),
'Canada to assist Central American victims of Hurricane Mitch',
November 8; *Amandala* (1998), 'A tragedy without precedent: Mitch
Victims face years of hardship', November 22.

55 *Amandala* (1998), 'Fields of death', November 15; *Amandala* (1998),
'Mitch's toll may hit 7000', November 8; *Amandala* (1998), 'Thousands
still missing in Honduras', November 8.

56 *Amandala* (1998), 'Mitch took everything from her but life', November 15.

57 *Amandala* (1998), 'Honduras lowers Mitch fatality figures', December 6.

58 *Amandala* (1998), 'Mitch and myth', November 8; *Amandala* (1998),
'Over 15,000 seek refuge in San Ignacio', November 8.

59 *Amandala* (1998), 'Belize escapes Hurricane Mitch', November 8;
Amandala (1998), 'All is not lost in the Bay Islands', November 18.

60 *Amandala* (1998), 'The Belize presence in Honduras', November
29; *Amandala* (1998), 'Minister Espat visits Honduras',
November 6; *Amandala* (1998), 'Our housing contractors should
go to Honduras', November 29.

61 *Amandala* (1998), 'Over 15,000 seek refuge in San Ignacio', November
8; *Amandala* (1998), 'Remember who built Belmopan!', November 8;
Amandala (1998), 'Carlos Fuller writes to *Amandala*', November 18.

62   Interview with Jeffrey Avilez, Membership Services, BTIA, Belize City,
     21.1.99; interview with Wende Bryan, Barracuda and Jaguar Inn and
     BTIA President (Placencia Chapter), Placencia, 11.1.99; interview with
     Deon Pascascio Assistant Minister of Tourism, Ministry of Tourism,
     Belmopan, 22.1.99; *Amandala* (1998), 'Ain't that a Mitch!', November 8.
63   Interview with Wieszman Pat, Executive Secretary, Mundo Maya
     Organization, Belmopan, 27.11.98; interview with Valerie Woods,
     Director of Tourism, Belize Tourism Board, Belize City, 26.11.98; inter-
     view with Deon Pascascio Assistant Minister of Tourism, Ministry of
     Tourism, Belmopan, 22.1.99.
64   Interview with Terry Clancy, Director, Discovery Expeditions Ltd, Belize
     City, 17.11.98; interview with Wende Bryan, Barracuda and Jaguar Inn
     and BTIA President (Placencia Chapter), Placencia, 11.1.99; interview
     with Deon Pascascio Assistant Minister of Tourism, Ministry of Tourism,
     Belmopan, 22.1.99; interview with Jeffrey Avilez, Membership Services,
     BTIA, Belize City, 21.1.99; *Amandala* (1998), 'Ain't that a Mitch!',
     November 8.
65   Interview with Dave Vernon, Toadal Adventures, Placencia, 15.1.99.
66   Interview with Al Westby, Housing and Planning Department, San Pedro,
     31.12.98; personal communication, Julie Seldon, Sales and Marketing,
     Sunbreeze Hotel, San Pedro, 29.12.98; interview with Dave Vernon,
     Toadal Adventures, Placencia, 15.1.99.
67   Interview with Jeffrey Avilez, Membership Services, BTIA, Belize City,
     21.1.99.

Chapter 5

1   Belize Audubon Society (2000), *Newsletter*, Jan–April, p1.
2   Punta Gorda Conservation Committee (1998), *Newsletter*, July.
3   Interview with Santiago Coc, Caretaker of Lubaantuun Mayan
    Archaeological Site, Lubaantuun, Toledo District, 9.1.99; also Juan Luis
    Bonor and Anouk van Opstal (2000), 'Stelae, bones and standing stones',
    The Courier, October–November, pp13–16.
4   Interview with Ray Hubbard, Fallen Stones Butterfly Ranch, Toledo
    District, 9.1.99.
5   Interview with Will Maheia, Director, TIDE, Punta Gorda, 8.1.99.
6   See www.ecotourism.org.
7   Interview with Rafael Cal, TEA Chair, Medina Bank, 10.1.99.
8   Interview with Chet Schmidt, TEA and Nature's Way Guesthouse, Punta
    Gorda, 8.1.99; also *Amandala* (1997), 'Toledo Ecotourism Association
    wins TODO 96 award', April 20; *San Pedro Sun* (1997), 'Punta Gorda:

176   A TRIP TOO FAR

Will Toledo learn what is right and what is wrong in conservation and
tourism?', May 3.

9   Interview with Rafael Cal, TEA Chair, Medina Bank, 10.1.99; also inter-
    view with Pio Coc, Toledo Maya Cultural Council, Punta Gorda,
    24.5.00.
10 Interview with Chet Schmidt, TEA and Nature's Way Guesthouse, Punta
    Gorda, 8.1.99.
11 Interview with Yvonne Villoria, Dem Dats Doin Sustainable Technology
    Farm, Toledo Visitor Information Centre, Punta Gorda, 9.1.99; Punta
    Gorda Conservation Committee (1998), *Newsletter*, July, p6.
12 Interview with Rafael Cal, TEA Chair, Medina Bank, 10.1.99; interview
    with Chet Schmidt, TEA and Nature's Way Guesthouse, Punta Gorda,
    8.1.99; Williams (1993a), pp9–11.
13 Interview with Gregory Ch'oc, Kekchi Council of Belize, Punta Gorda,
    23.5.00; interview with Reyes Chun, Toledo Ecotourism Association,
    Punta Gorda, 24.5.00.
14 Interview with Gregory Ch'oc, Kekchi Council of Belize, Punta Gorda,
    23.5.00.
15 *San Pedro Sun* (1997), 'Punta Gorda: Will Toledo learn what is right and
    what is wrong in conservation and tourism?', May 3; *Amandala* (1999),
    'Toledo's one-room hotels in financial trouble', November 21.
16 *Amandala* (1997), 'Toledo Tour Guide Association vexed with Ministry
    of Tourism', letter from the Toledo Tour Guide Association, April 13;
    Amandala (1997), 'TEA replies to Toledo tour guides', letter from TEA
    Executive Board, June 22.
17 Personal communication, Pio Saqui, Director of the Marine Research
    Centre, UCB, Belize City, 18.5.00.
18 Interview with Gregory Ch'oc, Kekchi Council of Belize, Punta Gorda,
    23.5.00.
19 *Amandala* (1999), 'Toledo Mayans "bex"', May 9.
20 Personal communication Pio Saqui, Director of the Marine Research
    Centre, UCB, Belize City, 18.5.00; *Amandala* (1999), 'Northern Maya:
    Mestizos support Valentino Shal's protest', October 17; *Amandala*
    (1998), 'Mayan student irate', letter from Valentino Shal, September 26.
21 Interview with Pio Coc, Toledo Maya Cultural Council, Punta Gorda,
    24.5.00; see Toledo Maya Cultural Council and Toledo Alcaldes
    Association (1997).
22 Interview with Chet Schmidt, Toledo Ecotourism Association, Punta
    Gorda, Belize 8.1.99. Other informants also talked about how they
    perceived the government's response to the Mayan eco-park, but they
    asked to remain anonymous.

23 Interview with Pio Coc, Toledo Maya Cultural Council, Punta Gorda, 24.5.00.
24 Interview with Pio Coc, Toledo Maya Cultural Council, Punta Gorda, 24.5.00; *Amandala* (1999), 'Indigenous immigrants', letter from Ed Shaw, August 8; *Amandala* (1999), 'Present state of affairs of Toledo Maya', November 21.
25 Interview with K Mustapha Toure, Project Manager, ESTAP, Punta Gorda, 25.5.00.
26 Anonymous interviewee.
27 *Amandala* (1999), 'Espat faces Musa', May 9; *Amandala* (1999), 'Musa visits Toledo', May 9; *Amandala* (1999), 'PG debates Toledo Development Corp bill', September 26.
28 Belize Audubon Society (2000), *Newsletter*, Jan–April, p10.
29 Interview with K Mustapha Toure, Project Manager, ESTAP, Punta Gorda, 25.5.00; interview with Gregory Ch'oc, Kekchi Council of Belize, Punta Gorda, 23.5.00.
30 Interview with K Mustapha Toure, Project Manager, ESTAP, Punta Gorda, 25.5.00; see ESTAP (2000).
31 *Amandala* (1999), 'PM Musa on the Toledo Development Corporation bill', October 19.
32 *Amandala* (1998), 'Erosion of democracy: the Malaysian logging concession', March 29; *Amandala* (1998), 'Maya lawsuit against GOB', April 5; *Amandala* (1998), 'Toledo Maya take government before Inter-American Commission on Human Rights', August 16.
33 *Amandala* (1999), 'Present state of affairs of Toledo Mayas', November 21; *Amandala* (1998), 'Erosion of democracy: the Malaysian logging concession', March 29.
34 *Amandala* (1999), 'Press release regarding the report on the Malaysian logging review committee', March 28; *Amandala* (1999), 'Civil society: Dangriga speaks', April 11.
35 *Amandala* (1998), 'Maya lawsuit against GOB still pending', April 5; *Amandala* (1998), 'Toledo Maya take government before Inter-American Commission on Human Rights', August 16; *Amandala* (1998), 'Rural Belizean "Toledoans" want to address the House of Representatives', October 11; *Amandala* (1998), 'Toledo Ecotourism Association pleased with reception in the city', October 18.
36 Interview with Chet Schmidt, Toledo Ecotourism Association, Punta Gorda, Belize, 8.1.99; *Amandala* (1998), 'Rural Belizean "Toledoans" want to address the House of Representatives', October 11; *Amandala* (1998), 'Toledo Ecotourism Association pleased with reception in the city', October 18.

37   *Amandala* (1999), 'Press release regarding the report on the Malaysian logging review committee', March 28; *Amandala* (1999), 'Civil society: Dangriga speaks', April 11.
38   Interview with Pio Coc, Toledo Maya Cultural Council, Punta Gorda, 24.5.00; Ix Chel (2000), 'Julian Cho Memorial Mass', *TMCC Newsletter*, May.
39   *Amandala* (1998), 'Maya leader dies alone!', December 6.
40   *Amandala* (1998), 'Respect Julian Cho RIP', December 6; *Amandala* (1998), 'Funeral Homily for Julian Cho', December 13; *Amandala* (1998), 'Julian Cho may have been murdered', December 20.
41   *Amandala* (1999), 'No new info on Julian Cho's death', January 17; *Amandala* (1999), 'Second pathologist says Cho's death accidental', February 7.
42   *Amandala* (1998), 'Friend who last saw Mayan leader alive', December 13; *Amandala* (1998), 'Mayan leader dies alone!', December 6.
43   Personal communication Reyes Chun, Toledo Ecotourism Association, Punta Gorda, 24.5.00.
44   Interview with Pio Coc, Toledo Maya Cultural Council, Punta Gorda, 24.5.00; *Amandala* (1999), 'Present state of affairs of Toledo Mayas', November 21; *Amandala* (1999), 'Toledo Maya comment on Bilal Morris article', letter from Pio Coc, November 28; *Amandala* (1999), 'Press release regarding the report on the Malaysian logging review committee', March 28.
45   Interview with Roberto Echevarria, tour guide, Toledo Institute for Development and Environment, Punta Gorda, 23.5.00.
46   Anonymous interviewee; *Amandala* (1999), 'Toledo eco politics: Maheia vs Espat', July 11.
47   Personal communications, anonymous informants.
48   Interview with Roberto Echevarria, tour guide, Toledo Institute for Development and Environment, Punta Gorda, 23.5.00; interview with Gregory Ch'oc, Kekchi Council of Belize, Punta Gorda, 23.5.00.
49   Anonymous informant.
50   Interview with Nicole Auil, Manatee Researcher, Coastal Zone Management Plan, Belize City, 23.11.98.
51   *Amandala* (1999), 'TIDE investigates dead manatees', October 17; *Amandala* (1998), 'Manatee slaughter illegal', September 6; see also Wildlife Preservation Trust International and Wildlife Conservation Society (1996), pp4–7.
52   Interview with Gregory Ch'oc, Kekchi Council of Belize, Punta Gorda, Belize, 23.5.00.

53   *Amandala* (1999), '17 testify in case of Guate shot by BDF', August 1; *Amandala* (1999), 'Statement by Minister Jorge Espat on June 12 1999 border incident', July 4.

54   *Amandala* (1999), 'Guatemalan forestry officials contemplate charges against Yalbac ranch', June 13.

55   *Amandala* (1999), 'Territorial uncertainty', October 17.

Chapter 6

1   Interview with Maria Vega, Vega Inn and BTIA, Caye Caulker, 21.1.98; see also Bureau for International Narcotics and Law Enforcement Affairs (1998c), Hampton (1996).

2   *The Times* (1999), 'Shadow over Tory Treasurer', July 13.

3   *The Times* (1999), 'A "mugging" and its consequences', July 14; *The Times* (1999), 'British diplomat tells Tories to launch Ashcroft enquiry', July 16.

4   *The Times* (1999), 'A "mugging" and its consequences', July 14; *The Times* (1999), 'Clamour grows for full-scale enquiry', July 16.

5   Anonymous interviewee.

6   *The Times* (1999), 'Some of these rumours about Ashcroft cast a shadow over his reputation', July 13; *The Times* (1999), 'The whiff of the casbah lingers', July 13; *The Times* (1999), 'He is off to Bournemouth and will be lobbying our politicians', July 13; *Guardian* (1999), 'Ashcroft sought aid from ministers to promote business interests abroad', July 15; *Guardian* (1999), 'Tory anger over Ashcroft leaks', July 14.

7   *Guardian* (1999), 'Caribbean jaunt landed MPs in hot water', July 13; *Guardian* (1999), 'Fury as MPs' trip to Belize revealed', July 23; *Guardian* (1999), 'Tory MP defends Ashcroft trip', July 24.

8   *The Times* (1999), 'Drugs Agency has Ashcroft on its files', July 17; *Guardian* (1999) 'Drip, drip, of disclosures', July 22.

9   *Guardian* (1999), '100 million wiped off shares', July 27; *Guardian* (1999), 'Ashcroft blocks US documents', October 5; *Guardian* (1999), 'Peace in our Times', December 13; *Guardian* (1999), 'The secret deal for the future of Conservatism', December 12; *Guardian* (1999), 'Why Rupert and Michael's compromise is a big deal', December 13.

10   *The Economist* (1999), 'A new class of trafficker', September 11–19, p66.

11   Bureau for International Narcotics and Law Enforcement Affairs (1998d), p1; *Guardian* (1997), 'Whose colony is this anyway?', June 17; *Amandala* (1997), 'US pressure in drug fight rankles some', January 19; *Amandala* (1997), 'Colombia and Mexico sign agreement to co-operate in anti drug fight', February 9; *San Pedro Sun* (1997), 'Drug traffic

increasing in the Caribbean', December 12. For further discussion of the global nature of the drugs trade see Stares (1996) and Nietschmann (1997), pp193–224.

12 *Amandala* (1997), 'Belize caught in the middle of a drug war', August 3; and Nietschmann (1997), pp193–224.

13 *Amandala* (1997), 'Belize by sea: much coast little guard', September 26, and anonymous interviewees.

14 Bureau for International Narcotics and Law Enforcement Affairs (1998a) p1; *Amandala* (1997), 'Defendants in Belize's biggest cocaine bust walk', September 28; *Amandala* (1997), 'Colombian drug trafficker pays fine, exits prison', October 5; *Amandala* (1997), 'Bad baby Belize says US', March 9.

15 *Amandala* (1997), 'Belize by sea: much coast little guard'. This was confirmed by a number of interviewees who wanted to remain anonymous.

16 Anonymous interviewees. This was a claim regularly made against the new owners of Blackbird Caye Resort and Manta Resort, which had previously been developed by Ray Lightburn, Ken Leslie and Al Dugan.

17 *Guardian* (1999), 'Tory MP reported to ombudsman as Belize affair widens', July 22; *Guardian* (1999), 'Mr Ashcroft's patronage', July 22.

18 *San Pedro Sun* (1997), 'Prime Minister Esquivel announces tourist village study', October 17; *Amandala* (1997), 'Tourist centre proposed for Fort Point', October 19.

19 *Amandala* (1998), 'Cutlack on tourist spending patterns', letter from Meb Cutlack, June 28; *Amandala* (1998), 'The tourism dollar', May 24.

20 Anonymous interviewee.

21 Anonymous interviewees.

22 Anonymous interviewees; also see Andreas (1996).

23 Anonymous interviewees.

24 *Amandala* (1998), 'Dept of Archaeology fights looting of Belizean artefacts', March 1.

25 Anonymous interviewees.

26 Interview with Ramon Silva, International Archaeological Tours, San Ignacio, 27.1.99. This was a common story told by tour guides in Mexico, Guatemala and Belize; see also Benz (1998) for further discussion of the ways that Mayan ruins have been reconfigured through archaeological excavations and restoration plans to make the ruins more pleasing for tourists rather than historically accurate.

27 *Amandala* (1998), 'Americans nabbed with antiquities at the airport', March 15; *Amandala* (1998), 'Four arrested for "hot" Mayan artefacts', December 16.

28 *Amandala* (1998), 'Americans nabbed with antiquities at the airport',
    March 15; *Amandala* (1998), 'Four arrested for "hot" Mayan artefacts',
    December 16.
29 Anonymous interviewees.
30 Anonymous interviewee.
31 Anonymous interviewee.
32 Interview with James Sanchez, Boat Captain, Marine Research Centre,
    UCB, and ex-Fisheries Officer, Calabash Caye, 29.1.98; *Amandala*
    (1997), 'Four Fisheries Department employees retrenched; more yet to
    go', October 5.
33 Interview with Dwight Neal, Director, Marine Research Centre, UCB,
    and ex-Fisheries Officer, Calabash Caye, 24.1.98; interview with Mito
    Paz, Director, Green Reef, San Pedro, 2.2.98.
34 Interview with Ellen McCrae, CariSearch Ltd, Siwa-Ban Foundation and
    BTIA, Caye Caulker, 3.1.98.
35 Personal communication, Hector Cunningham, Fisheries Officer,
    Calabash Caye, 29.1.98.
36 Interview with Victoria Collins, Editor of the *San Pedro Sun*, San Pedro,
    23.12.97.
37 *San Pedro Sun* (1997), 'Lobster season opens', June 27; *BAS News*
    (1998), 'September 30th marks end of closed season for the Queen
    Conch (Strombus gigas)'.
38 *Amandala* (1997), 'Chiste grants licence to catch undersized lobster',
    July 13; *San Pedro Sun* (1997), 'Fisheries regulations amended', August
    1; *San Pedro Sun* (1997), 'Lobster farming – who to believe?', August 1;
    Amandala (1997), 'Taiwanese mafia business at South Water Caye',
    August 10.
39 *Amandala* (1997), 'Belling the Chinese cat', August 31.
40 *Amandala* (1997), 'Dive Ship damages Belize Barrier Reef', July 13;
    Amandala (1997), '*Rembrandt Van Rijn*; *Fantome* offered "options"',
    August 10.
41 *Amandala* (1997), 'Windjammer Ltd apologises for reef destruction',
    August 10; *San Pedro Sun* (1997), 'MTE sanctions reef crunching
    vessels', August 8.
42 Interview with Mito Paz, Director, Green Reef, San Pedro, 2.2.98; inter-
    view with Tony Calderon, Park Ranger, Hol Chan Marine Reserve, San
    Pedro, 22.12.97; interview with Alberto Patt, Biologist, Hol Chan
    Marine Reserve, San Pedro, 2.2.98; *San Pedro Sun* (1997), '*Gypsy Queen*
    goes aground on the reef', October 14.
43 Anonymous interviewees; *San Pedro Sun* (1997), '*Gypsy Queen* goes
    aground on the reef', October 14.

44 Interview with Malcolm Hitchcock, Fido's Bar, San Pedro, 5.12.97.
45 *San Pedro Sun* (1997), 'Gypsy Queen goes aground on the reef', October 14.
46 Anonymous interviewees.
47 Anonymous interviewee.
48 Anonymous interviewees.
49 Interview with Victoria Collins, Editor of the San *Pedro Sun*, San Pedro, 23.12.97; *San Pedro Sun*, (1997), 'Lamanai Room Declaration issued by BTIA, Audubon and others', August 22.
50 Anonymous interviewees.
51 Green Reef (undated), *Contacts*, San Pedro, Belize.
52 Interview with Maria Vega, Vega Inn and BTIA, Caye Caulker, 21.1.98; interview with Ellen McRae, CariSearch Ltd, Siwa-Ban Foundation and BTIA, Caye Caulker, 3.1.98.
53 San Pedro Town Valuation Roll, 1996–2001; *San Pedro Sun* (1997), 'Open forum: a closer look at Sunset Coves, by UDP San Pedro Branch', October 28.
54 *Amandala* (19997), 'Sunset Coves Ltd sold', December 21.
55 McField, Wells and Gibson, (1996) pp88–93; interview with Janet Gibson, National Project Advisor, Coastal Zone Management Project, Belize City, 11.2.98; interview with Tony Calderon, Park Ranger, Hol Chan Marine Reserve, San Pedro, 22.12.97; *San Pedro Sun*, (1997), 'First phase of North Ambergris Caye development to start with Basil Jones airstrip says BIS press release, NACDC chairman', June 13.
56 San Pedro Town Valuation Roll 1996–2001. James Blake, a Belizean, was one of the other large land owners on the island. Also interview with Chocolate, Chocolate's Manatee Tours, Caye Caulker, 19.1.98.
57 Anonymous interviewees.
58 PUP (1998), *Set Belize Free: Manifesto of the PUP, 1998–2003*, p25.
59 Interview with Ellen McRae, Cari-Search, Ltd, Siwa-Ban Foundation and BTIA, Caye Caulker, 3.1.98; interview with Chocolate, Tour Guide, Chocolate's Manatee Tours, Caye Caulker, 15.12.97.
60 Anonymous interviewee. I also witnessed the activities of sand pirates.
61 Department of Environment (1998b), Compliance Monitoring Site Visit Report; interview with Janet Gibson, National Project Advisor, Coastal Zone Management Project, Belize City, 11.2.98,.
62 Anonymous interviewees. This was mentioned by a number of people who were interviewed, particularly those on Caye Caulker whose livelihoods had been directly affected by dredging.
63 Anonymous interviewee.
64 *Guardian* (1999), 'Mr Ashcroft's patronage', July 22.

REFERENCES

Abbott-Cone, C (1995) 'Crafting selves: The lives of two Mayan women', *Annals of Tourism Research,* vol 22, pp314–327

Adams, W (1990) *Green Development,* Routledge: London

Ades, A and di Tella, R (1996) 'The causes and consequences of corruption: A review of recent empirical contributions', *IDS Bulletin,* vol 27, pp6–11

Ahonsi, B A (1995) 'Gender relations, demographic change and the prospects for sustainable development in Africa', *Africa Development,* vol 20, pp85–114

Akama, J S, Lant, C L and Wesley, G (1996) 'A political ecology approach to wildlife conservation in Kenya', *Environmental Values,* vol 5, pp335–347

Amsden, A (1990) 'Third Word industrialisation: 'Global Fordism' or a New Model?', *New Left Review,* vol 182, pp5–32

Anderson, B (1991) *Imagined Communities: Reflections on the Origin and Spread of Nationalism,* revised edition, Verso, London

Andreas, P (1996) 'US drug control policy', *In Focus,* vol 1, no 12, *Foreign Policy in Focus,* joint project for the Institute for Policy Studies and the Interhemispheric Resource Center, Silver City, NM

Ap, J (1992) 'Residents' perceptions of tourism impacts', *Annals of Tourism Research,* vol 19, pp665–690

Ariel de Vidas, A (1995) 'Textiles, memory and the souvenir industry in the Andes' in Lanfant, M F, Allcock, J B and Bruner, E M (eds) *International Tourism: Identity and Change,* Sage, London, pp67–83

author unknown (1970) *Basic Considerations on the Planning of Human Settlement with High Tourist Development Potential: Case Study: The Island of Ambergris Caye, British Honduras,* Belize

Bacchus, M D (1986) 'Sociological indication and the visibility criterion of real world social theorising' in Garfinkel, H (ed) *Ethnomethodological Studies of Work,* Routledge and Kegan Paul, London and New York, pp1–19

Bach, S A (1996) 'Tourist-related crime and the hotel industry: A review of the literature and related materials' in Pizam, A, and Mansfeld, Y (eds) *Tourism,*

Crime and International Security Issues, J Wiley and Sons, Chichester and New York, pp281–296.

Ballantine, J L and Eagles, P F J (1994) 'Defining Canadian ecotourists', *Journal of Sustainable Tourism*, vol 2, pp210–214

Barbier, E et al (1994) *Paradise Lost? The Ecological Economics of Biodiversity*, Earthscan, London

Barclay, J and Ferguson, D (1992) 'Caught between the devil and the deep blue sea: The development of tourism in Cuba', *Community Development Journal*, vol 27, pp378–385

Barraclough, J (1992) 'Development tourists: Personal views of Oxfam's volunteers tours overseas', *Community Development Journal*, vol 27, pp396–401

Barrett, C B and Arcese, P (1995) 'Are integrated conservation development projects (IDCPs) sustainable? On conservation of large mammals in Sub-Saharan Africa', *World Development*, vol 23, pp1073–1084

BAS (1999) *Lighthouse Reef and Half Moon Caye Management Plan*, BAS, Belize City

Baxter, J and Eyles, J (1997) 'Evaluating qualitative research in social geography: Establishing "rigour" in interview analysis', *Transactions of the Institute of British Geographers*, vol 22, pp505–525

Bayart, J-F (1993) *The State in Africa: The Politics of the Belly*, Longman, London

Bayart, J-F, Ellis, S and Hibou, B (eds) (1999) *The Criminalisation of the State in Africa*, James Currey, Oxford

Beck, U (1995) *Ecological Politics in an Age of Risk*, Polity Press, Cambridge

Beck, U (1994) 'The reinvention of politics: Towards a theory of reflexive modernisation' in Beck, U, Giddens, A and Lash, S (eds) *Reflexive Modernisation: Politics, Tradition and Aesthetics and the Modern Social Order*, Polity Press, Cambridge, pp1–55

Beck, U, Giddens, A and Lash, S (eds) (1994) *Reflexive Modernisation: Politics, Tradition and Aesthetics and the Modern Social Order*, Polity Press, Cambridge

Beck, U, Giddens, A and Lash, S (1994) 'Replies and critiques' in Beck, U, Giddens, A and Lash, S (eds) *Reflexive Modernisation: Politics, Tradition and Aesthetics and the Modern Social Order*, Polity Press, Cambridge, pp174–215

Beckerman, W (1994) 'Sustainable development: Is it a useful concept?', *Environmental Values*, vol 3, pp191–209

Belize Fisheries Department/Mundo Maya/BTB (1995) *Belize Watersport Guide*, Mydan Publications, Belize City

Belize Institute of Management (1996) *Tour and Travel Guiding Serices Training Program: Participation Training Manual,* BTIA/BTB/ Ministry of Tourism and the Environment, Belize City/Belmopan

Ben-Ami, S, Peled, Y and Spetorowski, A (eds) (2000) *Ethnic Challenges to the Modern Nation-State,* Macmillan, Basingstoke

Benz, S (1998) *Green Dreams: Travels in Central America,* Lonely Planet Publications, Melbourne

Bevier, W (1995) 'Laughing Bird Caye National Park: Its relationship to the communities in the Placencia Lagoon Area of the Mango Creek Special Development Area', in *Proceedings of the Second National Symposium on the State of the Belize Environment,* NARMAP, Belize City, pp205–208

Blamey, R K and Braithwaite, V A (1997) 'A social value segmentation of the potential ecotourism market', *Journal of Sustainable Tourism,* vol 5, pp29–55

Blomstrom, M and Hettne, B (1984) *Development Theory in Transition: The Dependency Debate and Beyond: Third World Responses,* Zed Books, London

Bloom, J (1996) 'A South African perspective of the effects of crime and violence on the tourism industry' in Pizam, A, and Mansfeld, Y (eds) *Tourism, Crime and International Security Issues,* J Wiley and Sons, Chichester and New York, pp91–102

Boden, D and Zimmerman, D H (1991) 'Structure-in-Action: An introduction' in Boden, D and Zimmerman, D H (eds) *Talk and Social Structure: Studies in Ethnomethodology and Conversation Analysis,* Polity Press, Cambridge, pp3–22

Boden, D and Zimmerman, D H (eds) (1991) *Talk and Social Structure: Studies in Ethnomethodology and Conversation Analysis,* Polity Press, Cambridge

Bolin, B (1994) 'Science and policy making', *Ambio,* vol 23, pp25–29

Bolland, O N (1997) *Struggles for Freedom: Essays on Slavery, Colonialism and Culture in the Caribbean and Central America,* Belize City, Angelus Press

Berthold-Bond, D (2000) 'The ethics of "place": Reflections on bioregionalism', *Environmental Ethics,* vol 22, pp5–20

Boo, E (1990) *Ecotourism: The Potentials and the Pitfalls,* vols 1 and 2, WWF, Washington DC

Bookchin, M et al (eds) (1991) *Defending the Earth: A Dialogue Between Murray Bookchin and Dave Foreman,* South End Press, Boston

Booth, D (1985) 'Marxism and development sociology: Interpreting the impasse', *World Development,* vol 13, pp761–787

Bornschier, V, and Chase-Dunn, C (1993) 'Transnational penetration and economic growth' in Seligson, M A and Passe-Smith, J T (eds) *Development and Underdevelopment: The Political Economy of Inequality,* Lynne Rienner, London, pp239–266

Bottrill, C G (1995) 'Ecotourism: Towards a key elements approach to operationalising the concept', *Journal of Sustainable Tourism,* vol 3, pp45–54

Brack, D (1995) 'Balancing trade and the environment', *International Affairs,* vol 71, pp497–514.

Bramwell, B and Lane, B (1993) 'Interpretation and sustainable tourism: The potential and the pitfalls', *Journal of Sustainable Tourism,* vol 1, pp71–80

Broad, R (1994) 'The poor and the environment: Friends or foes', *World Development,* vol 22, pp811–822

Brohman, J (1996) 'New directions in tourism for Third World development', *Annals of Tourism Research,* vol 23, pp48–70

Brown, D (1996) 'Genuine fakes' in Selwyn, T (ed) *The Tourist Image: Myths and Myth Making in Tourism,* John Wiley and Sons, Chichester, pp33–47

Brown, N (1992) 'Beachboys as culture brokers in Bakau Town, The Gambia', *Community Development Journal,* vol 27, pp361–370

Bruntland, G H (1987) *Our Common Future,* World Commission on Environment and Development, Oxford University Press, Oxford

Bryant, R L (1997) 'Beyond the impasse: The power of political ecology third world environmental research', *Area,* vol 9, pp5–19

BTB (1993) *Tourism: A Historical Reference, A Challenge to the Future, from a Belize Tourist Board Prospective* (sic), BTB, Belize City

BTIA (1990) *Strategic Plan for the Medium Term 1990–1993,* BTIA, Belize City

BTIA (1989) *President's Report,* BTIA, Belize City

Bulmer, M and Warwick, D P (eds) (1993) *Social Research in Developing Countries,* UCL Press, London

Bulmer, M (1993) 'Interviewing and field organisation' in Bulmer, M and Warwick, D P (eds) *Social Research in Developing Countries,* UCL Press, London, pp215–219

Bureau for International Narcotics and Law Enforcement Affairs (1998a) *Country Certifications: The Certification Process,* US Department of State, Washington DC

Bureau for International Narcotics and Law Enforcement Affairs (1998b) *INL Mission Statement,* US Department of State, Washington DC

Bureau for International Narcotics and Law Enforcement Affairs (1998c) *International Narcotics Control Strategy Report, 1997: Money Laundering and Financial Crimes,* US Department of State, Washington DC

Bureau for International Narcotics and Law Enforcement Affairs (1998d) *International Narcotics Control Strategy Report, 1997: Canada, Mexico and Central America,* US Department of State, Washington DC

Burgess, R G (ed) (1982) *Field Research: A Sourcebook and Field Manual,* Allen and Unwin, London

Burgess, R G (1982) 'The unstructured interview as a conversation' in *Field Research: A Sourcebook and Field Manual,* Allen and Unwin, London, pp107–111

Calantone, R J and di Benedetto, C A (1991) 'Knowledge acquisition modelling in tourism', *Annals of Tourism Research,* vol 10, pp202–212

Calvani, S, Guia, E and Lemahieu, J L (1997) 'Drug resistance rating: An innovative approach for measuring a country's capacity to resist illegal drugs', *Third World Quarterly,* vol 18, pp659–672

Caricomp (1996) 'Contributed Caricomp Papers', *8th International Coral Reef Symposium,* June 24–29th 1996, Panama City, Panama

Cary, J (1993) 'The nature of symbolic beliefs and environmental behaviour in a rural setting', *Environment and Behaviour,* vol 25, pp555–576

Cater, E (1995) 'Environmental contradictions in sustainable tourism', *Geographical Journal,* vol 161, pp21–28

Cater, E (1992) 'Profits from paradise', *Geographical Magazine,* vol 64, pp16–21

Cater, E and Lowman, G (eds) (1994) *Ecotourism: A Sustainable Option,* John Wiley and Sons, London

Cater, E (1994) 'Ecotourism in the third world: Problems and prospects for sustainability' in Cater, E and Lowman, G (eds) *Ecotourism: A Sustainable Option,* John Wiley and Sons, London, pp69–86

Carson, R (1962) *Silent Spring,* Hamish Hamilton, London

Caulfield, H P (1989) 'The conservation and environmental movements: An historical analysis' in Lester, J (ed) *Environmental Politics and Policies,* Durham University Press, Durham, pp13–57

Chalker, L (1991) *Good Government and the Aid Programme,* ODA, London

Chambers, R (1983) *Rural Development: Putting the Last First,* Longman, Harlow, Essex

Chant, S (1992) 'Tourism in Latin America: Perspectives from Mexico and Costa Rica' in Harrison, D (ed) *Tourism and the Less Developed Countries,* Belhaven Press, London, pp85–101

Clapham, C (1996) *Africa and the Internal System: The Politics of State Survival,* Cambridge University Press, Cambridge

Coates, K (1993) 'Gales Point Manatee and ecotourism', unpublished MSc dissertation, School for International Training, University of Vermont

Cohan, M J (1999) 'Science and society in the historical perspective: Implications for social theories of risk', *Environmental Values*, vol 8, pp153–176

Columbia University (1990) *Organic Farming and Ecological Tourism: A Project Proposal for Belize*, School of International and Public Affairs, Economic and Political Development Workshop, Columbia University, New York

Coolidge, J and Rose-Ackerman, S (1997) *High-Level Rent Seeking and Corruption in African Regimes: Theory and Cases*, World Bank, New York

Coppin, A (1993) 'Recent evidence on the determinants of inflation in a tourism-oriented economy: Barbados', *Social and Economic Studies*, vol 42, pp65–80

Corbridge, S (ed) (1995) *Development Studies: A Reader*, Edward Arnold, London

Cotgrove, S and Duff, A (1980) 'Environmentalism, middle class radicalism and politics', *Sociological Review*, vol 28, pp333–351

Cothran, D A and Cole-Cothran, C (1998) 'Promise or political risk for Mexican tourism', *Annals of Tourism Research*, vol 25, pp477–497

Craik, J (1995) 'Are there cultural limits to tourism?', *Journal of Sustainable Tourism*, vol 3, pp87–98

Crouch, D (ed) (1999) *Leisure/Tourism Geographies: Practices and Geographical Knowledge*, Routledge, London

Crouch, G I (1992) 'Effect of income and price on international tourism', *Annals of Tourism Research*, vol 19, pp643–664

Cruise-Malloy, D and Fennell, D A (1997) 'Tourism and ethics: The form and function of organisational cultures', paper presented at the 1997 International Symposium on Human Dimensions of Natural Resource Management in the Americas, Canada, University of Regina

Cutlack, M (1993) *Belize: Ecotourism in Action*, Macmillan, London

Czyzewski, M (1994) 'Reflexivity of actors versus reflexivity of accounts', *Theory, Culture and Society*, vol 11, pp161–168

Daily, G C and Ehrlich, A H and P R (1995) 'Socioeconomic equity: A critical element in sustainability', *Ambio*, vol 24, pp58–59

Dann, G (1996a) 'The people of tourist brochures' in Selwyn, T (ed) (1996) *The Tourist Image: Myths and Myth Making in Tourism*, John Wiley and Sons, Chichester, pp61–81

Dann, G (1996b) *The Language of Tourism: A Sociolinguistic Perspective*, CAB International, Oxon

Davidson, D J and Freudenburg, W R (1996) 'Gender and environmental risk concerns: A review and analysis of available research', *Environment and Behaviour*, vol 28, pp302–339

Department of the Environment (1995) *Proceedings of the Second National Symposium on the State of the Belize Environment,* held at the Belize Biltmore Plaza Oct 5–6th 1995, Ministry of Tourism and the Environment, Belmopan, Belize

Department of the Environment (1998a) *Compliance Monitoring Site Visit Report: Caye Chapel,* DoE, Belmopan, Belize

Department of the Environment (1998b) *Compliance Monitoring Site Visit Report: San Pedro,* DoE, Belmopan, Belize

Devres Inc (1993) *Draft Report of the Tourism Industry Needs Assessment: Preliminary Survey Results,* Devres Inc, Washington DC

De Young, R (1993) 'Changing behaviour and making it stick: The conceptualisation and management of conservation behaviour', *Environment and Behaviour,* vol 25, pp485–505

De Young, R et al (1993) 'Promoting source reduction behaviour: The role of motivational information', *Environment and Behaviour,* vol 25, pp70–85

Dickson, B (2000) 'The ethicist conception of environmental problems', *Environmental Values,* vol 9, pp127–152

Dieke, P (1994) 'The political economy of tourism in The Gambia', *Review of African Political Economy,* vol 21, pp611–626

Dieke, P (1993) 'Tourism and development policy in The Gambia', *Annals of Tourism Research,* vol 20, pp423–460

Dobson, A (1996) 'Environmental sustainabilities: an analysis and typology', *Environmental Politics,* pp401–428

Dovers, S K and Handmer, J W (1995) 'Ignorance, the precautionary principle and sustainability', *Ambio,* vol 24, pp92–97

Drummond, I and Marsden, T K (1995) 'Regulating sustainable development', *Global Environmental Change,* vol 5, pp51–63

Duffy, R (2000a) 'Shadow players: Ecotourism development, corruption and state politics in Belize', *Third World Quarterly,* vol 21 pp549–565

Duffy, R (2000b) 'The politics of African and Central American peace parks: Environmentalism, state sovereignty and criminality', paper presented at the International Political Studies Association XVIII World Congress on World Capitalism, Governance and Community: Towards a Corporate Millennium, Quebec City, August 1–5 2000

Dunlap, R E and Van Liere, K (1978) 'The new environmental paradigm: A proposed measuring instrument and preliminary results', *Journal of Environmental Education,* vol 9, pp10–19

Dunlap, R E and Van Liere, K (1984) 'Commitment to the dominant social paradigm and concern for environmental quality', *Social Science Quarterly,* vol 65, pp1013–1028

Dryzek, J S and Lester, J P (1989) 'Alternative views of the environmental problematic' in Lester, J (ed) *Environmental Politics and Policies,* Durham University Press, Durham, pp314–330

Dwyer, W O, Leeming, F C, Cobern, M K, Porter, B E and Jackson, J M (1993) 'Critical review of behavioural interventions to preserve the environment: Research since 1980', *Environment and Behaviour,* vol 25, pp275–321

Eckersley, R (1992) *Environmentalism and Political Theory: Towards an Ecocentric Approach,* UCL Press, London

Economist Intelligence Unit (1993) *Tourism in the Caribbean: Special Report,* EIU, London

Eden, SE (1994) 'Using sustainable development: The business case', *Global Environmental Change,* vol 4, pp160–167

Edwards, E (1996) 'Postcards: Greetings from another world' in Selwyn, T (ed) (1996) *The Tourist Image: Myths and Myth Making in Tourism,* John Wiley and Sons, Chichester, pp197–221

Elliot, R and Gare, A (1983) (eds) *Environmental Philosophy,* Open University Press, Milton Keynes

Ellis, G (1995) 'Tourism and the environment: Some observations on Belize', in *Proceedings of the Second National Symposium on the State of the Belize Environment,* pp302–308

Elson, D (1988) 'Transnational corporations: Dominance and dependency in the world economy' in Corbridge, S (ed) (1995) *Development Studies: A Reader,* Edward Arnold, pp296–298. Reprinted from Crow, B, Thorpe, M et al (eds) (1988) *Survival and Change in the Third World,* Polity Press/OUP, Cambridge

Eltringham, P (1997) *Rough Guide to Belize and Guatemala,* Rough Guide Publications, London

Emmons, K et al (1996) *Cockscomb Basin Wildlife Sanctuary: Its History, Flora, and Fauna, for Visitors, Teachers and Scientists,* Belize Audubon Society, Belize City

Enriquez, J A (1993) '"Birds come, touris' come": The socio-cultural and socio-economic impact of ecotourism on rural Belizean communities: The case of Crooked Tree Village', unpublished research paper in partial fulfilment of MSc, Ministry of Tourism and the Environment, Belmopan, Belize

ESTAP (2000) *Regional Development Plan for Southern Belize,* ESTAP/GOB/Inter-American Development Bank, Belize City, Belize

Estrada-Claudio, S (1992) 'Unequal exchanges: International tourism and overseas employment', *Community Development Journal,* vol 27, pp401–410

Farrell, B H and Runyan, D (1991) 'Ecology and tourism', *Annals of Tourism Research,* vol 18, pp26–40

Fennell, D A (1999) *Ecotourism: An Introduction,* Routledge, London

Foote-Whyte, W (1982) 'Interviewing in field research' in Burgess, R G (ed) *Field Research: A Sourcebook and Field Manual,* Allen and Unwin, London, pp111–122

Ford, A (1998) *El Pilar Management Plan: El Pilar Landscape: Gateway Between Two Nations,* PROARCA/CAPAS BRASS/El Pilar Program/Ford Foundation/USAID, Rum Point, Belize

Ford, A (1997) *The Future of El Pilar: The Integrated Research and Development Plan for the El Pilar Archaeological Reserve for Flora and Fauna, Belize–Guatemala,* Bureau of Oceans and International Scientific Affairs, Virginia, US

Forsyth, T (1995) 'Business attitudes to sustainable tourism: Self-regulation in the UK outgoing tourism industry', *Journal of Sustainable Tourism,* vol 3, pp210–231

Gan, L (1993) 'The making of the Global Environmental Facility: An actor's perspective', *Global Environmental Change,* vol 3, pp256–275

Garfinkel, H (1967) *Studies in Ethnomethodology,* Prentice Hall, New Jersey

Garfinkel, H and Sacks, H (1986) 'On formal structures of practical actions' in Garfinkel, H (ed) *Ethnomethodological Studies of Work,* Routledge and Kegan Paul, London and New York, pp160–193

Garfinkel, H (ed) (1986) *Ethnomethodological Studies of Work,* Routledge and Kegan Paul, London and New York

Gelbard, R S (1996a) 'The globalisation of the drug trade', address at the John Jay College of Criminal Justice, Dublin, Ireland

Gelbard, R S (1996b) 'The threat of transnational organised crime and illicit narcotics', statement before the UN General Assembly, New York City

Ghai, D (1994) 'Environment, livelihood and empowerment', *Development and Change,* vol 25, pp1–13

Giddens, A (1994) 'Living in a post-traditional society' in Beck, U, Giddens, A and Lash, S (eds) *Reflexive Modernisation: Politics, Tradition and Aesthetics and the Modern Social Order,* Polity Press, Cambridge, pp56–109

Gnoth, J (1997) 'Tourism motivation and expectation formation', *Annals of Tourism Research,* vol 24, pp283–304

GOB (1994) *Belize National Environmental Report,* GOB, Belmopan

GOB (1995) *Tourism Consultation Report,* GOB, Belmopan

GOB/USAID (1992) *Amendment No 1 to the Project Grant Between the Government of Belize and the Government of the United States of America Acting through the Agency for International Development for the Tourism Management Project,* (project no 505–0044), USAID/GOB, Belmopan

Godfrey, G (1998) *Ambergris Caye: Paradise with a Past,* Cubola Productions, Belize City

Goff, W (1995) 'Gales Point community project', in *Proceedings of the Second National Symposium on the State of the Belize Environment,* NARMAP, Belize City, pp211–212

Gonzalez, V (1995) 'Keynote address', in *Proceedings of the Second National Symposium on the State of the Belize Environment,* NARMAP, Belize City, pp10–14

Goodall, B (1995) 'Environmental auditing: A tool for assessing the environmental performance of tourism firms', *Geographical Journal,* vol 161, pp29–37

Goodin, R (1983) 'Ethical principles for environmental protection' in Elliot, R and Gare, A (eds) *Environmental Philosophy,* Open University Press, Milton Keynes, pp3–21

Gorz, A (1980) *Ecology as Politics,* Billing and Sons, London

Grant, J (1995) 'Institutions: Their role in resource management', in *Proceedings of the Second National Symposium on the State of the Belize Environment,* NARMAP, Belize City, pp44–47

Grove, W (1995) 'The drug trade as a national and international security threat', paper presented at the Security 94 Conference at the Institute of Strategic Studies and the Security Association of South Africa, University of Pretoria, South Africa

Guimaraes, R P (1991) *The Ecopolitics of Development in the Third World: Politics and Environment in Brazil,* Lynne Rienner Publishers, Boulder and London

Hagvar, S (1994) 'Preserving the natural heritage: The process of developing attitudes', *Ambio,* vol 23, pp515–518

Hailwood, S A (2000) 'The value of nature's otherness', *Environmental Values,* vol 9, pp353–372

Hall, C M (1994) *Tourism and Politics: Policy, Power and Place,* John Wiley and Sons, Chichester and New York

Hall, C M and O'Sullivan, V (1996) 'Tourism, political stability and violence' in Pizam, A, and Mansfeld, Y (eds) *Tourism, Crime and International Security Issues,* John Wiley and Sons, Chichester and New York, pp106–122

Hall, D R (1992) 'Tourism development in Cuba' in Harrison, D (ed) *Tourism and the Less Developed Countries,* Belhaven Press, London, pp102–120

Hallin, P O (1995) 'Environmental concern and environmental behaviour in Foley, a small town in Minnesota', *Environment and Behaviour,* vol 27, pp558–578

Hammersley, M (1992) *What's Wrong with Ethnography,* Routledge, London and New York

Hampton, M P (1996) 'Where currents meet: The offshore interface between corruption, offshore finance centres and economic development', *IDS Bulletin,* vol 27, pp78–87

Hampton, M P and Levi, M (1999) 'Fast spinning into oblivion? Recent developments in money laundering policies and offshore finance centres', *Third World Quarterly*, vol 20, pp645–656

Hardin, G (1968) 'The tragedy of the Commons', *Science*, vol 162, pp1243–1248

Harrison, D (1994) 'Learning from the old South by the new South? The case of tourism', *Third World Quarterly*, vol 15, pp707–721

Harrison, D (1992a) (ed) *Tourism and the Less Developed Countries*, Belhaven Press, London

Harrison, D (1992b) 'International tourism and the less developed countries: The background' *Tourism and the Less Developed Countries*, Belhaven Press, London, pp1–18

Harrison, D (1992c) 'Tourism to less developed countries: the social consequences' in *Tourism and the Less Developed Countries*, Belhaven Press, London, pp19–34

Harrisson, L E (1993) 'Underdevelopment is a state of mind' in Seligson, M A and J T Passe-Smith (eds) *Development and Underdevelopment: The Political Economy of Inequality*, Lynne Rienner, London, pp173–181

Haysmith, L and Harvey, J (eds) (1995) *Nature Conservation and Nature Tourism in Central America*, University of Idaho Press, Moscow, ID

Hawkins, J P and Roberts, C M (1994) 'The growth of coastal tourism in the Red Sea: present and future effects on coral reefs', *Ambio*, vol 23, pp503–508

Healy, R G (1994) 'Tourist merchandise as a means of generating local benefits from ecotourism', *Journal of Sustainable Tourism*, vol 2, pp137–151

Herlihy, P II (1997) 'Indigenous peoples and the biosphere reserve conservation in the Mosquitia rain forest corridor, Honduras' in Stevens, S (ed) *Conservation Through Cultural Survival: Indigenous Peoples and Protected Areas*, Island Press, Washington DC, pp99–130

Herran, E (2000) 'Modernity, premodernity and the political: The NeoZapatistas of Southern Mexico' in Ben-Ami, S, Peled, Y and Spetorowski, A (eds) *Ethnic Challenges to the Modern Nation-State*, Macmillan, Basingstoke, pp221–235

Hettinger, N and Throop, B (1999) 'Refocusing ecocentrism', *Environmental Ethics*, vol 21, pp.3–22

Hitchcock, M and Teague, K (eds) (2000) *Souvenirs: The Material Culture of Tourism*, Ashgate Publishing, Aldershot

Hitchcock, M, King, V T and Parnwell, M J R (eds) (1993) *Tourism in South East Asia*, Routledge, London

Holloway, J and Pelaez, E (eds) (2000) *Zapatista! Reinventing the Mexican Revolution*, Pluto Press, London

Honey, M (1999) *Ecotourism and Sustainable Development: Who Owns Paradise?*, Island Press, Washington DC

Hultsman, J (1995) 'Just tourism: An ethical framework', *Annals of Tourism Research*, vol 22, pp553–567

Jackson, R (1990) *Quasi-States: Sovereignty, International Relations, and the Third World*, Cambridge University Press, Cambridge

Jackson, R H and Rosberg, C G (1986) 'Sovereignty and Underdevelopment: Juridical statehood in the African crisis', *Journal of Modern African Studies*, vol 24, pp1–31

Jacob, M (1994) 'Toward a methodological critique of sustainable development', *Journal of Developing Areas*, vol 28, pp237–252

Jacobs, N D and Castaneda, A (eds) (1998) *The Belize National Biodiversity Action Plan*, National Biodiversity Committee, Ministry of Natural Resources and the Environment, Belmopan, Belize

Johnson, V and Nurick, R (1995) 'Behind the headlines: The ethics of the population and environment debate', *International Affairs*, vol 71, pp547–565

Joyce, G P (1998) 'Bounding 'bout Belize', *Sport Diver Magazine*, vol 6, pp72–79

Judson, D H, Gray, L N and Candan Duran-Aydintung (1994) 'Predicting unique behavioural choices: Direct numeric estimation of rewards and costs and the satisfaction-balance decision model', *Social Psychology Quarterly*, vol 57, pp140–149

Karp, G D (1996) 'Values and their effect on pro-environmental behaviour', *Environment and Behaviour*, pp111–133

Kellerher, G and Kenchington, R (1991) *Guidelines for Establishing Marine Protected Areas: A Marine Conservation and Development Report*, IUCN, Gland, Switzerland

Khan, M H (1996) 'A typology of corrupt transactions in developing countries', *IDS Bulletin*, vol 27, pp12–21

Krause, D (1993) 'Environmental consciousness: An empirical study', *Environment and Behaviour*, vol 25, pp126–142

Krippendorf, J (1987) *The Holiday Makers: Understanding the Impact of Leisure and Travel*, Heinemann, London

Lanfant, J F (1995) "International tourism, internationalisation and the challenge to identity' in Lanfant, M F, Allcock, J B and Bruner, E M (eds) (1995) *International Tourism: Identity and Change*, London, Sage, pp1–24

Lanfant, M F, Allcock, J B and Bruner, E M (eds) (1995) *International Tourism: Identity and Change*, Sage, London

Langhelle, O (2000) 'Sustainable development and social justice: Expanding the Rawlsian framework of global justice', *Environmental Values*, vol 9 pp295–323

Lash, S (1994) 'Reflexivity and its doubles: Structure, aesthetics, community' in Beck, U, Giddens, A and Lash, S (eds) *Reflexive Modernisation: Politics, Tradition and Aesthetics and the Modern Social Order,* Polity Press, Cambridge, pp110–173

Lea, J P (1993) 'Tourism development ethics in the Third World', *Annals of Tourism Research,* vol 20, pp710–715

Lee, T H and Crompton, J (1992) 'Measuring novelty seeking in tourism' *Annals of Tourism Research,* vol 19, pp732–751

Lehman, A (1996) *Fodor's Guide to Belize and Guatemala,* Fodor's Travel Publications Limited, New York

Lengkeek, J (1993) 'Collective and private interests in recreation and tourism: The Dutch case: concerning consequences of a shift from citizen role to consumer role', *Leisure Studies,* vol 12, pp7–32

Leopold, A (1986) 'The land ethic', in Van De Veer, D and Pierce, C (eds) (1986) *People, Penguins and Plastic Trees,* Wadsworth Publishing Company, Belmont, pp73–82

Lester, J (1989) (ed) *Environmental Politics and Policies,* Durham University Press, Durham

Liebman Parrinello, G (1993) 'Motivation and anticipation in post-industrial tourism', *Annals of Tourism Research,* vol 20, pp233–249

Lindberg, Enriquez, K J and Sproule, K (1996) 'Ecotourism questioned: Case studies from Belize', *Annals of Tourism Research,* vol 23, pp543–562

Lindberg, K and Hawkins, D E (eds) (1993) *Ecotourism: A Guide for Planners and Managers,* Ecotourism Society, North Bennington VT

Lindberg, K (1991) *Policies for Maximising Nature Tourism's Ecological and Economic Benefits,* World Resources Institute, New York

Lovelock, J (1988) *The Ages of Gaia,* Oxford University Press, Oxford

Lovelock, J (1979) *Gaia,* Oxford University Press, Oxford

Luzar, E J, Diagne, A, Gan, C and Henning, B R (1995) 'Evaluating nature-based tourism using the new environmental paradigm', *Journal of Agricultural and Applied Economics,* vol 27, pp544–555

Lynn, W (1992) 'Tourism in the people's interest', *Community Development Journal,* vol 27, pp371–377

MacCannell, D (1989) *The Tourist: A New Theory of the Leisured Class,* Schoken Books, New York

Markwell, K (1997) 'Dimensions of photography in a nature-based tour', *Annals of Tourism Research,* vol 24, pp131–155

Marshall, B K (1999) 'Globalisation, environmental degradation and Ulrich Beck's perspective: Implications for social theories of risk', *Environmental Values,* vol 8, pp253–276

Matthews, H G and Richter, L K (1991) 'Political science and tourism', *Annals of Tourism Research*, vol 18, pp120–135

Maxwell Stamp Plc (1991) *Belize: Tourism Planning Stage 1*, prepared for the ODA on behalf of the Government of Belize, ODA, London

McCalla, W (1995) *Guide for Developers*, Ministry of Tourism and the Environment, Department of the Environment, Belmopan

McCalla, W (1995) 'Environmental legislation in Belize', in *Proceedings of the Second National Symposium on the State of the Belize Environment*, NARMAP, Belize City, pp14–21

McClelland, D C (1993) 'The achievement motive in economic growth' in Seligson, M A and J T Passe-Smith (eds) *Development and Underdevelopment: The Political Economy of Inequality*, Lynne Rienner, London, pp141–157

McCrone, D, Morris, A and Kelly, R (1995) *Scotland – The Brand: The Making of Scottish Heritage*, Edinburgh University Press, Edinburgh

McField, M, Wells, S and Gibson, J (eds) (1996) *State of the Coastal Zone Report Belize, 1995*, Coastal Zone Management Programme/Government of Belize, Belize City

McGann, J (1995) 'Financial mechanisms for natural resource and protected areas management', in proceedings of the *Second National Symposium on the State of the Belize Environment*, pp22–37

McIntosh, R (1996) 'The emperor has no clothes... let us paint our loincloths rainbow: A classical and feminist critique of contemporary science policy', *Environmental Values*, vol 5, pp3–30

McKercher, B (1993) 'Some fundamental truths about tourism: Understanding tourism's social and environmental impacts', *Journal of Sustainable Tourism*, vol 1, pp6–16

McRae, E (1995) 'The Caye Caulker Multihabitat Reserve: A community-based reserve: A voyage in time', in *Proceedings of the Second National Symposium on the State of the Belize Environment*, NARMAP, Belize City, pp187–204

Meadows, D H (1972) *The Limits to Growth*, Pan, London

Mendoza, J (1995) 'Environmental enforcement and compliance monitoring', in *Proceedings of the Second National Symposium on the State of the Belize Environment*, NARMAP, Belize City, pp67–71

Meyer, C A (1995) 'Opportunism and NGOs: Entrepreneurship and green North–South transfers', *World Development*, vol 23, pp1277–1289

Mill, J S (1863) *Utilitarianism*, reprinted 1987 by Everyman, London

Miller, C A (2000) 'The dynamics of framing environmental values and policy: Four models of societal processes', *Environmental Values*, vol 9, pp211–234

Ministry of Tourism and the Environment/Inter-American Development Bank (1998) *Tourism Strategy Plan for Belize*, Help for Progress/Blackstone Corporation, Belmopan, Belize/Toronto, Canada

Ministry of Tourism and the Environment (1994) 'Community-based tourism development in Belize: Government policies and plans in support of community initiatives', presented by Henry Young at the MT-sponsored Community-Based Tourism Gathering, Hopkins Village, Belize

Ministry of Tourism and the Environment (1994) *Guide to Community-Based Ecotourism in Belize*, MTE/BEST, Belmopan

Momtaz, D (1996) 'The United Nations and protection of the environment: From Stockholm to Rio de Janeiro', *Political Geography*, vol 15, pp261–271

Moran, J (1999) 'Patterns of corruption and development in East Asia', *Third World Quarterly*, vol 20, pp569–587

Morris, S D (1999) 'Corruption and the Mexican political system: Continuity and change', *Third World Quarterly*, vol 20, pp623–643

Moscardo, G, Morrison, A M and Pearce, P L (1996) 'Specialist accommodation and ecologically sustainable tourism', *Journal of Sustainable Tourism*, vol 4, pp29–52

Mowforth, R and Munt, I (1998) *Tourism and Sustainability: Dilemmas in Third World Tourism*, Routledge, London

Munt, I (1994a) 'The "other" postmodern tourism: Culture, travel and the new middle classes', *Theory, Culture and Society*, vol 11, pp101–123

Munt, I (1994b) 'Ecotourism or egotourism?', *Race and Class*, vol 36, pp49–60

Myers, N (1995) 'Population and biodiversity', *Ambio*, vol 24, pp56–57

Myerson, G and Rydin, Y (1996) *The Language of the Environment: A New Rhetoric*, UCL Press, London

Nietschmann, B (1997) 'Protecting indigenous coral reefs and sea territories, Miskito Coast, RAAN, Nicaragua', in Stevens, S (ed) *Conservation Through Cultural Survival: Indigenous Peoples and Protected Areas*, Island Press, Washington DC, pp193–224

Noguiera, J M and Dore, M (1994) 'The Amazon rain forest, sustainable development and the biodiversity convention: A political economy perspective', *Ambio*, vol 23, pp491–496

Nolan, M (1994) 'Balancing conservation with development', *Belize Review*, pp11–18

Norton, G (1994) 'The vulnerable voyager: New threats for tourism', *World Today*, vol 50, pp237–239

Obregon-Salido, F J and Corral-Verdugo, V (1997) 'Systems of beliefs and environmental conservation behaviour in a Mexican community', *Environment and Behaviour*, vol 29, pp213–235

ODI (1992) *Aid and Political Reform*, ODI Briefing Paper, ODI, London

Opperman, M (1993) 'Tourism space in developing countries', *Annals of Tourism Research,* vol 20, pp535–556

Orams, M B (1996) 'Using interpretation to manage nature-based tourism', *Journal of Sustainable Tourism,* vol 4, pp81–94

O'Riordan, T and Jordan, A (1995) 'The precautionary principle in contemporary environmental politics', *Environmental Values,* vol 4, pp191–212

Pattullo, P (1996) *Last Resorts: The Cost of Tourism in the Caribbean,* Cassell, London

Pearce, P L (1995) 'From culture shock and culture arrogance to culture exchange: Ideas towards sustainable socio-cultural tourism', *Journal of Sustainable Tourism,* vol 3, pp143–154

Pearce, D, Barbier, E and Markandya, A (1990) *Sustainable Development,* Edward Elgar, Aldershot

Perrine, D (1998) 'Divers and dolphins', *Sport Diver Magazine,* vol 6, pp40–47

Peterson, M J and T R Peterson (1996) 'Ecology: scientific, deep and feminist?', *Environmental Values,* vol 5, pp123–146

Petrucci, M (2000) 'Population: time bomb or smokescreen?', *Environmental Values,* vol 9, pp325–52

Picard, M (1995) 'Cultural heritage and tourist capital: Cultural tourism in Bali' in Lanfant, M F, Allcock, J B and Bruner, E M (eds) *International Tourism: Identity and Change,* Sage, London, pp44–66

Pizam, A, and Mansfeld, Y (eds) (1996) *Tourism, Crime and International Security Issues,* J Wiley and Sons, Chichester and New York

Pizman, A and Sussman, S (1995) 'Does nationality affect tourist behaviour?', *Annals of Tourism Research,* vol 22, pp901–917

Place, S E (1991) 'Nature tourism and rural development in Tortuguero', *Annals of Tourism Research,* vol 18, pp186–201

Poirier, R A (1997) 'Political risk analysis and tourism', *Annals of Tourism Research,* vol 24, pp675–686

Porter, M (1990) *The Competitive Advantage of Nations,* Macmillan, London

Primarck, R B, Bray, D, Galleti, H A and Ponciano, I (eds) (1988) *Timber, Tourists and Temples: Conservation and Development in the Maya Forest of Belize, Guatemala and Mexico,* Washington DC, Island Press

Prosser, R (1994) 'Societal change and the growth of alternative tourism' in Cater, E and Lowman, G (eds) *Ecotourism: A Sustainable Option,* John Wiley and Sons, London, pp19–37

Rabinow, P and Sullivan, W M, (1979) *Interpretive Social Science,* University of California Press, Berkeley

Redclift, M (1992) 'Sustainable development and global environmental change', *Global Environmental Change,* vol 2, pp32–42

Reno, W (1998) *Warlord Politics and African States,* Lynne Rienner, Boulder, Colorado and London

Reno, W (1995) *Corruption and State Politics in Sierra Leone,* Cambridge University Press, Cambridge

Richter, L K (1992) 'Political instability and tourism in the Third World' in Harrison, D (ed) *Tourism and the Less Developed Countries,* Belhaven Press, London, pp35–46

Rojek, C (1995) 'Veblen, leisure and human need', *Leisure Studies,* vol 14, pp73–86

Rydin, Y (1999) 'Can we talk ourselves into sustainability? The role of discourse in the environmental policy process', *Environmental Values,* vol 8, pp467–484

Sagoff, M (1994) 'Four dogmas of environmental economics', *Environmental Values,* vol 3, pp285–310

Salas, O (1995) 'Wildlife resources of Belize: Exploring utilizationist and decentralised approaches for their conservation and management' in *Proceedings of the Second National Symposium on the State of the Belize Environment,* NARMAP, Belize Cit,y pp106–114

Salvat, B (1992) 'Coral reefs: A challenging ecosystem for human societies', *Global Environmental Change,* vol 2, pp12–18

Sarkar, S (1999) *Eco-Socialism or Eco-Capitalism? A Critical Analysis of Humanity's Fundamental Choices,* Zed Books, London

Sarre, P (1995) 'Towards global environmental values: Lessons from western and eastern experience', *Global Environmental Values,* vol 4, pp115–127

Schahn, J and Holzer, E (1990) 'Studies of individual environmental concern: The role of knowledge, gender and background variables', *Environment and Behaviour,* vol 22, pp767–789

Schultz, P W and Stone, W F (1994) 'Authoritarianism and attitudes toward the environment', *Environment and Behaviour,* vol 26, pp25–37

Scott, D and Willits, F K (1994) 'Environmental attitudes and behaviour: A Pennsylvania survey', *Environment and Behaviour,* vol 26, pp239–260

Seligson, M A and Passe-Smith, J T (eds) (1993) *Development and Underdevelopment: The Political Economy of Inequality,* Lynne Rienner, London

Selwyn, T (ed) (1996) *The Tourist Image: Myths and Myth Making in Tourism,* John Wiley and Sons, Chichester

Selwyn, T (1992) 'Tourism society and development', *Community Development Journal,* vol 27, pp353–360

Sen, G (1995) 'Creating common ground between environmentalists and women: Thinking locally, acting globally?', *Ambio,* vol 24, pp64–65

Shackley, M (1992) 'Manatees and tourism in southern Florida: Opportunity or threat?', *Journal of Environmental Management*, vol 34, pp257–265

Sharrock, W and Anderson, B (1986) *The Ethnomethodologists*, Tavistock Publications, London

Shoman, A (1995) *Backtalking Belize*, Belize City, Angelus Press

Shrader-Frechette, K S and McCoy, E D (1994) 'How the tail wags the dog: How value judgements determine ecological science', *Environmental Values*, vol 3, pp107–120

Silva, E (1994) 'Thinking politically about sustainable development in the tropical forests of Latin America', *Development and Change*, vol 25, pp697–722

Silverman, D (1985) *Qualitative Methodology and Sociology: Describing the Social World*, Gower, Aldershot

Simmons, I G (1993) *Interpreting Nature: Cultural Constructions of the Environment*, Routledge, London

Sinclair, M T, Alizadeh, P and Onunga, E A A (1992) 'The structure of international tourism and tourism development in Kenya' in Harrison, D (ed) *Tourism and the Less Developed Countries*, Belhaven Press, pp47–63

Singdiga, I (1999) *Tourism and African Development: Change and Challenge of Tourism in Kenya*, Ashgate Publishing, Aldershot

Singer, P (1986) 'Animal liberation' in Van De Veer, D and Pierce, C (eds) *People, Penguins and Plastic Trees*, Belmont Press, California, pp24–32

Skocpol, T (1993) 'Wallerstein's world capitalist system: A theoretical and historical critique' in Seligson, M A and Passe-Smith, JT (eds) *Development and Underdevelopment: The Political Economy of Inequality*, Lynne Rienner, London, pp231–237

Smith, A (1776) *The Wealth of Nations*, reprinted 1970 by Pelican Books, London

Smith, M (1999) 'To speak of trees: Social constructivism, environmental values and the futures of deep ecology', *Environmental Ethics*, vol 21, pp359–376

Smith, R J (1996) 'Sustainability and the rationalisation of the environment', *Environmental Politics*, vol 5, pp25–47

Sonmez, S F and Graefe, A R (1998) 'Influence of terrorism risk in foreign tourism decisions', *Annals of Tourism Research*, vol 265, pp112–144

Sonmez, S F (1998) 'Tourism, terrorism and political instability', *Annals of Tourism Research*, vol 25, pp416–456

Sparks, P and Shepherd, R (1992) 'Self-identity and the theory of planned behaviour: Assessing the role of identification with "green consumerism"', *Social Psychology Quarterly*, vol 55, pp388–399

Spector, B I and Korula, A R (1993) 'Problems in ratifying international environmental agreements: Overcoming initial obstacles in the post-agreement negotiation process', *Global Environmental Change*, vol 3, pp369–381

Stares, P B (1996) *Global Habit: The Drug Problem in a Borderless World*, Brookings Institution, Washington DC

Steele, P (1995) 'Ecotourism: an economic analysis', *Journal of Sustainable Tourism*, vol 3, pp29–44

Sterba, J P (1994) 'Reconciling anthropocentric and nonanthropocentric environmental ethics', *Environmental Values*, vol 3, pp229–244

Stern, P C, Dietz, T and Guagano, G A (1995) 'The new ecological paradigm in social-psychological context', *Environment and Behaviour*, vol 27, pp322–348

Stern, P C, Dietz, T and Kalof, L (1993) 'Value orientations, gender and environmental concern', *Environment and Behaviour*, vol 25, pp322–348

Stevens, S (ed) (1997) *Conservation Through Cultural Survival: Indigenous Peoples and Protected Areas*, Island Press, Washington DC

Stiles, D (1994) 'Tribals and trade: A strategy for cultural and ecological survival', *Ambio*, vol 23, pp106–111

Stonich, S (1998) 'Political ecology of tourism', *Annals of Tourism Research*, vol 25, pp25–54

Stonich, S C, Sorensen, J H and Hundt, A (1995) 'Ethnicity, class and gender in tourism development: The case of the Bay Islands, Honduras', *Journal of Sustainable Tourism*, vol 3, pp1–28

Szerzynski, B (1999) 'Risk and trust: The performative dimension', *Environmental Values*, vol 8, pp239–252

Tangri, R (1999) *The Politics of Patronage in Africa: Parastatals, Privatization and Private Enterprise*, James Currey/Fountain/Africa World Press, Oxford/ Kampala/Trenton, New Jersey

Tarlow, P and Muesham, M (1996) 'Theoretical aspects of crime as they impact on the tourism industry' in Pizam, A, and Mansfeld, Y (eds) *Tourism, Crime and International Security Issues*, John Wiley and Sons, Chichester and New York, pp11–22

Tolba, M K (1995) 'Towards a sustainable development', *Ambio*, vol 24, pp66–67

Toledo Maya Cultural Council and Toledo Alcaldes Association (1997) *Maya Atlas: The Struggle to Preserve Maya Land in Southern Belize*, North Atlantic Books, Berkeley, California

Travel and Tour Belize Ltd (1998) *Proposal to the Government of Belize: Boca Chica Sea Park*, Belize City

Urry, J (1994) 'Cultural change and contemporary tourism', *Leisure Studies*, vol 13, pp233–238

Urry, J (1992) 'The tourist gaze and the environment', *Theory, Culture and Society*, vol 9, pp3–24

Urry, J (1990) *The Tourist Gaze: Leisure and Travel in Contemporary Societies*, Sage, London

Utting, P (1994) 'Social and political dimensions of environmental protection in Central America', *Development and Change*, vol 25, pp231–259

Van De Berghe, P L (1995) 'Marketing Mayas: Ethnic tourism promotion in Mexico', *Annals of Tourism Research*, vol 22, pp568–588

Van De Veer, D and C Pierce (eds) (1986) *People, Penguins and Plastic Trees*, Wadsworth Publishing Company, Belmont, California

Veijola, S and Jokinen, E (1994) 'The body in tourism', *Theory, Culture and Society*, vol 11, pp125–151

Vining, J (1992) 'Environmental emotions and decisions: A comparison of the responses and expectations of forest managers, an environmental group and the public', *Environment and Behaviour*, vol 24, pp3–34

Wall, G (1995) 'General versus specific environmental concern: A Western Canadian case', *Environment and Behaviour*, vol 27, pp294–316

Wallace, G N and Pierce, S M (1996) 'An Evaluation of Ecotourism in Amazona, Brazil', *Annals of Tourism Research*, vol 23, pp843–873

Walle, A H (1997) 'Quantitative versus qualitative tourism research', *Annals of Tourism Research*, vol 24, pp524–536

Wallerstein, I (1993) 'The present state of the debate in world inequality' in Seligson, M A and Passe-Smith, J T (eds) *Development and Underdevelopment: The Political Economy of Inequality*, Lynne Rienner, London, pp217–230

Warner, S, Feinstein, M, Coppinger, R and Clemence, E (1996) 'Global population growth and the demise of nature', *Environmental Values*, vol 5, pp285–301

WCED (World Commission on Environment and Development) (1987) *Our Common Future*, Oxford University Press, Oxford

Wearing, B and Wearing S (1992) 'Identity and the commodification of leisure', *Leisure Studies*, vol 11, pp3–18

Weaver, D and Elliot, K (1996) 'Spatial patterns and problems in contemporary Namibian tourism', *Geographical Journal*, vol 162, pp205–217

Weaver, D (1994) 'Ecotourism in the Caribbean Basin' in Cater, E and Lowman, G (eds) *Ecotourism: A Sustainable Option*, John Wiley and Sons, London, pp159–176

Weed, T J (1994) 'Central America's peace parks and regional conflict resolution', *International Environmental Affairs*, vol 6, pp175–190

Weinberg, B (1991) *War on the Land: Ecology and Politics in Central America*, Zed Books, London

Wheat, S (1994) 'Taming tourism', *Geographical Magazine,* vol 66, pp16–19

Wight, P (1994) 'Environmentally responsible marketing of tourism' in Cater, E and Lowman, G (eds) *Ecotourism: A Sustainable Option,* John Wiley and Sons, London, pp39–55

Wildlife Preservation Trust International and Wildlife Conservation Society (1996) *Field Research and Community-Based Ecotourism Development: A Multidisciplinary Approach to the Conservation of the West Indian Manatee and its Marine Habitat in Belize, Central America,* proposal for a preliminary implementation grant from the Center for Environmental Research and Conservation, Wildlife Preservation Trust International and Wildlife Conservation Society, Washington, DC

Williams, S (1993a) 'Tourism on their own terms: How the TEA blends with village ways', *Belize Review,* pp9–20

Williams, S (1993b), 'Pushing the boundaries of tourism', *Belize Review,* pp3–8

Wilkinson, P (1992) 'Tourism: The curse of the nineties? Belize: An experiment to integrate tourism and the environment', *Community Development Journal,* vol 27, pp386–395

Wilson, R J (1995) 'Towards a national protected area systems plan', in *Proceedings of the Second National Symposium on the State of the Belize Environment,* NARMAP, Belize City, pp49–54

Winpenny, J (1991) *Values for the Environment,* HMSO, London

World Bank (1997a) 'Corruption and good governance' *World Bank Group Issue Brief,* World Bank, New York

World Bank (1997b) 'Corruption: A major barrier to sound and equitable development', World Bank, New York

World Bank (1997c) 'Reducing corruption', *World Bank Policy and Research Bulletin,* vol 8, World Bank, New York

World Bank (1994) *World Development Report,* Oxford University Press, Oxford

World Bank/GEF (1997a) *Medium Sized Projects,* World Bank/UNDP/UNEP, New York

World Bank/GEF (1997b) *Operational Guidance for Preparation and Approval of Medium Sized Projects,* World Bank/UNDP/UNEP, New York

Wright, R (1989) *Time Among the Maya: Travels in Belize, Guatemala and Mexico,* London, Abacus

Wynne, B (1992) 'Uncertainty in environmental learning: Reconceiving science and policy in the preventive paradigm', *Global Environmental Change,* vol 2, pp111–127

Young, H (1994) 'Eco-cultural tourism in Belize: Reuniting man with the natural world', *Belize Review,* pp4–6

Zimmerman, ME (1994) *Contesting the Earth's Future: Radical Ecology and Post Modernity*, University of California Press, Berkeley

Zisman, S (1996) *The Directory of Belizean Protected Areas and Sites of Nature Conservation Interest*, NARMAP, Belize City

INDEX